ENGLISH POETRY IN THE
SIXTEENTH CENTURY

English Literature

—————

Editor
PROFESSOR BASIL WILLEY
formerly King Edward VII Professor of English Literature
in the University of Cambridge

ENGLISH POETRY
IN THE
SIXTEENTH CENTURY

Maurice Evans
Professor of English
McGill University, Montreal

HUTCHINSON UNIVERSITY LIBRARY
LONDON

HUTCHINSON & CO (*Publishers*) LTD
178–202 Great Portland Street, London W1

London Melbourne Sydney
Auckland Bombay Toronto
Johannesburg New York

★

First published 1955
Second (revised) edition 1967

Cover design by courtesy of
the Victoria and Albert Museum

This book has been set in Bembo, printed in Great Britain
on Smooth Wove paper by Anchor Press, and
bound by Wm. Brendon, both of Tiptree, Essex

CONTENTS

Author's Note   7

1   Cross-currents of the Renaissance   9

2   Poetic theory and practice   24

3   John Skelton and early Tudor
     poetry   39

4   Wyatt and Surrey   61

5   Shorter forms of Elizabethan
     poetry   83

6   Historical poetry   123

7   *The Faerie Queene*   135

8   Conclusion: the end of the century   157

Bibliography   171

Editions quoted   175

Index   179

AUTHOR'S NOTE

This book, originally published in 1955, has been rewritten in the light of recent scholarship and retains only the chapter on historical poetry and occasional short extracts from the original version. It has been impossible to acknowledge the multitude of debts to other writers on the period, but some indication of their scope is contained in the bibliographies compiled for each chapter. For reasons of space, I have had to be rigorously selective and to ignore many important aspects of sixteenth-century verse. For the same reason, I have not included any detailed treatment of the poetry of Shakespeare. All references are to the editions listed at the end.

June 1966   M.E.

I

CROSS-CURRENTS OF THE RENAISSANCE

The history of English poetry in the sixteenth century is the record of
the interaction between Renaissance Humanism and native traditions.
The terms 'Renaissance' and 'Humanism' are both modern coinages
around which much controversy has raged and to which a variety of
meanings have been attached. The nineteenth-century conception of
the Renaissance as a sudden rebirth of learning which liberated the
human spirit from the dark prison of medieval ignorance has long been
discredited, and the tendency nowadays is to see it as a development of
factors already present in the Middle Ages. Normally the term
'Renaissance' is used to describe a movement which began in medieval
Italy and had involved the whole of Europe by the end of the sixteenth
century. Its initial characteristic was a rejection of medieval for classical
Latin and a search for the lost texts of classical Latin and Greek literature, with results that ultimately penetrated far deeper than matters of
style and modified the whole current of European thought. Humanism, in the modern agnostic sense of the word, has little relevance to
anything in the Renaissance and the term can only be applied to the
period in the specialised sense which it carries when associated with the
'Humanities' at a university. A Renaissance Humanist was a person
who turned to the language and literature of classical Greece and Rome
and who saw in them a most fruitful basis for education.

The knowledge of the classics had, of course, never been wholly
lost. Throughout the Middle Ages western Europe knew and revered
its Virgil, Ovid, Seneca and many others, as well as Greek texts in
Latin translation; there was a Platonic revival at Chartres in the twelfth
century and the great Aristotelian renaissance of the thirteenth.

Nevertheless many Latin texts and even more Greek ones were lost under the drums and tramplings of the dark ages, or neglected where they were too stubborn to be absorbed by Christianity. When the Roman Empire broke up into its eastern and western halves, and the two churches were established at Constantinople and Rome, with Greek and Latin as their respective liturgical languages, the knowledge of Greek declined in the western world. Latin, on the other hand, remained a living language and, in the way of living languages, grew away from its origins to produce a new literature of its own. The Renaissance was a return to the fountain-head. The lost Latin and Greek texts were restored, the languages studied in their classical forms, though Greek was never very widely known in the Renaissance, and access to Greek texts was mainly through Latin translations. The Humanists rejected what Colet, in the Statutes for his new school, St Paul's, called 'All barbary, all corruption, all Latin adulterate which ignorant blind fools brought into this world, and with that same hath disdained and poisoned the old Latin speech and the very Roman tongue which in the time of Tully and Sallust and Virgil and Terence was used . . .' (Nugent, p. 41). In this process they brought about what C. S. Lewis has happily called the 'archaisation' of Latin, by which the fixed and dead literary language of Cicero drove out the living medieval tongue.

There must always have been Humanists, but Humanism as a conscious movement began in Italy early in the thirteenth century. Italy more than the rest of Europe had trade contacts with the east, and it had been absorbed less wholly into the fabric of feudalism than the countries of northern Europe. The Italian city states had developed out of the old cities of the Roman Empire, and as they grew in wealth and power they developed a civic pride in their origins and a desire to revive the ancient glories of Rome and of the Greek civilisation from which Rome had derived so much. By 1300 the search into monastic libraries had begun for manuscripts which had lain undisturbed for a thousand years, and by 1350 Petrarch had become the recognised father of Humanism, collecting, copying, editing manuscripts and tempting Greek scholars to teach their language in Italy. Chairs of Greek were created and filled by imported Greek scholars, the great Papal collections were being built up, and the fall of Constantinople to the Turks in 1453 which drove a flood of scholars to the west, bearing with them their precious manuscripts, was only a further step in a process which had been going on for a century and a half. The new printing press arose to meet the demand and Aldus' press in Venice systematically covered the whole field of the classics, especially in

Greek, or Greek in Latin translation. By 1515, when Aldus died, the whole range of classical texts as we now know it was substantially there, edited, printed and disseminated throughout Europe. The flood of books and the invasion of Italy by Charles VIII in 1494 helped the new humanist ideas to spread north, and turned Italy into the cultural Mecca for the whole of Europe. England had responded to the new ideas early in the fifteenth century, and Humphrey, Duke of Gloucester, for example, collected manuscripts and encouraged the study of Greek at Oxford; but the full impact was not felt until the end of the century when a generation of Oxford men went to Italy and brought Greek home with them. These were the so-called Oxford Reformers, Grocyn, Linacre, Lupset, Lily and the rest, from whose teaching and example Humanism spread into the bloodstream of English education. The sixteenth century is the period when Humanism really makes itself felt throughout northern Europe, and its influence is apparent in the poetry of the Pléiade in France or of the Elizabethans in England.

The literary results were, as we shall see, enormous; but the effects on modes of thought, though less tangible, were even more penetrating. Renaissance Humanism was not identified with any specific classical philosophy: a Humanist could be a Platonist, an Aristotelian, an Epicurean or a Stoic, or any possible combination of these. Whatever blend he chose, however, he would probably be a Christian in some degree; Humanism was mainly Christian Humanism and showed a strong vein of syncretism in its capacity to reconcile Christ with Plato, Aristotle, Hermeticism or the Jewish Kabbala. The ancient philosophies, especially that of the 'divine Plato', were often seen as anticipations of Christianity; they glimpsed as in a glass darkly the truths which Christ revealed in their full clarity: as Erasmus puts it through the mouth of a character in his colloquy, *The Religious Treat*:

The first place must indeed be given to the authority of the Scriptures: but nevertheless, I sometimes find some things said or written by the ancients . . . so chastly, so holily, and so divinely, that I cannot persuade myself, but that when they wrote them they were divinely inspired; and perhaps the Spirit of Christ diffuses itself farther than we imagine. . . . And therefore I can scarce forbear, when I read such things of such men, but cry out Sancte Socrates, ora pro nobis; Saint Socrates, pray for us.

From earliest times, the church had shown itself expert at incorporating the best of pagan thought with Christianity; and in the sixteenth century, reason and faith, the two wings on which the Christian mounted to heaven, often seem to be equated with the classics and the scriptures respectively, the former taking man as high as unaided reason could go, the latter ascending the final peaks. The two were partners, not opponents, and Browning's Bishop would not have been considered irreverent for praying to St Praxed for 'brown Greek manuscripts'.

Yet inevitably, under the pressure of Humanism, classical and Christian thought modified each other to produce a different synthesis from that of the Middle Ages. The idea of the fall of man constitutes the greatest difference between Christian and pagan: to the Christian, man is a fallen creature dependent on divine Grace and helpless without it, whereas in all classical philosophies he is potentially self-sufficient. To Plato the human body may have seemed more corrupt than it appeared to the Christian, whose estimate was modified by the fact that Christ had assumed the body of a man; but for Plato the mind was unfallen and could, without revelation or grace, transcend the flesh and mount to a union with God himself. Aristotle's *Ethics* similarly presents man as an unfallen creature for whom proper pride is no sin, and even the Stoics, while conceding man's helplessness in the face of fortune, credited him with a dignity which made him independent. Some of this pagan self-sufficiency rubbed off with the Renaissance and encouraged the Christian to rate himself more highly. It is for this reason, indeed, that Milton makes Greek philosophy the last and most dangerous of the temptations with which Satan confronts Christ in *Paradise Regained*, the temptation to feel self-sufficient. The Humanists were apt to see man as the measure of all things and to think geocentrally instead of theocentrally as the Middle Ages had done. Man is still a fallen creature, but at least his natural element is this world instead of the next. To the medieval church the fall of Adam had left the human race so weak that best safety lay in flight, and the monastic life of celibacy, self-denial and prayer was the theoretic ideal. The hero of medieval orthodoxy is not the noble Sir Launcelot but the saintly and virginal Sir Galahad who achieves his quest of the Grail and then is translated to heaven. Ascetic poverty rated more highly than civic usefulness, virginity than marriage, the contemplative than the active life.

This is no longer true for the Renaissance, and the fact constitutes one of the main differences between the medieval and the modern world. The ideal man of the Renaissance is secular and lives the active life: he is Sir Philip Sidney, or Spenser's Prince Arthur who may not get as near to the Grail as Sir Bors or Sir Percival in Malory's account, but who is more at home in the world and may perhaps do more towards repairing the ruins of the fall. The extreme statement of this

ideal is presented in Castiglione's *Book of the Courtier*, first published in
1528 and translated into almost every European language during the
next half-century. The book is a discussion of the qualities proper to a
public servant at an Italian court. He must have a 'comely shape of
person' and a consciousness of his own merit which he must not be
ashamed to acknowledge. His main function is to help his prince in all
matters of government, and for this he needs to be both orator and
soldier; but in his spare time he should be poet, painter and musician,
though careful to avoid those wind instruments which disfigure the
features in the playing. He should be able to converse gallantly with the
ladies, to dance, to make witty conversation and wear his clothes with
an air. It is an ideal of purely secular behaviour such as Lord Chesterfield would have understood, and a very far cry from the Poor Parson's
sermon; yet its influence can be seen in works with a specifically
Christian bent, such as Elyot's *Governor*, and the secular attitude which
it embodies colours even the conception of the religious life itself.
Calvinism was as intense in its religious fervour as the Roman Church
had ever been, and possessed an even stronger sense of Original sin;
yet Calvin founded a theocracy whose aim was to bring God down to
the level of the human state. On the other side, Thomas More's
Utopia carries the simplicities of the monastic retreat out into the
normal daily life and society of the world. Milton's famous defence of
active virtue in his *Areopagitica* spoke for the whole Renaissance and
not merely for those countries which had dissolved their monasteries:
'I cannot praise a fugitive and cloistered virtue, unexercised and
unbreathed, that never sallies out and seeks her adversary, but shrinks out
of the race where that immortal garland is to be run for not without
dust and heat.' Spenser's Belphoebe defines the way of virtue in almost
identical terms:

> In woods, in waves, in warres, she wonts to dwell,
> And wil be found with perill and with paine;
> Ne can the man, that moulds in idle cell
> Unto her happy mansion attaine:
> Before her gate high God did Sweat ordaine ...
>
> (II, III, 41)

The sweat of Adam's brow which came as a result of his fall may become the very means of salvation.

A symptom of the new values is the immense importance which the
Humanists attached to education, and their deep faith in what it could
achieve. Renaissance educators seem to anticipate Locke in their sense

of the purity of the child's mind, like an unsullied sheet on which we
may write what we will; as Ascham states it so lyrically in his *Scholemaster*: 'For, the pure cleane witte of a sweet yong babe, is like the
newest wax, most hable to receive the best and fayrest printing: and
like a new bright silver dishe never occupied, to receive and kepe
cleane, anie good thyng that is put into it' (p. 95). To such minds learning
will make its appeal without recourse to beating, and Renaissance
educators were unanimous in their condemnation of the old-style
schoolmaster and what Ascham called the 'butcherlie feare in making of
latines', just as the twentieth century has disowned the birching of the
Victorian age: knowledge will illuminate by its own virtuous light
without the need of force. For this reason and perhaps, also, because of
their novelty and accessibility resulting from the printing press, books
were credited with an infinite power to teach, whether by precept or
historical instance or by the feigned images of poetry. The debate in
Sidney's *Apologie for Poetrie* is about the kind of book which teaches
most effectively, but historian, philosopher and poet would all agree
that 'This purifying of wit, this enritching of memory, enabling of
judgment and enlarging of conceyt, which commonly we call
learning . . .' has, as its final end, 'to lead and draw us to as high a
perfection as our degenerate soules, made worse by theyr clayey
lodgings, can be capable of' (p. 160). Books such as *The Scholemaster*
were printed with little hands in the margin whose fingers point to
the profitable maxims, and Elyot and Ascham alike claimed that books
are better and less painful instructors than experience itself. For the
Humanist, learning and the good life were almost synonymous; to
know the best is to pursue it—indeed to know the best is in part to be
it, for we cannot know anything in whose nature we do not share.
Because man is capable of conceiving of God, he must himself be
divine.

Of all Renaissance schools of philosophy, the great Platonic revival
in Florence during the latter half of the fifteenth century was probably
the most specific source of this idealism. Cosimo de Medici established
his Platonic academy in 1459 and placed in charge of it Marsilio Ficino
who, for the next forty years, taught, edited and translated the whole
body of Plato's works and those of later Neo-Platonists. The Christian-
Platonic doctrines of the school were disseminated throughout
Europe through such widely read books as Ficino's own *Commentary
on Plato's Symposium*, Castiglione's *Courtier* and the popular omnibus
of Platonic lore, *The Philosphy of Love* by the Jewish writer, Leone.
Renaissance Platonism had moved a long way from Plato's original
teaching, under the influence of Aristotelian, Christian, Neo-Platonic

and Arabic thought in the intervening centuries. It was still based on
Plato's Theory of Ideas and the conception of a universe created by the
fusion of form and first matter, but the system had become more
elaborate and the emphasis modified. Instead of a single Chaos out of
which everything was formed, Ficino postulates three, one for the
formation of each of the three levels into which the universe was
traditionally divided. These levels are first that of the heavenly hier-
archies, the pure intelligences and the fixed stars, which is both im-
material and incorruptible; secondly, the level of incorruptible matter
which comprises the planets and their spheres, and lastly that of the
earth, which is both material and corruptible. The universe was
created because generation is an intrinsic quality of divine perfection.
God first contemplated his own infinity, and the Platonic forms are his
awareness of the infinite diversity of his own being. Simultaneously
his love flowed out and kindled in the topmost chaos a desire for these
divine forms which, being imprinted there, produced the angelic
world. From here the divine love emanated downwards, inflaming each
succeeding chaos with a love of the divine forms as they exist at the
level above, so that each chaos took on form as far as its nature would
allow and each level of existence came into being. In this way the one
reached the many and the whole universe expressed in its diversity
what God himself comprises as a unity. The theory itself goes back as
far as Plotinus and was a commonplace of the Middle Ages. Theseus
at the end of Chaucer's *Knight's Tale* draws on it when he explains how
that which 'parfit is and stable' descends 'til it be corrumpable', and for
that reason earthly things have to achieve their eternity 'by successiouns'
instead of being eternal as God is (3003–15). It constitutes Theseus'
defence of the marriage with which the tale ends. The Renaissance,
however, presents the same theory with a very different emphasis: the
cycle of decay and rebirth which for Chaucer's Theseus was the best a
fallen world could do to replace its lost perfection was, for the Platonist, less of a falling off and the expression of a more positive idealism.
Death and birth occur because the lowest chaos burns with a divinely
implanted love of form, but is prevented by its corruptible nature from
retaining any one form permanently. Hence, in the words of Leone,
'first matter, in its insatiable desire to partake of divine beauty by the
reception of forms, moves continually from one form to another in
the unceasing circular motion of generation and corruption' (p. 337).
The simple need to survive is transmuted into the source of a fuller, more
diversified being and a truly Lucretian plenitude. It is for this reason
that Nature declares Mutability to be the means by which all things
'their being doe dilate' at the end of *The Faerie Queene* (VII, VII, 58).

A cosmology such as this, based on a belief in the immanence of the divine form within the material cover, implies a deep sense of the divine love which implanted it there. The Platonists were especially conscious of God's overflowing love which kindled a mutual love in form and chaos, so that the descent of the one was met by the willing embraces of the other. From this comes the beautiful conception of the circle of love, which is described with such lyricism by Leone, for example:

so love originates from the primal Father of the universe, and from Him is successively imparted, like the gift of a father to his child, from the greater to the less and from the perfect to the imperfect, or more properly, from the more beautiful to the less beautiful, that the perfection and beauty of the Godhead may be diffused in the highest measure possible throughout every degree of being ... and this process is continued throughout the whole of the first half-circle down to chaos, the least of all being. And thence love begins to ascend through the second half circle, from the lower to the higher and from the imperfect to the perfect that it may achieve its perfection, and from the less to the more beautiful that it may enjoy its beauty.   (p. 451)

It is God's overflowing love which brings and holds form and first matter together, and if that love were withdrawn the whole universe would crumble back into its constituent formless atoms. There is a magnificent and tragic arrogance in Othello's assertion that:

> ... when I love thee not,
> Chaos is come again.
> (III, III, 91)

For the Platonist especially, love forms the motive of everything: the stone falls to the earth out of its love of its mother; the fire rises through love of the higher sphere; the Ptolemaic spheres which carry the planets in their courses revolve within each other through their desire to touch each other as completely as possible, and make their music because of their pleasure in the process; the lamb flees the wolf not out of hatred of the wolf but out of love of itself (Ficino, III, IV, p. 153). It is an extreme form of idealism which springs from a profound sense of the immanence of God in his universe, the divine just below the surface of each created thing; and a favourite image was that of the statue standing complete within the rough block of stone, only waiting for the sculptor to set it free. Inevitably, therefore, the Platonists were conscious of the beauty of the creation, and raised a new hymn in its praise, of which Castiglione's words in the *Courtier* are typical:

Beside other things therfore it giveth a great praise to the world, in saying that it is beautifull. It is praysed, in saying the beautifull heaven, beautifull earth, beautifull sea, beautifull rivers, beautifull woodes, trees, gardens, beautifull cities, beautifull churches, houses, armies. In conclusion, this comely and holy beautie is a wondrous setting out of everie thing.   (p. 310)

Some of this religious idealism inevitably coloured and ennobled the concept of human love. If beauty is, by definition, the 'splendour of the divine forms', and love the desire which all chaos feels for it, then human love springs from the same sacred impulse and is the inevitable human reaction to the glimpse of divinity manifested in its most transparent image, the beauty of a woman's face. 'All true love is honourable and every lover virtuous,' says Ficino, and Berowne's impassioned defence of the ennobling power of love in *Love's Labour's Lost*, (IV, III, 300–50) is grounded on the same Platonic assumptions. The hyperboles of love, therefore, the lover's sleepless agonies, his idealisation and worship of his mistress, are all fitting, since it is God he is seeking within the mortal mistress, and she is a goddess in more than name alone. In this way the traditional behaviour of the lover in terms of the old Courtly code received a new philosophical sanction and Cupid gained in sanctity. In this metamorphosis Petrarch played a vital role: his account of his love for Laura is conceived in terms of the worship and fidelity belonging to the Courtly code, but Petrarch stopped, so to speak, at Book III of *Troilus and Criseyde*, preferring to explore the psychology of romantic frustration rather than to carry on to the physical conclusion on which Courtly love insisted. For this reason his sonnets were in harmony with the new Platonic idealism and formed a bridge between old and new. One can see this relationship between Courtly and Platonic love in the last two books of the *Courtier*. Book III discusses the perfect woman of the court, the complement of the perfect courtier; and her image involves the idealism and reverence common to both the Courtly and the Platonic traditions, as well as the secrecy which belongs only to the former. Book IV, however, gives a purely Platonic picture of love. The theme of Bembo's great speech in defence of love is the holiness of beauty: 'I say that beautie commeth of God, and is like a circle, the goodnesse whereof is the Centre' (p. 308). The lover begins with his mistress' beauty but uses it 'for a stayre (as it were) to climbe up to another farre higher than it', by which means he ultimately transcends the physical altogether and climbs to an ecstatic union with God which renders even the most perfect earthly beauty contemptible. 'Whereupon being made dimme with this greater light, he shall not passe upon the lesser, and burning in a more excellent flame, he shall litle esteeme it, that hee set great store by at the first' (p. 318). The mistress of the sonnet or of Courtly love would scarcely be gratified by a lover who seeks universal beauty because he recognises 'what a straight bond it is to bee alwaies in the trouble to behold the beautie of one bodie alone' (p. 317). But Bembo, it must be remembered, is describing the love proper to an old man, and even that originates in physical fulfilment. He admits that young men neither can nor should be so philosophical about the passion. Neo-Platonism, though idealistic, had a place for the body: as God first contemplated his own beauty and then propagated it, so too may the lover propagate the divine beauty once he has recognised it. There are two Venuses, the elder Venus Urania, the heavenly Venus who contemplates the divine beauty, and her younger sister, Venus Dione, the Venus Genetrix who follows with generation (Ficino, II, VII, p. 142). They are sisters and both of them holy because they represent related aspects of the same divinity. It is in terms of this that Shakespeare reproaches his young man of the sonnets for 'having traffic with thyself alone' (IV) and not handing on the largesse which Nature gave him; and Donne gives the conception a typically ironic twist when he writes that 'Love sometimes would contemplate, sometimes do' (*Loves Growth*). For the Platonist, contemplation implies generation, and both are distinct from lust, which is carnal desire without the justifying idealism. Leone's Platonic philosophy of love is nearer to Christianity than is Courtly love in that it bids the lover be fruitful and multiply.

There is little sense of the Fall in Renaissance Platonism, and this is the source of such claims to human greatness as are made in Pico della Mirandola's famous *Oration on the Dignity of Man* of 1486. Man was created last of all things, says Pico, and having a mind, a soul and a body, he contains the whole of creation within himself and has the freedom to live at whatever level of the universe he chooses, whether at that of the animals or at that of God himself:

When man came into life, the Father endowed him with all kinds of seeds and with the germs of every way of life. Whatever seeds each man cultivates will grow and bear fruit in him. If these seeds are vegetative, he will be like a plant; if they are sensitive, he will become like the beasts; if they are rational, he will become like a heavenly creature; if intellectual, he will be an angel and a son of God. And if, content with the lot of no created being, he withdraws into the centre of his own oneness, his spirit, made one with God in the solitary darkness of the Father, which is above all things, will surpass all things.

(*Renaissance Reader*, p. 479)

These ideas had a profound influence in northern Europe, especially after the middle of the sixteenth century, but they were rarely accepted so completely as in Italy, and it is a commonplace that northern Humanism from the beginning was more orthodoxly Christian. Erasmus used his Greek to produce his new Greek Testament which challenged the authority of the Latin Vulgate, and most of the Oxford reformers were in Holy Orders: they saw in Humanism and particularly in Greek philosophy a means of overthrowing the aridities of late scholasticism and allowing the true primitive christianity to bloom again. The initial results of Humanism in England were less literary than educational, in the form of new schools and colleges designed to promote the Christian way of life. It is important to recognise, how-ever, that there was little sense of a conflict between Humanism and Christianity at this stage, but that the two gave each other support. Thomas More, for example, attacked the so-called Trojans who formed the hard core of scholastic resistance to Greek and humanist studies at Oxford. 'No one has ever claimed than a man needed Greek and Latin, or indeed any education in order to be saved', he admits; 'Still, this education which he (his opponent) calls secular does train the soul in virtue' (Nugent, pp. 68–9). In the same way, Bishop Fox insisted in the statutes of Corpus Christi College, Oxford, which he founded in 1517, that it should be a bee-garden wherein were three skilful herbal-ists: the teacher of Latin, the reader of Greek, 'whom we place in our bee-garden expressly because the holy ordinaunces have established and commanded most suitably for good learning and Christian litera-ture'; finally, the reader of sacred Divinity 'whom it behoves the other gardeners to obey, wait on, and serve' (Nugent, pp. 32–4). The liberal Christian quality of early Tudor humanism set its stamp on sixteenth-century education, and Elyot's *Governor* or Ascham's *Scholemaster* are typical products later in the century.

The Reformation, however, disturbed this state of harmony. Luther and Calvin were not anti-Humanist, and many of their criticisms of the Catholic church were accepted by Humanists such as More and Erasmus within the church itself. All agreed, for example, that the living scriptures were lost under the weight of scholastic disputation, the spirit obscured by the letter, and that the sale of indulgences for sins before they were even committed reduced atonement to some-thing entirely mechanical. The necessity of reform was everywhere accepted, but Luther was more radical in his programme. The medieval Catholic church had absorbed too much of classical thought to see man as totally corrupt. The Fall, by God's Grace, was only a partial one, and all Adam's seed still inherited some degree of reason and free will, some innate potentiality for good by virtue of which man could earn salvation. For the Catholic, Justification was by Merit as well as by Faith, and the Christian on his pilgrimage through life could co-operate with God in the achievement of his own redemption. The medieval Everyman, it will be remembered, took his good deeds with him beyond the grave. Luther, however, obsessed by his own personal sense of sin and sceptical of the value of a merit which could be bought and sold, denied the orthodox conception of the Fall. For him it was total, rendering man utterly corrupt in mind and will, unable by his own powers to perform or even desire any act of virtue. There can be no Justification by Merit, because man is incapable of merit by his own efforts, and only those can be saved whom God takes by the hand and re-fashions out of his own goodness. This is the faith which justifies, but it comes from God alone and man can have no say in its achievement. In his debate with Luther about free will Erasmus held the orthodox Catholic doctrine which 'leaves to the human will, when it does not lack divine grace, a certain place in the unfolding of the act' (*Renaissance Reader*, p. 686, *On Free Will*). In reply, Luther asserts the bondage of the will and insists that there can be no hope for man until 'he comes to know that his salvation is utterly beyond his own powers, counsel, endeavours, will and works and absolutely depending on the will, counsel, pleasure and work of another, that is God only' (*The Bondage of the Will, Renaissance Reader*, p. 700). The human will, he continues, is like a beast: 'If God sit thereon, it wills and goes where God will . . . If Satan sit thereon, it wills and goes as Satan will. Nor is it in the power of his own will to choose to which rider it will run' (Ibid., p. 703). Luther does not, of course, deny the fact of good works. Those who are 'sweetly breathed on' by the spirit of God are changed in will and do good' not from compulsion but responsively, from pure willingness, inclination and accord; so that it cannot be turned another way by anything contrary' (Ibid., p. 702). But such virtue is a result of salvation, not a cause of it, and can have no merit in the medieval sense. The Thirty-Nine Articles of the Elizabethan church insist that good works performed before Justification are not pleasant to God and partake of the nature of sin. Calvin too starts with these assumptions and develops out of them logically his own statement of the great doctrines of Predestination and Election. If there is nothing man can do towards his own salvation, then God must have chosen from the beginning of time those whom he will save and those to be damned. It demanded a desperate faith or an astonishing certitude to trust one's soul to God in this way, and to most Catholics the reformed religion seemed an abrogation of human responsibility, leading either to despair or to licentiousness. Thomas More gives an amusing picture of a protestant sect for whom Justification by Faith without the need of Merit was only too easy a process:

... they have found out so easy a way to heaven as to take no thought but make merry nor take no penance at all, but set them down and drink well for our Saviour's sake, set cock a-hoop and fill in all the cups at once, and then let Christ's Passion pay for all the scot.   (*Dialogue of Comfort*, p. 231)

The assumptions of Luther and Calvin about the fallen nature of man were opposed to those of Neo-Platonism and of classical philosophy in general; and by the end of the sixteenth century the harmony between Classic and Christian was less stable than it had been a century before. A comparison between More's *Utopia* and Marlowe's *Dr Faustus* or Book II of *The Faerie Queene* will indicate the development. More's Epicurean Utopeans become Christians as soon as they are shown the Gospels, without needing to make any essential change in their way of life; but Marlowe and Spenser alike weigh the classical ideal of self-sufficiency against the Christian conception of the Fall and brand the former a deadly sin. Humanism itself poses a moral problem, and the Protestant Humanist of the later sixteenth century was faced with a dilemma which the new Anglican church gave him little help in solving. Elizabeth's church settlement was an instrument of policy designed to admit all except the extremists rather than to give a precise definition of orthodoxy. The Thirty-Nine Articles insist on Justification by Faith and not by Works, for example, but are evasive concerning Free Will, Predestination, Election, and the extent to which the Christian can be responsible himself for achieving a faith which justifies. The articles reiterate that good works spring from and are a sign of a true and lively faith; but they warn the Christian at the same time not to try to prove his faith to himself by the commission of Works of Supererogation—in other words, good works in excess of what God's commandments demand. The final sanction for all our actions must be the Scriptures: 'that Will of God is to be followed, which we have expressly declared unto us in the Word of God'; but this was no easy matter, as we can see from Bunyan's struggles to reconcile conflicting texts, in the next century. The very accessibility of the scriptures threw a new responsibility on to the individual in forcing him to test his daily actions by the touchstone of the Bible with a rigour which had not previously been demanded of the layman. For those who were conscious of being numbered among the Elect, the reformed creeds offered a fresh and personal assurance of the love of God; but the less confident followers found some cause for uneasiness in a religion which predestined the greater part of mankind to eternal damnation, irrespective of their actions. The new protestant had a more difficult path to tread than the medieval Catholic. Whereas the medieval man had the way of the monastery open to him if he chose the religious life, and every kind of ecclesiastical and theological support to help him through the secular life, the protestant had to thread his uncertain way through the world by the light of his own interpretation of the scriptures, no longer sheltered in the bosom of a ghostly community which safeguarded him from the minute of his birth to the last moment of Extreme Unction and even beyond. The medieval Everyman has the dignity and restraint of basic security; the sins are clearly known, the recognised remedies available at the right time and in the right order. He has no need to ask Bunyan's agonised question, ' What shall I do to be saved?'

The poetry of the later sixteenth century reflects this moral incertitude, at its most serious, and seeks to cure it. The Renaissance conception of poetry was a very elevated one: the poet was no longer the purveyor of honest recreation which had been his primary role in the Middle Ages; the humanists credited the Serious poet with possession of the Divine Fury and looked up to him as to the vates, the divinely inspired Maker civilising barbarous nations with his eloquence. In Book VI of *The Faerie Queene* the poet, Colin, pipes to the dancing of the Graces but they vanish at the approach of an ordinary mortal; and Sidney's *Apologie* is based upon this conception of poet as seer and rhetorician combined. The 'right' poet can see beyond the material cover to the divine forms within creation and, like Nature herself, creates a golden world which is nearer to the unfallen world of Eden than that in which we live. This new creation mingles delight with instruction and by this means draws men inevitably towards virtue:

... our Poet ... dooth not only show the way, but giveth so sweete a prospect into the way, as will intice any man to enter into it ... hee commeth to you with words sent in delightful proportion ... with a tale forsooth he commeth unto you, with a tale which holdeth children from play, and old men from the chimney corner. And, pretending no more, doth intende the winning of the mind from wickednesse to vertue.   (p. 172)

For this reason men turned to poetry and looked for moral guidance from it perhaps more than at any other period. The moral interpretations which Sir John Harington appended to his translation of the more doubtful portions of the *Orlando Furioso* should not be dismissed as

hypocrisy; they are a response to the need which the age felt to justify
the active life in terms of morality and theology. Renaissance secular
poetry is more didactic than that of the Middle Ages, and the degree
of change can be measured by the difference between the *Canterbury Tales*
and *The Faerie Queene*: the Renaissance poet pronounces with greater
authority on moral affairs, and does so by right of his own calling as a
poet; he does not need to speak through the mouthpiece of the poor
parson or to be the voice of religious orthodoxy. Poetry lacking this
serious moral purpose was enjoyed but not taken very seriously; but
poetry possessing it aroused an almost Arnoldian reverence as the
arbiter and touchstone of values. Daniel's great poem *Musophilus* is
an argument between a lover of poetry and a practical man of affairs
who prefers action to thought:

> Whilst timorous knowledge stands considering,
> Audacious ignorance hath done the deed. (490)

The lover of the Muses replies in terms which are a curious anticipation
of *Culture and Anarchy* in the nineteenth century. The times, he says,
are full of confusion, with everyone busy, but to what end or by what
criteria of values nobody knows:

> Gath'ring, incroching, wresting, joining to,
> Destroying, building, decking, furnishing,
> Repairing, altring, and so much a do
> To his soules toile, and bodies travailing:
> And all this doth he little knowing who
> Fortune ordaines to have th' inheriting.
> (111–16)

Poetry alone can separate the true from the false and give to human
action coherency and moral value, taking the true degree:

> Of the just height of swolne mortalitie
> Right as it is, not as it seems to be.
> (615)

It is a proud boast, but one of which Elizabethan poetry showed itself
worthy.

2

POETIC THEORY AND PRACTICE

We have seen that the Renaissance began with the patriotism of the Italian city states, and spread through Europe on the rising tide of national self consciousness. This is apparent in the patriotic concern for the quality of the vernacular tongue which found explicit expression in Italy as early as Dante's *De Vulgari eloquentia* but became a major issue in northern Europe only in the sixteenth century. It is difficult for us nowadays to think in terms of any language but our own, but it must be remembered that the great mantle of Latin had covered Christendom for fifteen hundred years, and that even by the sixteenth century it was still the accredited medium of scholarship. The vernaculars, although they had become the language of government and the law, were still to win their spurs in the fields of literature and learning, and the achievement of this patriotic ideal was a main Renaissance preoccupation.

The first need of the vernaculars was to widen their vocabularies, and the fifteenth and sixteenth centuries saw a great expansion of their range, as new words were coined or old ones appropriated from outside sources. This indeed is one of the explicit aims of Elyot's *Governor*, to provide English with an adequate vocabulary for the discussion of moral philosphy, and he borrows words from Latin, finds English forms for them and explains their meaning. One of the great controversies of the period raged over the question of where the new words should come from, and sixteenth-century England was torn between the factions of those who wanted to keep the language pure and those who were prepared to borrow what their opponents contemptuously called 'Inkehorne Termes' out of Latin, Greek or living European languages. With our after-knowledge, we are apt to laugh at sixteenth-century purists like Sir John Cheke who preferred the clumsiest coinages from the native stock to any foreign imports; but his attitude was not unreasonable. One has only to read *The Governor* or Ben Jonson's *Poetaster* to see that many of the imported words dropped out of circulation at once because there was no necessity for them, and Shakespeare's Osric demonstrates that much inkehorne language was no more than affectation. Moreover, the new printing presses were concentrated in London, Oxford and Cambridge, which naturally gave preference to the south-eastern dialect of English, 'the usuall speach of the Court, and that of London and the shires lying about London within lx myles, and not much above' (Puttenham, III, iv, p. 145). As with the spread of the King's English by means of the BBC, so the monopoly of print enjoyed by the London dialect tended to discredit other dialects and cause many good old words either to be dropped altogether or relegated to the level of slang. Caxton, when he began to translate at the end of the fifteenth century, was faced with the problem of a language already rapidly changing in this way, as exemplified in the curious story he tells in his Preface to the *Eneydos* of the merchant who tried to buy eggs from the country-woman who knew them only as old English 'eyren'. But the new words were often stranger than the old, and the anonymous author of the Preface to Spenser's *Shepheardes Calender* voices a just complaint of his age when he argues that English is giving away with one hand what it takes in with the other. Many 'good and natural English words', he argues, have been 'cleane disherited', and the gap filled by words of foreign origin which makes a 'hodgepodge' of the language. For this reason the sixteenth century was acutely aware of the distinction between current and obsolete words, and conscious archaism became a constituent of both the heroic and the pastoral styles.

The same spirit of nationalism is apparent in Renaissance attitudes towards the vernacular literature. The early Humanists tried to emulate the classics in the classical languages, and there were the great Latinists such as Valla or Mantuan, who wrote Eclogues like Virgil or orations like Cicero. By 1500, however, the sterility of this aim had become apparent, and the writers sought increasingly to emulate in the modern vernaculars what the ancients had achieved in theirs. The new romantic epic of Ariosto and the enormous popularity of Petrarch's vernacular love poems mark the change. In France Du Bellay's *La Defense et Illustration de la langue Francoyse*, which forms the manifesto of the Pléiade in the middle of the century, asserts the potential literary greatness of the French language and calls for the wholesale imitation of the classics

in French. In England, where the full impact of this literary Humanism was not felt for another twenty-five years, Sidney surveys English
literature to date in his *Apologie for Poetrie* and asks sadly 'why England
(the Mother of excellent mindes) should bee growne so hard a step-
mother to Poets' (p. 193). Puttenham's *Arte of English Poesie*, printed
in 1589 but begun back in the sixties, has as the heading of its second
chapter, 'That there may be an Art of our English Poesie as well as
there is of the Latine and Greeke', and goes on to ask, 'why should not
Poesie be a vulgar Art with us as well as with the Greekes and Latines,
our language admitting no fewer rules and nice diversities than theirs?'
(p. 5). The Italian Humanist felt that Latin literature was, in a sense, his
own and by 1550 was conscious that Italy had already produced a
vernacular literature which could stand comparison with the classics.
The northern countries, however, were less confident; in England
only Chaucer was generally accepted as a major writer and even his
language was out of date, and Nashe dismisses the whole of English
medieval literature in a typical hyperbole: 'Chaucer, Lydgate, Gower
with such like, that lived under the tirranie of ignorance' (Gregory
Smith, I, p. 318). However great the native poets were, they wrote in a
rude and barbaric language, so that most Englishmen suffered from an
inferiority complex when faced with the manifest superiority of
classical literature.

It is important to recognise, also, that through printing, classical
literature was presented suddenly, in its entirety, accompanied by a
body of authoritative criticism which included Horace, Aristotle's
Poetics and the great mass of literary criticism of the Italian Renaissance
based on them. This produced in the sixteenth-century writer a very
self-conscious, analytical approach to his work; he turned to the great
writers of the past and to their critics to see how a thing should be
done and shaped his own work accordingly. For this reason, perhaps,
the Horatian doctrine of the literary 'kinds' made an especial appeal,
with its tidy division of literature into the general categories of high,
mean and low, and the further subdivision of these into the traditional
poetic genres. The first book of Puttenham's *Arte* is largely concerned
with defining these poetic 'kinds', each with its appropriate range of
subject-matter, level of language and rules for composition. Beginning
with a chapter 'Of poemes and their sundry formes . . .' (p. 25)
Puttenham goes on to consider 'The forme of Poeticall rejoysings',
'The forme of Poeticall lamentations', 'Of the Shepheards or pastorall
Poesie called Eglogue', 'In what forme of Poesie the amorous affections
and allurements were uttered', and many others. It is on the basis of
these traditional categories that Sidney rejected tragi-comedy as

'neither right tragedies nor right comedies', and Shakespeare mocked the rigidity of the system in Polonius' catalogue of 'tragical-comical-historical-pastoral'. In Chaucer's most original work the poetic form is organic, rising out of the subject itself: *Troilus and Criseyde* reproduces in the curve of the story 'From wo to wele, and after out of joie' the turning of Fortune's wheel which is its subject; and the *Canterbury Tales* is panoramic in structure because its subject is all mankind. In contrast, the Elizabethan poet starts with a set of pre-fabricated moulds, such as eclogue, ode, elegy or satire, and, selecting the one traditionally associated with his poetic intention, pours his material into it. The Renaissance brought an enclosing, not a liberation, of literature, but this was no bad thing. Elizabethan poetry rarely suffers from the formlessness which afflicts much medieval literature; and the traditional forms carried with them the whole authority of classical practice, together with the admiration which it inspired, so that they seemed the natural and inevitable means of expression. The pastoral convention was a release and a stimulus to Milton's genius when he wrote *Lycidas*; it is not until a convention becomes worn out, as the Pastoral convention had by the time of Dr Johnson, that it ceases to be a conductor of emotion and seems artificial; and this was far from being the case in the sixteenth century. At that stage the 'kinds' offered the poet a greater variety of modes of expression than had been known in England before.

The recognised method of mastering the new techniques was Imitation, a term familiar to poets and rhetoricians since classical times. The writer turns to his chosen model but without the obligation to reproduce it faithfully which belongs to the translator. Du Bellay defines the method in his *Defence*: the imitator must project himself into the situation from which the original poem sprang, and then develop it in the same way and with the same degree of detail, but in terms of his own personality and background—what Du Bellay calls 'devouring . . . digesting . . . converting into blood and nurture' (I, VII, p. 171). To change the metaphor, the poet breaks up his model into its basic bricks and then rebuilds them into a new building with the same number of rooms and serving the same purpose, but of his own personal design. Imitation thus transfers a literary form out of one civilisation into the terms of another without destroying the original pattern. A very great part of Elizabethan poetry consists of 'imitation' in this sense, taken from Theocritus or Virgil, Petrarch, Ariosto or Mantuan. Because the full impact of Humanism came late to England, often by a circuitous route through Italy and France, English poetry is often an imitation of an imitation, modelling itself on

those continental poets who had already imitated the classics, or who
had achieved an equal greatness in their own right. The gods of the
English poetic Renaissance were Petrarch, Ariosto and Ronsard as
much as Theocritus or Virgil. The point is illustrated by the poetry of
Spenser, which epitomises this as well as so many other aspects of the
Renaissance. His *Shepheardes Calender* is built out of Marot, Mantuan,
Virgil and Theocritus; his *Complaints* out of Petrarch and Du Bellay,
and for *The Faerie Queene* he has devoured and digested the whole
range of previous heroic poems, from Homer to Tasso.

This is a result both of the circulation of books and of the cosmopoli-
tan nature of English society, especially in the second half of the century.
The Grand Tour, taking in France and Italy, was the usual way of
finishing off one's education, and in this way Sidney, for example,
gained his first-hand knowledge of French and Italian culture. At home,
too, London, as a growing centre of commerce, was full of foreigners—
Italians like Florio, refugee Huguenots, French courtiers concerned
with the Anjou marriage, or Flemings in flight from the Low Countries,
such as Van der Noodt, who gave Spenser his first commission. In
addition, the endless military and diplomatic missions to the continent
and the flood of foreign books made the teaching of foreign languages
almost a major industry. English literature has never been more cosmo-
politan than it was in the last twenty years of the sixteenth century, to
its own undoubted profit.

The Elizabethan poet, then, had a great variety of forms to assimilate,
and in this way the ode, the elegy, the sonnet, the satire, the eclogue,
the epigram and the heroic poem were all absorbed into the English
tradition in a surprisingly short time. The process was even extended
beyond foreign literatures to include earlier periods of England.
Spenser occasionally imitated Chaucer and was in his turn imitated by
such writers as Barnefield. Hardin Craig in his book *The Enchanted
Glass* has compared Elizabethan literature to a cannibal chief who
throve by absorbing the bodies of his rivals, and indeed the literature
of the whole century is composed of the digested scraps of other modes
and periods. One has only to compare the simple songs and sonnets of
which the early *Tottel's Miscellany* is composed with the variety of
madrigals, eclogues, pindarics, anacreontics, epigrams and elegies
which make up Davison's *Poetical Rhapsody* of 1602 to see how far
poetry had moved.

A literature of this kind presupposes an attitude to poetry very
different from our own, and the Renaissance had little interest in
originality as it is understood and prized today, although most of the
poetic 'Imitations' did, in fact, take on a profoundly original colouring

in the process of transformation. Yet it is doubtful whether the Elizabethans prized their writing for this quality. They seem rather to have delighted in the echoes of other literatures in which their poetry abounds, finding in them a proof that English was at last able to do what the more polite and advanced nations had done already. Francis Meres' famous *Palladis Tamia* shows an almost obsessive precision in coupling contemporary names with those of their classical parallels. The reader enjoyed the sense of solidarity with the past which an imitation of Virgil or Juvenal gave him, and the poets built upon the ability to recognise verbal echoes. In consequence the new and the old agreed together well and shaded imperceptibly into each other. The formal satire took over from the great tradition of native satire from Chaucer onwards; the new pastoral had behind it both the realism of the medieval shepherd plays and the perpetual spring of the gardens of Courtly love; the Petrarchan sonnet developed out of the medieval love poem. The great strength of sixteenth-century English poetry lies in its ability to fuse the native and the humanist strains.

The especial importance of rhetoric to poetry in the sixteenth century is a further point to be recognised. Aristotle had distinguished poetry from rhetoric by their different functions, poetry being an art of imitation for the purpose of giving pleasure and having the creation of fiction as its very essence; rhetoric being concerned with persuasion and tied to literal truth. Both, however, employed the same basic verbal techniques of the rhetorical figures and tropes, though poetry used a selection appropriate to its particular function. By Horace's time poetry had been drawn more into the orbit of oratory and had taken on some of its functions; Horace's famous dictum that the job of poetry is to teach by pleasing represents a fusion between poetic and rhetorical theory. From thereon the two arts stayed very close together. In the Middle Ages rhetoric declined in importance as oratory ceased to play a major part in public life and the conduct of the state; the logic which in Aristotle or Quintilian formed the basis of its persuasive power was absorbed into the separate study of dialectic, and rhetoric itself became increasingly synonymous with mere verbal embellishment. Poetic theory goes the same way: the standard medieval poetic, Geoffrey de Vinsauf's *Poetica Nova*, is mainly concerned with the figures of speech, the 'colours' of rhetoric by which the poet may embellish his tale. With the Renaissance, however, rhetoric once more became a public art, and skill in oratory a necessity for anyone who would get on in the new world of public debate. 'The utility that a nobleman shall have by reading these orators is that when he shall hap to reason in counsel, or shall speak in a great audience or to strange

ambassadors of great princes, he shall not be constrained to speak words
sudden and disordered, but shall bestow them aptly and in their
places', says Elyot (p. 35), and makes a training in classic rhetoric an
essential part of the education of his Governor. The rediscovery of
Quintilian and the full texts of Cicero showed the part which rhetoric
had once played in society and revealed again the full range of its
possibilities. The new rhetorics, of which there are many in the
sixteenth century, mark a return to the original classical standards.

The best of these in English is Thomas Wilson's *Art of Rhetoric*
published in 1553, and a word about its contents and terminology is of
help in the study of sixteenth-century poetry. Wilson treats rhetoric
under its five traditional divisions. The first and main part is Invention,
literally the finding out of the materials and arguments relevant to
the particular oration. For this the orator needs a training in logic and a
knowledge of the Aristotelian 'places', the categories under which the
subject of any enquiry may be classified—the genus, the species, the
time when, the place where, things similar, things contrary, etc. They
offer the orator a drill by means of which he can investigate the subject
under consideration and select those aspects of it which are relevant
to his purpose. The second part of rhetoric, Disposition, is concerned
with the presentation of the materials which invention has discovered,
and the selection of the best methods in each particular instance.
These will be dictated by the function of the speech, the nature of the
audience, the type of occasion for which it is designed and so forth.
A speech in the Queen's Council will be more judicial than one
designed for a court of law; a speech designed to persuade a judge will
need more logic and less emotion than one designed to dazzle a jury.
It was at the level of Disposition that Brutus failed and Mark Antony
succeeded. Elocution, the third part, is concerned with the choice of
language once invention and disposition have done their work, and
provides the orator with the figures and tropes from which he may
produce the high or low, the plain or flowery style appropriate to his
task. The remaining two divisions of Rhetoric, Memory and Utterance, though relevant to the art of the orator and the actor, are not of
direct concern to the poet; the first three, however, are, for poetry is
seen as a special type of rhetoric, different in intention but using the
same fundamental techniques. Puttenham defines poetry in terms of
rhetoric; it is, he says:

a maner of utterance more eloquent and rethoricall than the ordinarie prose,
which we use in our daily talke: because it is decked and set out with all maner
of fresh colours and figures, which maketh that it sooner invegleth the judge-

ment of man, and carrieth his opinion this way and that . . .   (I, iv, p. 8)

His *Arte of English Poesie* is in essence a textbook of rhetoric, in which
the emphasis falls on style because poetry, persuading primarily by
pleasure and not tied to literal truth, will necessarily luxuriate in the
beauties of fine language. Underneath, however, one can trace the
standard rhetorical divisions. The opening section dealing with the
functions and subjects of poetry corresponds to Invention; the analysis
of the poetic 'kinds' which follows is Disposition, and the long third
book dealing with figures of speech is Elocution. Throughout, the
figures of speech are continually related back to the rhetorical intentions
of the poem as a whole. Many of them, for instance, are figures of
logic; such are 'Etiologia, or the tell cause', 'Paramologia, or the
figure of admittance', a figure 'much used by our English pleaders in
the Star Chamber and Chancery'; 'Dialesis, the dismembrer . . . not
unlike the *dilemma* of the Logicians', and many more. Some of the
figures are not simple verbal structures at all but techniques for
strengthening an argument: 'Parecnasis, or the straggler', for example,
is delaying the main point of your argument so that you may produce
it later when it is least expected; and Procatalepsis, 'the figure of
Presupposal', is anticipating your opponent's argument before he has
time to state it. Figures such as these abound not only in the poetry of
genuine argument but in the sonnet too which, as we shall see later,
was more concerned with the witty presentation of ideas than with
the expression of love longing. Spenser, for example, often begins his
sonnets with a dilemma, such as 'Is it her nature, or is it her will . . .'
(XLI) or 'Shall I then silent be, or shall I speake? . . .' (XLIII) and
solves it by a process of argument in which logic is put to strange uses.
Sidney loves to follow a thread of logic through to a paradoxical
conclusion: when Stella declares that out of her great love for Astrophil
she will give him up rather than spoil his career, he replies: 'Deare,
love me not, that you may love me more' (62). With similar logic he
argues that the double negative of Stella's refusal, 'No, No!' is really
an acceptance, 'For Grammer says . . . That in one speech two Nega-
tives affairm' (63). Or Constable, being told that it is an impossibility
for his Diana ever to love him, proves by a syllogism that she may, for
'Gods only doe impossibilityes' and thus, 'A goddesse thou shalt prove
and happie I' (*Diana*, p. 134). The Elizabethan sonnet owes its close-
knit texture to this use of rhetoric.

It should be remembered, too, that 'things like' form one of the
places of logic by means of which a definition can be established; a
comparison places the things compared into a more general category

which, through the common point of likeness, defines some aspect of
their nature. Rosamond Tuve has shown, in her *Elizabethan and
Metaphysical Imagery*, the extent to which logic contributes to the
defining quality of Elizabethan metaphor and its extended form,
allegory. Puttenham's title for it—Metaphora, or the figure of trans-
port—and his example of allegory, 'as for example if we should call the
commonwealth, a shippe; the Prince a Pilot, the Counsellours mariners,
the stormes warres ...' (III, xviii, p. 187), draw attention to this
quality. When Shelley compares the grief of the lonely heart to 'sad
dirges/Like the wind through a ruined cell' he is not seeking to
establish a precise analogy between an empty heart and a hollow cave
so much as to present a roughly analogous object which shall convey an
appropriate emotion in a more intense form. When, however, Barnefield describes a woman's painted face he does so in images which
define with great precision the deceitfulness and prostitution which
he associates with woman's painting:

> Ill-worshipt Idoll, false Imagerie,
> Ensign of vice, to thine own selfe a lier,
> Silent Inchaunter, mindes anatomie,
> Sly Bawd to Lust, Pander to Infamie ...
> (*Complaint of Chastitie*)

In the same way, Shakespeare's row of images defining the 'innocent
sleep' in *Macbeth*, or Donne's comparison of lovers to compasses,
pinpoint with great accuracy those aspects with which the poets are
concerned. The writer is always conscious of the two sides of his
comparison—the object which he is describing and the image in terms
of which he is describing it—and seeks, by exploring the inter-relation-
ship, to illuminate the natures of both, or, in more flippant forms of
verse, to show off his wit by the invention of ingenious parallels.
Sidney, for example, draws a comparison between himself riding his
horse and himself ridden by love. 'A horsman to my horse, a horse to
Love' (49). Starting from this comparison he establishes a most accurate
and logical series of analogies between himself and the animal: the
reins and bit which control the horse's motions are 'in me, poore
beast', the humble and reverent thought which control his passion;
the curb is his fear,

> ... but with guilt bosse above
> Of Hope, which makes it seeme faire to the eye.

Love's whip is Sidney's own desire, the saddle, his fancy; the girths which hold it in place, his memories; and by this means, love 'spurres with sharpe desire my hart'. The allegory allows Sidney to demonstrate his wit, and at the same time expresses his sense of the slightly ridiculous role he feels himself to be playing.

All good Elizabethan extended metaphor depends upon the power of subject and image to maintain the relationship to each other at all stages of their parallel development, so that with each new cross-reference, the identity of the two becomes more complete. In this way, for example, Donne's comparison of lovers to the legs of a pair of compasses in his *Valediction: forbidding Mourning* begins as a simile:

> If they be two, they are two so
> As stiffe twin compasses are two ...

but develops inevitably into the complete fusion of metaphor:

> Thy firmnes makes my circle just,
> And makes me end, where I begunne.

Often the writers show a special virtuosity in linking the two sides of a comparison by the use of terms common to both, so that the relationship is cemented by means of a pun. In this way, Barnes compares his mistress' face to a calendar which shows, in the variety of its expressions, all the days of the year: the Sundays are her smiles, the working days her frowns, numbering 'six to one more than the rest', and in conclusion, he looks forward to his Leap Year:

> When all my cares I overleap and feast
> With her, fruition....
> (Parth, LXXXIV)

The audacious pun on 'leap' brings the two sides of the comparison together with a snap, just as the pun on 'strait' does in Donne's medical voyage over his own sick body—'*Per fretum febris*, by these streits to die'. Such an attitude towards metaphor, and such virtuosity in its handling, springs from the training in Rhetoric on which the art of poetry was grounded.

The Elizabethan poet, therefore, for whom these rhetorical techniques were second nature, approached the writing of a poem as if it were a special kind of oratory. There is a statement to be made and he invokes the appropriate aids. Invention helps him to examine the nature of his subject; Disposition, to choose the best method of presentation and so the poetic 'kind' in terms of which it should be

B

treated; and Elocution, to select the fitting level of style. The guiding
principle is Decorum, a key term in Renaissance criticism, implying
the matching of means to ends within the framework of rhetorical
practice. Puttenham describes in detail 'which matters be hie and loftie,
which be but meane, and which be low and base, to the intent the
stiles may be fashioned to the matters and keep their decorum and
good proportion in every respect' (III, V, pp. 149–50). There is little
room for the spontaneous overflow of powerful feelings in the
Elizabethan art of poetry; a poem is a highly deliberate and formal
artefact in which vocabulary, style and logic are all harnessed to a
specific end, whether of praising a mistress, denigrating a vice, or telling
a story.

On the surface, this dominance of the concept of decorum might
seem to imply a cold and mechanical attitude towards poetry, but in
practice this was not the case; Decorum offered not rules but principles
capable of the most flexible application. The figures of rhetoric,
though formal, are only the formalisations of normal speech patterns,
as Puttenham points out: '. . . all your figures Poeticall or Rhethoricall,
are but observations of strange speeches, and such as without any arte
at al we should use, and commonly do, even by very nature without
discipline . . . so as we may conclude, that nature herselfe suggesteth
the figure in this or that forme: but arte aydeth the judgement of his
use and application, . . .' (III, XXIV, p. 298). At his most rhetorical,
the poet is holding the mirror up to nature, even though his mirror
may be a highly polished one. Furthermore the way in which figures
are used is dictated by the logic of their function, not by a set of arbitrary rules, and here an examination of the three styles at work may make
the point more forcibly. Let us begin by examining the decorum of the
High style, as exemplified by the passage describing the first appearance
of Prince Arthur in *The Faerie Queene*:

> His haughtie helmet, horrid all with gold,
> Both glorious brightnesse, and great terrour bred;
> For all the crest a Dragon did enfold
> With greedie pawes, and over all did spred
> His golden wings: his dreadfull hideous hed . . .
> . . . Like to an Almond tree ymounted hye . . .
>
> (I, VII, 31–2)

The needs of the heroic poem are in the first place an exalted style set
above the level of ordinary speech, so that its tone is not dragged down
by colloquial associations from everyday life, and it is not identified
with anything temporary or local. It also needs a strongly pictorial

quality, aimed at the sight, the highest of the senses, and serving to imprint the details of a sustained narrative firmly in the mind. Spenser attains the first of these ends by the creation of an artificial language based on archaic heraldic terms such as 'close-couched', 'greedie', 'adowne', together with words carrying their original Latin meaning, such as 'horrid' in the sense of 'bristling'. By tapping the vocabulary both of the Virgilian epic and the Heroic Romance he creates an exalted literary language which places the poem in the heroic tradition to which it properly belongs. The use of carefully patterned alliteration further emphasises the deliberate lack of naturalism. As for the visual quality which is necessary to such a narrative, Spenser achieves this by what Puttenham calls 'Hypotiposis, or the counterfait representation', the aim of which is to 'set foorth many things, in such sort as it should appeare they were truly before our eyes'. The close detailed description of the helmet followed in the next stanza by the beautiful simile of the almond tree to describe the crest give the necessary pictorial quality, and make this important moment of the poem a memorable one. Such rhetoric is essentially functional; the heroic poem is too serious an art form to allow of verbal fireworks for their own sake.

The 'mean' or middle style, in contrast, allows more latitude, and there is more scope for virtuosity in diction where the content is more flippant. A sonnet will best illustrate the full range of Elizabethan rhetoric, for the sonnet was not taken very seriously and the poet was free to indulge in word play without offending Decorum.

> I Doe not now complaine of my disgrace,
>   o cruell fayre one, fayre with cruell crost:
>   nor of the hower, season, time nor place,
>   nor of my foyle for any freedom lost;
> Nor of my courage by mis-fortune daunted,
>   nor of my wit, by over-weening strooke,
>   nor of my sence, by any sounde inchaunted,
>   nor of the force of fierie poynted hooke.
> Nor of the steele that sticks within my wound,
>   nor of my thoughts, by worser thoughts defac'd,
>   nor of the life I labour to confound;
>   But I complaine, that beeing thus disgrac'd,
> Fyerd, feard, frantick, fetterd, shot through, slaine,
> My death is such as I may not complaine.
>   (*Diana*, 1594. Fifth Decad, sonnet II, p. 198)

This, like the majority of sonnets, is not so much a statement of serious feeling as an expression of witty paradox, and the whole sonnet leads up to the final contradiction in terms, 'but I complaine ... as I may not complaine'. Since the theme is merely witty and the mood light, Decorum demands as much rhetorical virtuosity as the poet can muster, and the variety of figures employed is bewildering, although the types proper to the high style do not appear. The principal figures around which the sonnet is constructed are Merismus and Anaphora. Merismus is what Puttenham calls the Distributor ... 'a figure very meete for Orators or eloquent perswaders such as our maker or Poet must in some cases shew him selfe to be', and it consists of taking a general statement and then dismembering it into its component parts. In this case, the general statement is 'I Doe not now complaine of my disgrace', which is broken down into its constituent details, the time and freedom lost, the courage and wit destroyed, the wounds received, and so on, all of which are implied in 'being thus disgrac'd'. With Merismus goes Anaphora, 'when we make one word begin, and as they were wont to say, lead the daunce to many verses in sute': 'nor of ....' fulfils this function. Among the minor figures of rhetoric in the sonnet, 'O cruel fayre one, fayre with cruell crost' is an example of Antimetavole or the Counterchange 'which takes a couple of words to play with in a verse, and by making them to chaunge and shift one into others place they do very pretily exchange and shift the sense ... '. Parimion or the figure of like letter—in other words, alliteration—is used consistently throughout to achieve a balance in every line; Ploche or the doubler, the 'speedie iteration' of a word with a few others between, appears in the line:

Nor of my thoughts, by worser thoughts defac'd;

and the progression 'Fyerd, feard, frantick ...' exemplifies both Brachiologia, or the cutted comma, where single words are separated by commas, and also Traductio or the translacer, which is a play on words of similar sounds—fyerd, feard. 'I complaine ... complaine' is an instance of Epanalepsis or the Eccho, and there is, of course, Allegoria, 'a long and perpetuall Metaphore', in 'steele ... wound' and 'fetterd ... slaine'. Even the final couplet which sums up the whole is itself a figure of rhetoric known as Epithonema or the Surclose. There are probably other figures in this poem which a rhetorician could identify, but even this incomplete analysis shows both the proficiency which a minor poet could attain in the use of rhetoric, and the purpose which it served.

The low style has fewer figures of rhetoric, yet its very plainness is part of rhetorical decorum. It is a style proper to the pastoral because shepherds are an uncouth race, and elaborate rhetoric would be indecorous on their lips: it is also used for satire, whose object is to degrade; and the proper style, therefore, is a rugged unpolished colloquialism with little show of art, and the choice of mean and undignified images which degrade in describing. The metres are often rough and irregular, designed to suggest something barbaric and uncontrolled in the nature of the subject. In the *Mirror for Magistrates*, for example, the ragged verse in which the wicked Richard makes his complaint is solemnly justified by the editors, on the grounds that 'it were agaynst the decorum of his personage to use eyther good meter or order' (Trag. 24).

To understand and enjoy poetry of this kind, we must rid ourselves of many of our modern assumptions about spontaneity and sincerity in poetry which would have had little meaning to a man of the Renaissance and, in fact, only sprang up with the Romantic revival. The term 'rhetorical' nowadays is apt to be used as a term of abuse. The Elizabethan, in contrast, took his rhetoric for granted; it was the medium of poetry, the basic technique to be mastered by the poet, just as fingering has to be mastered by the musician, or the various positions by the ballet dancer. 'Our maker,' says Puttenham, 'may both use, and also manifest his arte to his great praise, and need no more be ashamed thereof, than a shomaker to have made a cleanly shoe, or a Carpenter to have buylt a faire house' (III, xxv, pp. 302–3). The poet must, of course, use his rhetoric to say something, and will be judged ultimately on the quality of his meaning; art without nature is empty, but equally, nature without art is inarticulate and barbarous. The Elizabethan, in the flush of new discovery, loved to flaunt his art and had little use for the art which conceals itself. Art was one of the things distinguishing man from beast, and the art of rhetoric clothed the naked language as gorgeous clothes distinguished man from the bare forked animal. Puttenham's figures of ornament and the elaborations of Euphuism alike are the equivalent in language of the pageantry of Court life, the ritualistic wooing of the sonnet, or the bombast and decoration of Elizebathan costume. It is not an accident that Puttenham, writing of 'Ornaments Poeticall', compared them to clothes:

And as we see in these great Madames of honour, be they for personage or otherwise never so comely and bewtifull, yet if they want their courtly habillements or at leastwise such other apparell as custome and civilitie have ordained to cover their naked bodies, would be halfe ashamed or greatly out of countenance to be seen in that sort ... Even so cannot our vulgar Poesie

shew itselfe either gallant or gorgious, if any lymme be left naked and bare
and not clad in his kindly clothes and coulours.   (III, 1, p. 137)

The word 'kindly' refers, of course, to the poetic 'kind' which dictates
the nature of the rhetoric. The Elizabethan insistence on poetry as an
'arte' is synonymous with their insistence on the need to be civilised;
and unless we can enjoy the notes which the anonymous E.K. added
to the *Shepheardes Calender* and share in some degree his enthusiasm
for the 'prety Epanorthosis . . . and withall a Paranomasia or playing
with the word' which he admires in the first eclogue, we shall not only
miss a whole dimension of Elizabethan poetry; we shall misunderstand
the fundamental sensibility of the age.

3

JOHN SKELTON AND EARLY TUDOR POETRY

The Tudors brought domestic peace and a settled court after a century
of intermittent civil war, and English poetry which, in the fifteenth
century, had depended on the security of the church, as in the case of
Lydgate, or on the patronage of the City, as with Hoccleve, returned to
the court again from which it had been absent since the time of
Chaucer. To this fact it owes a new sophistication which finds its first
notable outlet in the poetry of Skelton. In the intervening century,
however, between the death of Chaucer and the accession of the
Tudors, the principles of English prosody became unsettled and confused, and the new poets were faced with the task of building poetry
anew almost from first principles. There have been two great systems
of prosody in English verse. The first, the accentual system of Old
English and much middle English verse, was based on a line of indeter-
minate length in which the pattern was established by a fixed number
of strongly accented syllables linked by alliteration and divided by a
strong Caesura in the middle of the line. The second is the foot and
syllable system perfected by Chaucer and forming the basis of most
English poetry ever since. English, however, is an accentual language
with great flexibility of stress depending on the importance of a word
in its particular context; and for this reason the foot, which derives
from classical quantitative verse, has never been used in English with
the regularity which is normal in Latin. Good English verse has always
been a compromise between quantity and stress: the expectation of the
formal pattern of feet sets up in the mind a basic rhythm to which the
natural accent of the language forms a counterpoint—like the two
hands on the piano, when the one beats out the rhythm and the other

syncopates. Chaucer's verse has this fugal effect, with a pattern of four stresses superimposed on the basic five-foot line:

Whán that/Aprílle/with his/shóures/sóte

It is, as Professor Northrop Frye has shown, a basic quality of English verse (*Anatomy of Criticism*, p. 251 ff.).

In the fifteenth century, however, for reasons which are still not wholly clear, Chaucer's mastery of prosody was not maintained by his successors. One reason may have been the patriotic revival of Old English accentual verse which had begun in the previous century and probably helped to deflect poetry from the Chaucerian mode. Its influence was very widespread and can still be seen in the heavy alliteration which lingers on until the end of the sixteenth century. Another reason was undoubtedly the rapid changes in pronunciation and the anglicisation of words of French origin, once French ceased to be the language of the court. The loss of the final 'e', and the movement of stress from the final to the penultimate syllable, threw pronunciation into confusion and disrupted the traditional verbal patterns of verse. At the same time, the literary phenomenon which Dunbar christened 'aureation' made poetry especially vulnerable to these uncertainties. Aureation represents the first impact of Renaissance nationalism and sprang from a desire to make the vernacular sound as elevated as the classics; it is an attempt to heighten style by the inclusion of as many polysyllabic words of French and Latin origin as possible. Stephen Hawes both defines and exemplifies it in his *Pastime of Pleasure* published in 1509, the last great exemplar of what had been the typical 'high' style of Lydgate:

> So that elocucyon doth ryght well clarify
> The dulcet speche frome the langage rude
> Tellynge the tale in termes eloquent
> The barbary tongue it doth ferre exclude
> Electynge wordes whiche are expedyent
> In Latyn or in englysshe after the entent
> Encensynge out the aromatyke fume
> Our langage rude to exyle and consume.

Hawes recognises clearly the humanist nature of what he is advocating, and traces it back to the 'well of fruytfulnesse' 'Claryfyed' by Virgil and Tully (1160). He uses such 'aromatik' words as facundyous, sentencyous, tenebrous, contynuance, brevacyon, perambulat, equypolent, and is quite arbitrary in their pronunciation, a fact to which the increased circulation of books and manuscripts probably contributed: poetry written for silent reading such as Lydgate's *Fall of Princes* or Hawes' own *Pastime* is inevitably more uncertain in its prosody as soon as it loses its contact with the spoken word. The early Tudor poets inherited these growing pains as verse ceased to be aural and became literature; and the only really confident prosody of the period is that of song, where the music enforces and steadies the metre.

The sixteenth-century writers seem to have had little conception of what in fact was happening, and Chaucer's decasyllabic line, its final 'e' forgotten, was read as an irregular four-stress line generally known as 'Ryding Rhyme' after the supposed metre of the Prologue to the *Canterbury Tales*. Gascoigne in his *Certain Notes of Instruction* tried to scan Chaucer on the principles of the Latin Hexameter, while Crowly, in his Preface to *Piers Plowman*, 1550, failed to recognise the accentual nature of the metre and mistook it for a sort of rugged blank verse. The very principles of scansion were in debate, and the sixteenth-century critics who sought to restore them were all concerned with the most elementary mechanics of verse-making. Webbe, Gascoigne and Puttenham alike found it necessary to deal with such matters as the need to keep the same number of syllables in a line, or the nature of a foot. We should bear this state of things in mind when we come to estimate the significance of Skelton's rapid and irregular 'Skeltonic' line, or Wyatt's prosodic experiments in his sonnets, or the astonishing popularity of Surrey's monotonous but regular Poulter's Measure.

Hawes, who was Skelton's contemporary, is of interest if only because he exemplifies all that Skelton reacted against; but a poet of more positive relevance is Alexander Barclay, chaplain at the College of St Mary Ottery in Devon. He was chiefly known, in his time, for his translation in 1508–9 of the *Narrenschiff*, *The Ship of Fools* by the German writer Sebastian Brant; and the fact that he turned to this popular satire is of significance to our understanding of the period. Whenever the accepted ideals of society become seriously divorced from its realities, satire appears, as in the later Middle Ages, when the feudal system and the medieval Catholic church were in actual decay while still keeping their hold on men's minds. Chaucer's satire sprang from these conditions, and for the same reason, the first twenty-five years of the sixteenth century, on the very eve of the Reformation, form an important period of English satire. In prose there are Erasmus' *Colloquies* and *The Praise of Folly* and More's *Utopia*; and in verse, Barclay, Skelton and even Wyatt in some degree. The influence of

Brant's *Ship of Fools* is apparent on Skelton's *Bouge of Court* (1498), ten years before Barclay translated the poem; although in Skelton's poem it is all the rogues of court, not the fools, who go aboard.

Of special relevance to Skelton, also, is Barclay's translation and adaptation of a group of Renaissance Eclogues in 1513–14. The pastoral Eclogue has a long history, and what began with Theocritus as the expression of the town man's nostalgia for the simple life was invested by Virgil with a more serious purpose and crossed, during the Middle Ages, with the Biblical conception of the 'Good Shepherd'. By the Renaissance, the form had become capable of a variety of functions. It could still present the simple country idyll of shepherds watching their flocks and competing in singing matches; but it could also take on allegory, in which the shepherd as the generic singer could voice the problems of poetry, or as the generic priest, could criticise the abuses of church and state. Barclay's Eclogues attack life at court, borrowing their pastoral form from the Italian Humanist, Mantuan, and their content from the earlier Humanist, Aenius Sylvius; and the interesting Prologue shows that Barclay understood the humanist nature of what he was doing. He begins by describing the traditional poetic 'kinds', and traces the Eclogue through from Theocritus to his own day, at the same time defining the range of its subject matter— 'Sometime disputing of courtly misery,/Sometime of Venus disceatfull tiranny . . .' His own Eclogues are to be imitations of 'other Poetes olde', written in the low style 'fitting a heard or man rurall. . . . So teacheth Horace in arte of poetry.' The first three of the poems, therefore, are discussions between two shepherds about the miseries of life at court; the fourth deals with the neglect of poets by rich men, and the fifth is a debate about life in town and country. The first three in particular are very effective in their calculated roughness. They describe the sycophancy of court life, the 'uncleane penury' of court meals where 'Thy potage is made with wedes and with ashes' (II, 745), and where ten knives all meet in the common dish as each hungry courtier fights for his share, so that the unwary one who forgets his gauntlet may well lose a finger:

> On a finger gnaweth some hasty glutton,
> Supposing it is a piece of biefe or mutton
> (II, 983)

The third Eclogue gives an even more horrible picture of the unclean sleeping accommodation, with twenty in a room and the most unsavoury bed-fellows:

> So foule and scabbed, of harde pimples so thin,
> That a man might grate hard crustes on his skin
> (III, 89)

Barclay's Eclogues show that the humanist conception of the satire as a distinct art form had entered into England and been understood. They help us to see Skelton's greater satires in a truer perspective, and to recognise also that his was not a solitary voice, but that others were speaking out as loudly, if not with such topicality.

Skelton himself was born about 1460, and by 1490 was acknowledged as a scholar 'late created poet laureate'. A Laureate in the normal sense of the term was a graduate in the faculty of rhetoric, and with this qualification Skelton was employed at the court of Henry VII as one of the little band of scholars and orators with which a progressive Renaissance monarch was expected to surround himself. He was tutor to the young prince, Henry, and tells us proudly that 'The honour of England I learned to spell' (*Against Garnesche*); but when the eldest son Arthur died and Henry became heir to the Throne, Skelton was dismissed with the rich living at Diss in Norfolk as the reward for his services. When his late pupil came to the throne as Henry VIII, Skelton petitioned to be re-employed at court, and by 1512 was established at Westminster as Orator Royal, celebrating English victories in verse and, for the next ten years, protecting his king from evil counsellors, in particular Wolsey, against whom he launched his great series of satires. He seems to have made his peace with Wolsey after 1523, and died peacefully in 1529, shortly before the Cardinal fell from power.

To the sixteenth century Skelton was known as a satirist and, even more, as a jester and buffoon. He was one of those characters to whom all the floating legends of his generation seem to attach themselves, and the *Merry Tales of Skelton* with its accounts of insanity, jokes at the expense of friars and innkeepers was one of the most popular books of the century. Most of the tales are probably apocryphal, although the famous story of how Skelton outfaced his scandalised congregation by holding up his new-born child in the pulpit and challenging anyone there to produce a better, has the ring of truth. Skelton certainly anticipated the Reformation in respect of the marriage of the clergy, which was one reason for his popularity later. But whatever the literal truth of these tales, there is in Skelton's poetry a strain of buffoonery which helps to explain the popular estimate of his character. A poet who could parody the service of the dead so gaily, as in *Philip Sparrow*, or write shocking epitaphs in rhyming

Latin and English on a deceased member of his congregation:

> *Jam jacet hic* stark dead
>   Never a tooth in his head.
> Adieu, Jayberd, adieu . . .
>   I pray you all
>   And pray shall,
>   At this trental
>   On knees to fall
>   To the football;
>   With 'Fill the black bowl
>   For the Jayberd's soul . . .'
>   With 'Hey, ho, rumbelow!'
>   *Rumpopulorum*
>   *Per omnia secula seculorum!* Amen
>   *Requiem* etc . . .
> (*A Devout Trental for old John Clarke*, p. 57)

a poet who could so enjoy his slanging match with Garnesche, or introduce the names of his enemies in cryptograms into the middle of serious poems, or invent the sophisticated riddles of which *Speak Parrot* is composed, must have been the sort of character around whom a legend will inevitably spring up.

Nevertheless, Skelton's jesting has more than a merely personal significance. It represents a reaction against the solemnity of much fifteenth-century verse, particularly that of Lydgate, and a turning towards Chaucer in the gayer, bawdier moods of the *Canterbury Tales*. The Scottish Chaucerians had already led the way and Dunbar, in particular, with his flyting and his earthy humour, has the closest affinity with Skelton. It is significant that Jane Scrope, the heroine of *Philip Sparrow*, prefers Chaucer to Lydgate and criticises the latter on the grounds that:

> some men find a faute,
> And say he writeth too haut.

Not that Skelton himself does not use Aureate Diction; there is plenty of it where the occasion demands, as in the early elegy on Northumberland or the more exalted parts of *The Garland of Laurel*. For Skelton, Aureate Diction still constituted the ideal of the high style, but on the whole he avoids situations in which it is necessary, and turns for choice to whatever is colloquial and popular. Where he can bring the traditional high style down to a lower level, he does so. One of his favourite metres, for example, is Rhyme Royal, the metres of *Troilus and Criseyde* or the *Fall of Princes*, yet, as used by Skelton, it has the dramatic fluency of the comic Interlude. The description of Riot beating time upon his tankard and bragging of his amorous conquests is far from aureate:

> Counter he could *O Lux* upon a pot,
>   An Ostrich feather of a capon's tail
> He set up freshly upon his hat aloft.
>   'What revel rout!' quod he an 'gan to rail
>   How oft he had hit Jennet on the tail,
> Of Phyllis fetis, and little pretty Kate,
> How oft he knocked at her clicket-gate.
>   (*Bouge of Court*, p. 48)

In a similar fashion, Skelton turns to the popular medieval song rather than to the courtly lyric, and the realism of his love poetry is unspoiled by the earlier conventions of Courtly love or the later clichés of Petrarchism. His two beautiful lyrics, *Mannerly Margery* and *My Darling Dear*, which Cornysshe, the court musician, set to music, treat sex with a frankness common in the Middle Ages but almost destroyed by the influence of Petrarch in the sixteenth century. *Mannerly Margery, Milk and Ale*, is a dialogue between a man and a maid in which the girl is won and left as in so many popular medieval songs. *My Darling Dear* corrects the picture with the tale of the wife who kisses her amorous husband to sleep and then runs off to her lover:

> My darling dear, my daisy flower,
>   Let me, quod he, lie in your lap.
> Lie still, quod she, my paramour,
>   Lie still hardely, and take a nap.
>   His head was heavy, such was his hap,
> All drowsy dreaming, drowned in sleep,
> That of his love he took no keep.
>   With hey lullay, lullay, like a child,
>   Thou sleepest too long, thou art beguiled. . . .

The four-stress beat of accentual verse can still be heard underneath the stanza form; and Humanism has not yet transformed the Kate of the popular lyric into the pastoral Phyllida. The court poet can still write a lyric in the popular mode.

Skelton's rebellion against the aureate style finds its completest expression in the famous metre which is named after him. The origin of the 'Skeltonic' has never been finally settled; it has been identified with the half line of old English verse or traced back to the metre of medieval Latin poetry or rhyming latin prose. Whatever its origin, however, the important thing is that it broke with the clogged, halting metres of much fifteenth-century verse and let in speed and movement again. In this respect it provided Skelton with a medium of remarkable range and flexibility. At one extreme it can throw words like stones in pithy offensive doggerel; it can hammer away at a point with a cluster of epithets all bound together by a single recurring rhyme which can be maintained for as long as the poet chooses. At the other end, it is capable of the delicate expression of feeling and the precise matching of its movement to the nature of its content. In Jane Scrope's description of her sparrow, for example, the metre seems to hop with the very movements of the bird itself.

> Sometime he would gasp
> When he saw a wasp;
> A fly or a gnat,
> He would fly at that;
> And prettily he would pant
> When he saw an ant.
> Lord, how he would pry
> After the butterfly!
> Lord, how he would hop
> After the gressop!
> And when I said 'Phip, Phip!'
> Then he would leap and skip,
> And take me by the lip. . . .
> (*Philip Sparrow*, pp. 63–4)

As in form, so in idiom and allusion, Skelton turns wherever possible to the colloquial source. His poetry is full of popular euphemism, such as the example already quoted from the *Bouge of Court*, and proverbial sayings like 'Dun is in the mire', or 'Mock hath lost her shoe', or 'By the right of a rame's horn'. There is a wealth of traditional lore behind his poetry which gives it a provocatively allusive quality:

> But when the friar fell in the well,
> He could not sing himself thereout
> But by the help of Christian Clout.
> (*Colin Clout*, pp. 275–6)

The very metaphors are often only half out of the Interlude, and one can see the popular Morality figure in process of shrinking into a figure of speech:

> Our sheep are shrewdly shorn,
> And truth is all to-torn;
> Wisdom is laughed to scorn,
> Favel is false forsworn ...
> Havel and Harvey Hafter,
> Jack Travel and Cole Crafter. ...
> (*Why come ye not to Court?*, p. 311)

Characters very like these form the actual cast of *Magnificence*. His vocabulary supports this general picture—though caution is necessary here because a modern reader naturally notices the obsolete medieval words but takes for granted those still in use. It has been estimated that Skelton's poems record for the first time over a thousand of the new words which were first introduced into English during the fifteenth and sixteenth centuries. Nevertheless, he obviously draws deeply on the stock of fine old English dialect words which have survived only as slang, or passed away altogether under the pressure of King's English and the spread of the London dialect. Blinkard, blowbowl, bowsy, blo, cawry-mawry, doddypate, frumple, gup, pode, titivel, and many others attest the native wealth of the English language and make the attempts of Sir John Cheke and his fellows to prevent the incorporation of new words from foreign sources less ridiculous than might otherwise appear. Many of these words are not recorded before Skelton and in some cases are not found after him, but many of them are related to words in common medieval use, and it is probable that Skelton was bringing dialect words into literary usage rather than inventing new ones himself. Often they are terms of abuse and they make a very picturesque catalogue: blommer, bibble, blother, cockwat, fizgig (a particularly vivid term for a loose woman; it will be remembered that Alfred Jingle was loved by Donna Christina Fizzgig), gorbellied, lampatran, prendergest, reasty, skirgalliard, whipslovens, wretchocks—the list could be prolonged indefinitely. Many have the repetitive onomatopoeic quality which seems to be an instinctive way of expressing obscenity—tirly tirlow, whim wham, trim tram, flip flap are terms whose meaning had better be left undefined, and it is noteworthy that Dunbar has his own varieties, of which tyrlie myrlie, crowdie mowdie, are instances. This is the language which Skelton hurls at his enemies with a conviction which makes the more deliberately decorous abuse of the Elizabethan pamphleteers seem pale. The one is Skelton's own native language; the other, a self-conscious exercise following on a century of discussion about the English language and how to use the low style.

The picture of Skelton which so far emerges is of a man who looks backward into the Middle Ages whose ideals he hopes to keep living, rather than forward into the Renaissance. He sees, for example, the new passion for Greek, introduced by the Oxford Reformers and shared by Wolsey and the King, but he is sceptical about its value. It is still an amateur's language, not yet 'conned perfitely, and after the rate, As *lingua Latina* . . .' (*Speak Parrot*, p. 293); its devotees may know the name of a straw mat in Greek, but they cannot use it for so practical a purpose as to say, riding by the way:

> Ho Hostler, fetch my horse a bottle of hay! (p. 293).

It is a dead language not a living one. In the same way he opposes the new humanist insistence on the importance of literature which would relegate grammar to a lower status, as merely a means to an end:

> Plautus in his comedies a child shall now rehearse
> And meddle with Quintilian his *Declamations*
> That Petty Cato can scantly construe a verse . . .
> (p. 294)

We should not expect such a man to be at ease in the new Tudor world, and Skelton disliked and misunderstood many of the things going on around him. The Tudor court was a new type of phenomenon with its centralisation and its dependence on counsellors of relatively low birth but possessing professional skills; and to Skelton it seemed merely a place where upstarts struggle for position. His attack, therefore, can draw on the same tradition of anti-court poetry as that of Barclay, but it does so with a deeper conviction which springs from first-hand experience. The evils of the court form the subject of much of Skelton's poetry. In the *Bouge of Court*—'bouge' meaning rewards, or rations—Drede, young and innocent, sets sail in the great ship of Court, encouraged by Desire and trusting in Good Luck; but no sooner is he aboard than he is surrounded by a band of rogues, Flattery, Suspect, Deceit, Dissimulation—the Osrics and Oswalds who haunt the courts of the later drama—until Drede almost jumps overboard for very fear:

> Methought I see lewd fellows here and there
> Come for to slay me of mortal intent . . .
> (p. 53)

In the Interlude, *Magnificence* (1516), the same ill-favoured crew appear again under the guise of Counterfeit Countenance, Crafty Conveyance,

Cloaked Collusion and Courtly Abusion who strip Magnificence, their monarch, bare of his wealth and dignity. In *Why come ye not to Court* (1522-3), all these parts are played by Wolsey alone who by guile and violence has worked himself into the King's ear, so that the old nobility go in fear of their lives:

> Our baron's be so bold
> Into a mousehole they wold
> Run away and creep,
> Like a meiny of sheep:
> Dare not look out at door
> For a dread of the mastiff cur,
> For dread of the butcher's dog . . .
>   (p. 317)

Skelton harps continuously on Wolsey's 'greasy genealogy', his low birth that:

> . . . came of the sang royall
> That was cast out of a butcher's stall.
>   (p. 322)

He failed to realise the deliberate Tudor policy of centralisation which Wolsey was encouraged to develop: he failed to understand the inevitable reshuffle in rank which followed the Wars of the Roses, though it must be admitted that half the writers of the sixteenth century followed him in his lament that 'Jack would be a gentleman' (*Against a Comely Coistrown*).

In the same way, he was as aware as anyone of the Church's need for reform, but he wanted, like Chaucer and Langland and Thomas More, to patch the old fabric rather than build anew. When, in 1518, Wolsey was empowered, in the interests of efficiency, to shut down some of the smaller religious houses, Skelton treated the action to a tirade of abuse against the turning of abbeys to granges and monasteries to water-mills. The philosophy behind all this is not, however, essentially reactionary; Skelton believed in gradual changes and his ideal is the Aristotelian Mean. In *Magnificence* all is well as long as Measure is the King's counsellor; it is only when Liberty gains a free hand that the state is swept by an orgy of lawlessness in which all respect for degree is lost. Life, to Skelton, was the age-old struggle between wit and will, between reason and the instinct for lawless liberty. On the individual level, the triumph of will produces the unbridled ambition which is the characteristic of the Comely Coistrown or the new courtier; on the social level, it is exemplified by Wolsey and everything he

stood for. It is 'Will, will will will will', which rules at court, and in
its train follow all the Aristotelian excesses:

> Too hasty of sentence,
> Too fierce for none offence,
> Too scarce of your expense,
> Too large in negligence,
> Too slack in recompence ...
> (*Why come ye not to Court?*, p. 308)

The damning word 'too' is a constant ingredient of Skelton's descriptions of evil. Music gives him a fine metaphor with which to describe
his conception of wrong. The mean is a musical term describing the
middle voice which carries the tune while the others perform the
descant, and the pun on Aristotle's use of the word serves Skelton's
purpose and opens up all sorts of further puns connected with singing
too high or too base:

> He cannot find it in rule nor in space:
>   He solfas too haute, his treble is too high;
> He braggeth of his birth, that born was full base;
>   His music without measure, too sharp is his *Mi*;
>   He trimmeth in his tenor to counter pardee;
> His descant is busy, it is without a mean. ...
>   (*Against a Comely Coistrown*, p. 35)

The puns on mean, measure, base, counter, and mi are an amusing
device for describing someone who is getting above himself.

There is no room in a book of this size to consider in detail any but
the finer of the individual poems, and we may begin, therefore, with
that curiously complementary pair of opposites, *Philip Sparrow* and
The Tunning of Elinour Rumming. *Philip Sparrow* was written at Diss
between 1504 and 1508, and was addressed to Jane Scrope, a young
lady living in a religious house near Norwich, whose pet sparrow had
been killed by the cat Gib, a 'cat of carlish kind'. In its mock heroic
curse upon the cat and its high-pitched laments for the dead bird which
are said to rival those of Andromache for Hector, the poem resembles
Chaucer's parody of the rules of Geoffrey de Vinsauf in the *Nonne
Preestes Tale*. But the essential quality of the poem springs from the use
it makes of the service for the dead, from the initial Placebo, through
Vespers and Matins, the Mass and Introitus to the final commendation
of the soul to God. Skelton weaves the solemn phrases, together with
the chants which accompany them, into the pattern of his poem:

> *Pla ce bo*
> Who is there, who?
> *Di le xi!*
> Dame Margery.
> *Fa, re, my, my.*
> Wherefore and why, why?
> For the soul of Philip Sparrow
> That was late slain at Carrow ...
> (p. 60)

The Mass for the dead is appropriately one of the bird Masses which were popular in the Middle Ages and of which *Who Killed Cock Robin* is the sole modern survivor. There is a bewildering list of birds and their habits:

> The raven, called Rolfe,
> His plain-song to sol-fa ...
> The bittern with his bumpe,
> The crane with his trumpe....
> (pp. 71–2)

the cock will tell the time, the phoenix can provide the incense, the eagle shall be the sub-dean and even the ostrich is to be the bell-man,

> And let him ring bells,
> He can do nothing else.
> (p. 74)

Skelton gives an amusing picture of the ostrich trying in vain to sing the top notes and being corrected like a choir-boy out of tune:

> Fa, lorrel, fa, fa
> (p. 74)

Jane wants an epitaph for her sparrow but finds difficulty in writing one, and Skelton makes this fact an excuse to comment on the contemporary problems of English literature. Jane knows the *Tales of Canterbury* and of King Arthur, and Dame Gaynor, his queen, who 'Was somewhat wanton, I ween', and of Cresseid who 'was much to blame'; but she is no Humanist: she 'can but little skill/Of Ovid or Virgil/Or of Plutarch/Or Francis Petrarch': and to add to her difficulties:

> Our natural tongue is rude,
> And hard to be ennewed
> With polished termes lusty ...
> (p. 82)

Gower's English 'is old', and people 'bark' at Chaucer's English, while
that of Lydgate is 'diffuse'. For this reason, Skelton provides her with
the epitaph 'In Latin plain and light' (p. 83), in the absence of any
adequate native tradition. The poem returns to the form of the church
service and ends with the traditional commendation, not however of
the soul of the dead to heaven, but of the beauty of Jane herself.
Skelton writes a long parody of the medieval icon, beginning at the
top with her 'eyen grey and steep', working down past her wart 'set so
womanly', to her foot upon which 'How often I did toot'. It is a very
charming and delicate fancy, full of the tenderness and humour which
little girls seem always to inspire in Skelton. The lyrics to Mistress
Margery Wentworth and Mistress Margaret Hussy in *The Garland
of Laurel* possess the same mixture.

   The Tunning of Elinour Rumming, written in all probability soon after
Philip Sparrow, might have been designed as a counterblast to it. It is a
description of the old ale-wife who lived 'Beside Leatherhead', and
in its account of her habits and those of her clientele is one of the
finest pieces of gross realism in the language. We see her brewing
under the hen-roost so that the dung drops into the ale and makes it
'flower the thicker', while, near by, the old sow and her litter wander
in and out of the room and frig their rumps against the bench. The
gossips come in, bringing their pots and pans, their bacon, their hoods
or their beads to exchange for ale, and there they sit in a row on the
bench or tumble to the floor, talking, drinking or vomiting according
to their needs. They pour into the alehouse in an endless stream until
the whole world seems to be there in one vast milling crowd; and
the ability of the Skeltonic to keep going without a pause for breath
contributes largely to the total effect of movement and confusion
which the poem gives:

> Another set of sluts:
> Some brought walnuts,
> Some apples, some pairs,
> Some brought their clipping shears,
> Some brought this and that,
> Some brought I wot ne'er what;
> Some brought their husband's hat,
> Some puddings and links,
> Some tripes that stinks. . . .
>   (p. 124)

The poem gives an impression of spontaneity, as if Skelton were there
describing the people just as they come in, but the poem is in fact far

from artless. The line just quoted—'Another set of sluts:'—for example, points to the fact that Skelton is composing and assembling deliberately a sequence of vignettes which add up to a single overwhelming image. It is the traditional image of Drunkenness, as we see it in the Pardoner's Sermon, but taken out of the larger context in which Chaucer treated it and handled by itself to form a satire, within the framework of the humanist literary kinds. The fact that Skelton pictures only women clients, for instance, indicates the very deliberate selection of material within the poem. Whether he did this because the thought of so many drunken women is more sobering than the equivalent picture of men, in whom such behaviour is more to be expected; or whether he was mocking the idealism of Courtly love, as Dunbar does in his *Tretis of the tua mariit Wemen and the Wedo*, we cannot know; but the poem is undeniably a very calculated piece of art in astonishingly exuberant language—'All foggy fat she was'; 'They are sheer shaking nought'.

We should be careful, in the same way, not to mistake the great satires written between 1521 and 1523 for the simple artless primitives which the last two of them, at least, might appear to be. We are not likely to make this mistake with the first one, *Speak Parrot* (1521), which is an ostentatiously learned poem, a laureate satire in which the poet looks down on Wolsey from the pinnacle of his own learning. *Elinour Rumming*, written at Diss, is a homily as much as a satire, and could justify its uncouthness on the grounds that Skelton was writing as a parish priest to save the souls of his parishioners, as George Herbert was to do later. But, back at court, Skelton may have been more conscious of his laureate dignity, and for this reason his first satire is an enormous academic sneer at Wolsey whose 'Latin tongue doth hobble' (*Why Come ye*). The poem describes a Parrot in its cage:

> With my beke bent, my little wanton eye,
> My feathers fresh as is the emerald green,
> About my neck a circulet like a rich ruby ...
> (p. 288)

and reproduces the medley of phrases and names in many languages which a well-trained parrot might be expected to have picked up. But as the phrases flow, they begin to assume a pattern, and much covert satire emerges from under the cloak of apparently random chatter. The clues have all the ingenuity of a *Times* crossword puzzle, and their solution depends upon a knowledge of contemporary history and of the Vulgate Bible. A few instances may be given to illustrate the

method. Anything referring to butchers may be taken as a euphemism
for Wolsey who was reputed to be a butcher's son, a fact which
Skelton could not forgive in a person who had achieved so high a
rank: he is the golden calf, 'Vitulus in Horeb'; he is 'Og that fat hog of
Bashan' and 'Moloch the merciless', the bull-headed god. A deceptively
innocent sentence such as 'In Afric tongue byrsa is a thong of leather'
coming apparently at random in the poem reveals layer upon layer of
meaning when fully analysed. To cut thongs of other men's leather
was a well-known proverb describing the sort of unscrupulous greed
which Skelton saw in Wolsey, while the word 'byrsa' suggests the
Burse, the official container for the Great Seal which Wolsey possessed
and paraded with so much ostentation. All this is mixed up with a pro-
fusion of tags in Latin, Greek or Italian, mostly of a cautionary nature
and containing some reference to the value of the golden mean—
'Moderata juvant', 'Myden agan', 'Ne tropo sanno, ne tropo mato', for
example. By this means Skelton demonstrates his Humanism and reminds the reader that he is speaking with the sacred voice of divine
poetry as the humanists conceived of it. The parrot is his mouthpiece
because, as tradition asserts, 'When parrot is dead, she doth not
putrefy', and thus she is a fitting symbol for poetry. Skelton therefore
identifies himself with the parrot—'Parrot is my own dear heart
and my dear darling'—and claims the right of the poet to speak
out:

> Melpomene, that fair maid, she burnished his beak:
> I pray you, let Parrot have liberty to speak!
> (p. 295)

The poet may hide his meaning under riddles:

> But that *metaphora, allegoria* with all,
> Shall be his protection, his paves, and his wall.
> (p. 295)

but there is nothing unworthy in this. Skelton is quoting the traditional
defence of poetry from Aristotle onwards when he insists that 'Parrot
nothing has surmised,/No matter pretended, no nothing enterprised';
Sidney is making the same point when he argues that 'The poet
nothing asserteth and therefore nothing lieth'. Through his fiction,
Skelton asserts the divinity of poetry; and it is a conception he believed
in deeply, for he reiterated it more plainly in his curious poem *A
Replication*, written at the very end of his life:

... With me, ye must consent ...
How there is a spiritual,
And a mysterial,
And a mystical
Effect energial,
As Greekes do it call ...
Of heavenly inspiration
In laureate creation ...
By whose inflammation
Of spiritual instigation
And divine inspiration
We are kindled in such fashion
With heat of the Holy Ghost
... That he our pen doth lead ...
(p. 427)

Speak Parrot both in form and content, therefore, is an explicitly humanist poem though not in any of the recognised humanist genres.

Colin Clout (1522) is spoken by a countryman who, by his imagery in the poem, would seem to be a shepherd. Certainly when Spenser took over the name, he made of Colin the generic shepherd of pastoral, able to satirise church and court or be the mouthpiece of the poet himself. Skelton uses Colin in the former role, warning the reader at the beginning of the poem that he is writing a serious poem:

For though my rhyme be ragged,
Tattered and jagged,
Rudely rain-beaten,
Rusty and moth eaten,
If ye take well therewith,
It hath in it some pith.   (p. 251)

and at the end rounding off with the traditional defence of satire as it is to be found in Horace or Ben Jonson:

Wherefore take no disdain
At my style rude and plain;
For I rebuke no man
That virtuous is: why then
Wreak ye your anger on me?
(p. 282)

The language is accordingly uncouth and 'moth-eaten', the metre Skeltonic as befits the decorum of the literary kind. Skelton's specific references to the pastoral rudeness of the poem show, therefore, that he was writing within the framework of humanist satire.

It is not, however, the pastoral satire as Barclay knew it; Skelton is simultaneously tapping a native tradition of satire, that of Piers Plowman, the countryman, who comments on the vices of the world around him. In this way he avoids the artificiality which always strikes the reader when pastoral shepherds begin to talk of state affairs, and at the same time provides himself with a protecting screen. Skelton's shepherd only repeats what he hears the people say:

> Thus I Colin Clout
> As I go about,
> And wandering as I walk
> I hear the people talk
> (p. 258)

Who can possibly blame Colin for repeating what everybody says, especially as he is careful to insist that 'Full falsely on you they lie', before he goes on to give the next instalment of slanderous gossip. Skelton thus has it both ways: in fusing the humanist and the medieval traditions, he combines the realism of first-hand reporting with the convention of allegory which allows the poet to speak through his pastoral mouthpiece. By the end of the century, Spenser's Colin Clout has lost his medieval realism and become a purely literary figure of the pastoral. Skelton's poem is a scathing attack on the clergy for their lack of learning, their money-making and neglect of their flock; and underneath its homely colouring it is a highly sophisticated piece of satire with very subtle verbal effects. The bishops are pilloried as metaphorical and as literal shepherds for their general rapacity and their activities as sheep farmers:

> Layman say, indeed,
> How they take no need
> Their silly sheep to feed,
> But pluck away and pull
> The fleeces of their wool ...
> (p. 252)

The failure of all but 'two or three' to keep the wolf from the door and to separate the sheep from the goats is twisted into a witty attack on the lechery of the friars in their woollen cloaks:

> ... The wolf from the door
> To werrin and to keep
> From their ghostly sheep,
> And their spiritual lambs,

> Sequestered from the rams
> And the bearded goats
> With their hairy coats.
>
> (p. 254)

The poem ranges in tone from the Chaucerean irony of his description
of the begging friars:

> Sometime a baconflick,
> That is three fingers thick
> Of larde and of grease,
> Their convent to increase
>
> (pp. 274–5)

to the almost Gilbertian virtuosity with which he describes the
irregularities of the ecclesiastical courts:

> In their provincial cure
> They make but little sure,
> And meddle very light
> In the Church's right;
> But *ire* and *venire*
> And sol-fa so a-la mi-re
> That the praemunire
> Is like to be set afire.
>
> (p. 253)

The poem shows a great mastery of innuendo and the power to hint a
fault almost by the tone of voice. It is a most professional piece of work
and totally devoid of the amateurism which C. S. Lewis believes to be
Skelton's greatest fault.

The same cannot be said of the last of the great satires, *Why come
ye not to Court* (1522–3), which is perhaps the most personal but certainly
the least controlled of the three. Like *Colin Clout* it exploits the
anonymity of the common people, and is written as if it were the
utterances of so many messengers rushing in from all parts of the
country with their news—'What newes, what newes ... What hear
ye of Lancashire ... What hear ye of Cheshire?' It is like the stop-
press column of a newspaper, with pauses for rest until the next report
comes in:

> But now upon this story
> I will no longer rime
> Till another time,
> Till another time.
>
> (p. 315)

The poem is an undiluted attack on Wolsey for his lechery and disease, his deficiencies 'In Tully's faculty/Called humanity', on his diplomatic failures:

> Fie on this winning alway!
> Now nothing but pay, pay!
> (p. 335)

on his methods of financing his abortive wars which weighed so heavily on rich clothiers like 'Good Spring of Lavenham'. The new palace of Hampton Court with its unseemly tapestries had already been attacked in *Colin Clout* (pp. 277–8); now we are asked the challenging question which forms the title of the poem:

> *Why come ye not to court?*
> To which court?
> To the kings court,
> Or to Hampton court?
> (p. 320)

Once more we have the renaissance theme of the Court treated in explicit satire: it is 'At Juvenal's request' that Skelton feels constrained to write 'Of this vainglorious beast' (p. 343); but the attack is crude after the verbal subtlety of *Colin Clout*. Perhaps Skelton was too personally involved to be capable of the degree of detachment necessary for irony; the poem reads like a personal duel and opens, significantly, with a complaint that the court is no place for old men, and a plea for restitution:

> For age is a page
> For the court full unmeet,
> For age cannot rage,
> Nor buss her sweet, sweet,
>   But when age seeth that rage
> Doth assuage and refrain,
> Then will age have corage
> To come to court again.
> (p. 309)

Skelton was over sixty at this time and perhaps out of tune with the merry monarch. It is difficult not to hear his voice upbraiding his old pupil for neglecting the advice of his mentor and laureate.

It is on this personal level, I think, that we may find the explanation of the last great poem which Skelton wrote, *The Garland of Laurel* (1523). Whether out of nostalgia for the past, or whether out of a need to defend himself publicly after his long duel with Wolsey, Skelton returns to the earlier mode of the dream vision, and writes a long justification of himself as Laureate which is modelled on Chaucer's *House of Fame*. Like Chaucer's poem, *The Garland* contains a good deal of comedy: Skelton dreams that he is transported to the House of Fame and joins the procession of all the laureates as they parade past their deity. They are a very mixed collection of famous people, all jumbled together with a freedom which must have offended Skelton's humanist contemporaries:

> Plutarch and Petrarch, two famous clerkes.
>
> (p. 359)

Moreover, as they go past, arm in arm, tankard in hand, one has the uneasy suspicion that they are all a little drunk:

> But blessed Bacchus, the pleasant god of wine,
> Of clusters engroséd with his ruddy floates
> These orators and poetes refreshéd their throates!

Skelton is welcomed as an equal by the three great English masters, Gower, Chaucer and Lydgate, and does not conceal his preference for Chaucer—the treatment of Lydgate, as in *Philip Sparrow*, contains more than a touch of parody. Finally the list of works which constitute his claim to fame is read out and a very curious catalogue it is, ranging from *Colin Clout* to 'Of Tully's Familiars the translation'; from *Magnificence* to 'The grunting and the groigning of the gronning swine'. Yet it is enough, and Skelton, showing less diffidence than Chaucer in the same situation, is crowned with the Laureate wreath embroidered for him by his patron, the Countess of Surrey, and her maidens. It is a funny poem but contains a serious plea; it is directed 'Against envy/ And obloquy' (p. 395), and expresses a hope for better times—'Good luck this new year! the old year is past' (p. 393). It is clearly a reflection of the difficulties in which Skelton found himself at court.

I have dealt with Skelton at some length because he is so much more than the brilliant eccentric for which we are apt to mistake him. He is perhaps the most considerable poet between Chaucer and Spenser and comes at the point of intersection between the medieval and the humanist traditions. The great range of modes comprised within the *Canterbury Tales* is to be found equally in the works of Skelton, but split up into separate and tentatively humanist kinds, so that Skelton points both forward and back. His materials are Chaucerean, but his underlying assumptions are much closer to those of Spenser. *The Garland of Laurel* is more than a defence of himself; it is a plea for the high dignity of Laureat verse, a reminder that even Virgil had to bear the same indignities. It is an assertion that Skelton himself has put on Chaucer's mantle of fame. The Latin address to his own book near the end of the poem bids it 'Say Skelton was your Homer; though barbarous, you now run an equal race with Latin verse. And though the greater part is woven of British words, our Thalia is not too uncouth, nor my Calliope too unlearned' (p. 394). This is the unmistakable voice of the new age, and for all his grumbles against the new learning, Skelton himself is a part of it. His very conception of his own role as a court poet and laureate is a case in point: he saw himself as the King's guide and counsellor, the watch dog guarding Magnificence from the snares of flattery; and no doubt the fact that he had taught Henry as a boy gave him a personal feeling of being *in loco parentis*. But it is more than this; the poet is bringing wisdom and philosophy to court, trying to unite the philospher and the king as Plato had done. Skelton is a more ambitious educator than Sir Thomas Elyot, for the governor he seeks to fashion is the King himself, and he is giving practical application to Erasmus' *Education of a Christian Prince*. We must read his poetry, therefore, with the values of Spenser as well as those of Chaucer in mind, and recognise in Skelton the great bridge between the two.

4

WYATT AND SURREY

In the latter end of the same kings raigne sprong up a new company of courtly
makers, of whom Sir Thomas Wyat th' elder and Henry Earle of Surrey were
the two chieftaines, who having travailed into Italie, and there tasted the
sweete and stately measures and stile of the Italian Poesie as novices newly
crept out of the schooles of Dante, Arioste and Petrarch, they greatly pollished
our rude and homely maner of vulgar Poesie, from that it had been before, and
for that cause may justly be sayd the first reformers of our English meetre and
stile.   (Puttenham, *Art of Englishe Poesie*, I, xxxi, p. 60)

So George Puttenham contrasts the second generation of Tudor poets
writing in the later years of Henry VIII with the earlier Skelton '(I wot
not for what great worthines), surnamed the Poet Laureat.' Wyatt and
Surrey are 'Courtly' poets, with both the refinement and the limitation
which the term implies. The 1530's, were dangerous times and did not
encourage the poet to attempt sweeping satires: even Skelton had been
muzzled after 1523, and the new generation had to be more careful.
Wyatt himself was more at home in the Tudor world than Skelton
had ever been, since he belonged to the families who had risen with the
new dynasty. His father had fought at Bosworth field with Richmond
and had later earned a knighthood and an honoured position in the
government. Thomas Wyatt, born in 1503, came to court in the early
1520's and had risen high in the royal service as a diplomat by the time
of his death in 1542; yet even with these advantages, he was twice in
the Tower and in some danger of his life. In contrast Surrey, born in
1517, belonged to the pre-Tudor nobility and started life, therefore,
with the scales weighed against him. His father was Thomas Howard,
Duke of Norfolk, who had made himself useful to the King for his

skill in soldiering; and the family rose high in the King's favour when
Henry married Catherine Howard, only to suffer eclipse with her fall.
Father and son were imprisoned for treason, and Surrey himself was
executed in 1546, shortly before the death of the King. In dangerous
times like these, poets had to avoid the big political themes in which
Skelton had delighted; and their verse, mainly written for private
circulation, is very much concerned with matters of technique, and
more cautious about public issues except as they impinge directly on
the personal lives of the poets. The poetry of Wyatt and Surrey is
largely private and more closely geared to their private lives than that
of Skelton.

This is especially true of Wyatt whose personal career had a deep
influence on his poetic development. The most illuminating account
of this will be found in the recent study by Miss Thomson. He received
his first official employment in a government office in 1524 and, after
the early break-up of his own marriage, became in some degree
involved with Anne Boleyn in 1525, when she was at court as Catherine
of Aragon's maid-of-honour. We have no means of knowing how
far the affair went, but we know that Wyatt wrote a riddle on her
name:

> What wourde is that that chaungeth not,
>   Though it be tourned and made in twain?
> It is myn aunswer, god it wot,
>   And eke the causer of my payn . . .
>
>   (no. 50)

In 1526–7, however, he was away on diplomatic missions in France
and Italy, and by the time he had returned Henry had become interested
in Anne whom he married in 1533. Tradition has it that Henry
warned Wyatt off, and it is generally agreed that the fine and bitter
sonnet, 'Who so list to hount . . .' (7) adapted from Petrarch's sonnet
CXC, 'Una candida cerva', represents the poet's reaction to Henry's
new interest in her. The deer that he has followed with such 'vayne
travaill' is now finally out of his reach because:

> . . . graven with Diamonds, in letters plain
> There is written her faier neck rounde abowte:
> *Noli me tangere*, for Cesars I ame . . . (no. 7)

The diamonds are taken from Petrarch's sonnet, but Wyatt's reference
to them would suggest that Henry had signalled his royal favour with
the gift of a diamond necklace. Later, when the affair was far behind,
and Wyatt had turned to Elizabeth Darrell with whom he lived

happily until his death, he seems to be commenting on it all in his sonnet, 'If waker care, if sodayne pale Coulor' (95). If the usual symptoms of love mean anything he says:

> ... then do I love agayne,
>   If thow aske whome, sure sins I did refrayne
>   Brunet, that set my welth in such a rore,
> Th' unfayned chere of Phillis hath the place
>   That Brunet had: she hath and ever shal.

Anne Boleyn was certainly a brunette; and Wyatt made the reference more specific in an earlier version of the poem where, instead of the comment on Brunet's extravagance, he wrote: 'Her that ded set our country in a rore.'

Whatever the nature of Wyatt's relationship with Anne, it did him no immediate harm with his monarch and he continued to rise in the royal favour. He was Marshal of Calais in 1529, chief Ewer at Anne's coronation in 1533, and was knighted two years later. But when Anne fell in 1536, he was thrown into the Tower, probably at the instigation of his enemy, Suffolk; and from there he appears to have watched 'out of a grate' the execution of the five men who were arraigned, probably on trumped-up charges, for adultery with the Queen. He may even have seen the execution of Anne herself on May 19th. The record of this experience is the great and moving poem recently identified by Professor Muir in the Blage Manuscript, 'Who lyst his welthe and eas Retayne' (XLIII). In it Wyatt describes what the experience meant to him:

> These blodye days have brokyn my hart;
>   My lust, my youth dyd then departe,
>   And blynd desyre of astate;
>   Who hastis to clyme sekes to reverte:
>   Of truthe, *circa Regna tonat.*
>
> The bell towre showed me suche syght
>   That in my hed stekys day and nyght;
>   Ther dyd I lerne out of a grate,
>   Ffor all valuore, glory or myght,
>   That yet *circa Regna tonat.*

His Chaucerean sonnet exhorting lovers to arise and 'do May some observance' may well refer to the same occasion: a May morning can

invite other lovers to 'live in lust and joyful jollitie', but for him in the
Tower there is no such joyful rising:

> In May my welth and eke my liff, I say,
> Have stonde so oft in such perplexitie:
> Rejoyse! Let me dreme of your felicitie.
> (no. 92)

Wyatt was spared and went home to his father at the family castle
of Allington in Kent; but the experience stuck in his mind and seems
to have transformed him from a young and ambitious courtier into a
thoughtful and disillusioned man. His three satires directed against life
at court and the ambitions of those who go there are of this period.
As a loyal Tudor servant he never questions:

> The powar of them, to whome fortune hath lent
> Charge over us, of Right, to strike the stroke:
> (no. 196, ll. 8-9)

but the court now appears to him as it appeared to Drede in Skelton's
Bouge of Court, and he is able to treat the stock themes of Renaissance
satire with a sincerity which Barclay had lacked. In the first satire, he
protests his inability to practise the sycophancy on which success at
court depends:

> I cannot crowche nor knelle to do so grete a wrong,
> To worship them, lyke gode on erthe alone,
> That ar as wollffes thes sely lambes among.
> (no. 196, ll. 25-7)

he prefers instead to live his quiet country life 'in Kent and Christen-
dome', as he puts it with fine irony. In the second, he tells the old fable
of the country mouse who went to the town dwelling of her sister,
foolishly expecting great wealth, until 'The traytor Catt had caught
her by the hippe' (197). The way to happiness is not through ambition
but through that stoicism which finds contentment in those things within our own control:

> Thy self content with that is the assigned,
> And use it well that is to the allotted.
> Then seke no more owte of thy self to fynde
> The thing that thou haist sought so long before,
> For thou shalt fele it sitting in thy mynde.
> (no. 197, ll. 95-9)

The Tudors, however, rarely destroyed a loyal servant who could still be of use, and Wyatt was soon back in favour once more. From 1537 to 1540 he was in France, Spain and the Netherlands on difficult and unrewarding diplomatic missions: in 1540 his friend and protector, Cromwell, fell from power, and soon afterwards he turned towards religion with his verse paraphrases of the Penitential Psalms. At this juncture, his old enemy, Suffolk, and Bishop Bonner, with whom he had been associated in Spain, took the opportunity to settle old scores, and in 1541 Wyatt found himself back in the Tower. Once more he was freed, possibly at the intercession of Henry's new queen, Catherine Howard, only to die of a fever in 1542 on his way to meet the French ambassador at Dover. His life is that of the typical Tudor servant, honest and loyal but not for that reason out of the reach of danger. His poetry records his development from witty and ambitious youth to mature and possibly religious middle age.

Wyatt's personal development is accompanied by corresponding changes in literary method, as he developed his own personal contacts with humanism. The precise order in which his poems were written is by no means certain, but he began with lyrics in the fifteenth-century mode and continued writing these until the end of his life, although he turned to sonnets after his visit to Italy in 1526–7, and to satires at the time of his trouble in 1536. Recent studies of Wyatt, notably those of Mr Lever and Mr Mason, have concentrated on the sonnets and have relegated the lyrics to an inferior position, on the grounds that they are entirely conventional. Their conventionality cannot be denied: they are in the tradition of the fifteenth-century courtly lyric—not the popular lyric of Skelton—and their subject-matter is made up of the conventional situations of courtly love, the wooing of the obdurate lady, the fidelity promised and broken. Wyatt plays endlessly with these traditional themes in the short-line metres so common in the previous century. Here is part of a typical fifteenth-century lyric addressed to *An Inconstant Mistress* and quoted by Professor Robbins in his collection of Secular Lyrics:

> O Mestres, whye
>   Owtecaste am I
> all utterly
>   from your pleasaunce?
> Sythe ye and I
> or thys, truly,
> famyliarly
>   have had pastaunce ...

But sythe that ye
So strange wylbe
As toward me,
   & wyll not medyll,
I truste, percase,
to fynde some grace
to have free chayse,
   & spede as welle!

(no. 137)

The attitude to the mistress is typically un-Petrarchan; the metre is the old ballad with its eight-syllable line divided into fours. Here now is Wyatt doing just the same thing, though with considerably more neatness and polish!

Wyth serving still
   This have I wone,
For my godwill
   To be undone;

And for redresse
   Of all my payne,
Disdaynefulnes
   I have againe. . . .

Wherefore all ye
   That after shall
Bye fortune be,
   As I am, thrall,

Example take
   What I have won,
Thus for her sake
   To be undone!

(no. 157)

Most of these lyrics were designed to be sung, as can be assumed from Wyatt's freqent references to his lute:

Now cesse, my lute, this is the last
Labour that thou and I shall wast . . .

(no. 66)

and to enjoy the full flavour of them, it is necessary to imagine them in their original setting, at a court where the King himself was both composer and performer and informal music of this kind was a staple entertainment. Like Castiglione's courtier, those who served Henry VIII had to be able to turn and to sing a courtly love lyric; and a conventional and ostensibly quite impersonal love song can take on a wholly new dimension when sung in the presence of a mixed company of courtiers and ladies who all know one another and are familiar with the current *affaires de cœur*. In the right company, a wholly traditional lyric such as the following can become very personal if aimed, so to speak, in the right direction:

> Lyke as the Swanne towardis her dethe
> Doeth strayn her voyse with dolefull note,
> Right so syng I with waste of breth,
> I dy! I dy! and you regarde yt note....
>
> (no. 70)

Perhaps the real vitality of Wyatt's lyrics springs from the fact that the courtly attitudes they express were not merely conventional but were still produced inevitably by the conditions of the court in which he was writing. Courtly love itself grew in the first place out of the nature of the little feudal court, where the sexes are constantly together but separated by tabus of rank and convention. There are the noble ladies and the young men of breeding undergoing their education in court service; marriage depends on rank and dowry, so that love is forced into a separate compartment, its gratification often outside the marriage bond. For this reason, Courtly love demands adultery and secrecy, the private bargain faithfully observed in place of the official binding of the marriage service. In such a society, as Dr Stevens has shown, sexual awareness exerts a constant pressure; and the songs of courtship, the debates on love, the elaborate code of gallantry between the sexes, are the means by which this explosive instinct can be acknowledged and, through ritual, made relatively safe. Love is turned into a sophisticated parlour game, a public currency between the sexes which allows an outlet for emotions which are thereby made more safe because the display is public and traditional. The court of Henry VIII was not essentially different from that of Eleanor of Aquitaine; Anne Boleyn, for example, was in close proximity to Wyatt and yet, in terms of rank, his superior. It is for this reason that he can speak with the generic voice of courtly lovers and bring new conviction to old themes. The lover had always asked:

> What menythe thys? When I lye alone,
> I tosse, I turne, I syghe, I grone;
> My bedd me semys as hard as stone ...

but Wyatt can add a new authentic touch of realism which suddenly brings the convention to life:

I syghe, I playne contynually;
The clothes that on my bedd do ly
Always methynks they lye awry:
    What menys thys?   (no. 110)

At the same time, a simple love lyric can gain in intensity by evoking
the whole courtly tradition which is behind it. Wyatt's lyric 'And
wylt thou leve me thus?' for example, by minute variations from
stanza to stanza, turns a simple plea into a just demand backed by the
authority of centuries of courtly lovers:

And wylt thow leve me thus?
Say nay, say nay, for shame,
To save the from the Blame
Of all my greffe and grame . . .

And wylt thow leve me thus
That hathe lovyd the so long . . .

And wylt thow leve me thus,
That hathe gevyn the my hart,
Never for to Depart . . .

And wylt thow leve me thus
And have nomore Pyttye
Of hym that lovythe the?
                    (no. 113)

Each verse carries the demand a stage further, in terms of the logic of
the code which insists that faithful service must have its reward.
Wyatt's special power, indeed, is to invest the traditional crises of the
courtly relationship with a fresh dramatic immediacy: the moment
when the lovers make their bargain:

Madame, withouten many wordes
    Ons I ame sure ye will or no;
And if ye will, then leve your bordes,
    And use your wit and shew it so. . . .

Yf it be yea I shalbe fayne;
    If it be nay, frendes as before;
Ye shall an othre man obtain,
    And I myn owne and yours no more.
                    (no. 34)

the anger when the mistress proves unfaithful:

What shulde I saye
Sins faithe is dede,
And truthe awaye
From you ys fled?
Shulde I be led
With doblenesse?
Naye, naye, mistresse!
(no. 143)

the lover's protestation of his own innocence:

Perdye I saide yt not
Nor never thought to do
(no. 134)

or the sweet reconciliation after the quarrel which has blown up and miraculously subsided, as the stanza form itself expands and collapses to embody the occasion:

Ys yt possyble
That so hye debate,
So sharpe, so sore, and off suche rate,
Shuld end so sone and was begone so late?
Is it possyble? (no. 111)

These are all familiar lyric situations which Wyatt captures and sharpens until they have the clarity of an emblem. His greatest originality, however, lies in his power to develop the dramatic moment into the dramatic sequence, and make the emotion both grow and resolve itself within the framework of the single poem. This is his achievement in his fine lyric 'In eternum' (71), where the 'In eternum' of his initial love has changed to one of hate by the end of the poem, and the refrain has become an organic part of the whole:

In eternum then from my herte I kest
That I had furst determined for the best;
Nowe in the place another thought doeth rest,
In eternum. (no. 71)

It is even more the case with his great anthology piece, perhaps the finest of all his lyrics:

They fle from me that sometyme did me seke

> With naked fote stalking in my chambre . . .
> (no. 37)

The poem is full of nostalgia and of bitterness at the memory of
favours once granted but now withheld: the astonishing juxtaposition
of 'naked' and 'stalking' suggests Yeats' women 'proud and stiff/When
on love intent,' yet leads on, at the same time, to Wyatt's favourite
metaphor of the deer, once 'gentill tame and meek' but now wild and
no longer willing to 'take bred at my hand'. The past and the present,
the gratitude and the contempt, are simultaneously there in Wyatt's
mind, and are reflected in the consistent ambiguity of the language.
'Gentill', for example, carries both its modern meaning and its older
one of 'nobly born' and hence out of reach. Skelton uses the word with
the same ambiguity in his lyric to Mistress Margaret Hussy—'Gentle
as Falcon/Or hawk of the tower' (p. 380): and Wyatt's whole sequence
is reminiscent of the deer in his sonnet, 'Whoso list to hount,' who is
'wylde for to holde, though I seme tame'. (7) Another word used with
double meaning is 'daunger'—'they put theimself in daunger/To take
bred at my hand'. We think of the danger into which the ladies thrust
themselves by coming to Wyatt's hand, but we are also reminded of
Daunger in the *Romance of the Rose*, that sinister medieval character
and arch-enemy of lovers who now bars the gate against him. Yet in
the past Wyatt has penetrated into the rose garden on at least one
occasion:

> . . . ons in speciall,
> In thyn arraye after a pleasaunt gyse,
>   When her lose gowne from her shoulders did fall,
>   And she me caught in her armes long and small;
> Therewithall swetely did me kysse,
> And softly saide, *dere hert, howe like you this?*

The hint of the conventional description of the medieval literary
mistress with her arms 'long and small' further places the sequence in
the *Rose* tradition and serves to remove the memory to the world of
Romance and Dream Vision; and for this reason Wyatt has to assure
himself that 'It was no dreme: I lay brode waking'. But the thought of
'waking' brings him with a rush out of his world of reverie, where
memory and desire are mixed, back to the present and the real, from
which the mistress has vanished with her 'straunge fasshion of for-
saking'. The comfort of memory has gone and only the pain is left,
which Wyatt expresses in the colloquial language and the angry
lurching metre of the final couplet:

But syns that I so kyndely ame served,
I would fain knowe what she hath deserved.

The double meanings are still there, in 'kyndely', but now both pull
the same way and express the same anger: the simple irony of 'kyndely'
used in its modern sense is reinforced by the older and, in this case,
more insulting implications of the word, that infidelity is part of her
sexual nature. The poem has moved from an initial statement of simple
grief to a conclusion of simple anger, but with the most subtle combinations of emotion in between. Wyatt has crossed the love lyric with
the deeper psychological realism of Chaucer and transferred the
interest from the outer situation to the inner drama of the mind.

Wyatt rescued the medieval courtly lyric from the decadence into
which it had fallen and gave it a new profundity: at the same time he
launched English poetry upon a new career in the field of the sonnet.
The accredited humanist model for love poetry was Petrarch; twenty
years after Wyatt began writing sonnets, Du Bellay in his famous
Defense of the French Language bade all French poets abandon the
rondeaux, ballades, virelays and chansons in favour of 'these beautiful
sonnets, the learned and pleasant invention of the Italians'. Like Chaucer
earlier, Wyatt returned from Italy fired with a love of the literature
he found there and brought the sonnet form with him. He wrote over
thirty in all, twenty-five of them derived directly from Petrarch, and
they are the first sonnets to be written in English. The form was not
an easy one to acclimatise: Wyatt usually stays close to the Petrarchan
pattern with an octave all on two rhymes, but splits the sestet up into
a quatrain and a final couplet. The result is something radically
different from the smooth flow and balance of the Italian original:
the units of thought in Wyatt's sonnets still tend to be large ones,
following the basic grouping of ideas into a balancing octet and sestet,
but the final couplet insists on an epigrammatic summing up or final
volte face which is not there in Petrarch. Moreover Wyatt's tone is
colloquial and dramatic rather than formal, and there is within his
sonnets a struggle between the dramatic explosiveness of the human
voice and the formal structure imposed by the elaborate rhyme scheme,
which is shut in by the final couplet instead of being released through
the more flowing Petrarchan structure. As a result, Wyatt's sonnets
give a unique sense of concentration and of pressure generated within
a little space, together with a roughness which has often been mis-
interpreted. Miss Foxwell, for example, assumed that Wyatt was
struggling to attain the smooth and regular form of Surrey and the
later sonneteers, and that he too achieved it after early trials and

misses. She therefore suggested a system of elisions and muted syllables by means of which even the most irregular of Wyatt's sonnets could be forced into the Procrustean bed of regular scansion.

Wyatt could, on occasion, write a wholly regular sonnet, such as 'The piller pearisht' (no. 173), or 'Dyvers dothe use' (no. 145)—although we cannot always say with certainty whether such sonnets were written early or late. We know, too, that in the lyric, he had an impeccable ear, both for regularity and for the calculated irregularity of a line such as, 'It was no dreme: I lay brode waking,' whose strange lingering quality was so ruined by Tottel's attempt to smooth it out—'It was no dreame, for I lay broad awaking.' We are entitled to assume, I think, that when Wyatt wrote irregular lines, he intended to do so; and some of the movements he achieved were obviously aimed at something quite different from the normal decasyllabic sonnet line:

> I abide and abide and better abide,
>> And after the olde proverbe, the happie daye;
>> And ever my ladye to me dothe saye:
>> 'Let me alone and I will provyde'. (no. 160)

this seems an attempt to combine the sonnet with the old song, just as the opening lines:

> Who so list to hount, I knowe where is an hynde,
>> But as for me, helas, I may no more: (no. 7)

contain a suggestion of ballad metre. Sometimes Wyatt seems to be attempting a line in which the five feet also contain five stresses:

> A swete languor, a great lovely desire . . .
> Or else in my sperklyng voyse lower or higher
> Which nowe fere, nowe shame, wofully doth tyer . . .
>> (no. 12)

He is always trying out ways in which the tone of voice and the natural stresses of speech can reinforce and clarify the meaning within the compressed rhetoric of the sonnet form:

> Withoute Iyen, I se; and withoute tong I plain;
>> I desire to perisshe, and yet I aske helthe;
>> (no. 26)

> My galy charged with forgetfulnes
>> Thorrough sharpe sees in wynter nyghtes doeth pas

> Twene Rock and Rock; and eke myn ennemy, Alas,
> That is my lorde, sterith with cruelnes;   (no. 28)

The voice, groping for regularity, is forced to linger on 'Iyen', 'tong', 'Perisshe' 'helthe', 'ennemy', 'lorde', all key words upon which the central antitheses of the lines depend. We should not read Wyatt as if he were a failed Surrey, but as if he were trying to be a Donne; and we should recognise that he is attempting to convey the dramatic immediacy of the lyric through a poetic form which we have come to associate with formal regularity, but which in Wyatt's own day, at a time when the principles of prosody were so unfixed, evoked no such assumption.

In recent years, attention has been directed more to the contents of Wyatt's sonnets than to their prosody. Wyatt was so different in temperament from Petrarch that his treatment of the Petrarchan material reveals more of him than does his treatment of the traditional lyric, with the basic attitudes of which he had more natural affinity. He has none of Petrarch's rhapsodical idealism of his lady, no sense of her physical beauty or of the unity of human love with the great seasonal awakenings of nature. When Petrarch remembers Laura it is a memory of her surrounded by the green leaves, her hair entwined with pearls and gems which she spreads out and gathers up so lightly and gently (CXCVI: 'L'aura serana'). When Wyatt remembers his mistress it is as she comes to his chamber 'in thyn arraye . . . when her lose gowne from her shoulders did fall,' (no. 37). The two memories epitomise the difference between the romantic idealist and the practical wooer, a difference which is immediately apparent whenever Wyatt allows himself any freedom in the treatment of his model. At first he was content to translate, though even when he is most close to Petrarch, he introduces modifications which make the resulting poems his own. His sonnet 'My galy charged with forgetfulnes' (no. 28) for example, translated from Petrarch's 'Passa la nave' (CLXXXIX), replaces Petrarch's rather literary Scylla and Charybdis with the more vague and sinister 'Twene Rock and Rock', and Petrarch's rather imprecise 'dolci usati segni' with the more concrete and evocative line 'The starres be hid that led me to this pain'. What in the original is a literary conceit, the familiar ship metaphor extended throughout the sonnet, becomes in Wyatt's version something of a deeper psychological import, the projection of a powerful and agonised hopelessness.

More commonly, however, Wyatt 'imitates' Petrarch in terms of current literary theory, and keeping close to the original wording produces something totally different. In Petrarch's 'Una Candida

Cerva' (CXC), the white doe which the lover pursues, until he sees
written around her neck in diamonds and topaz, 'Touch me not, for it
is Caesar's will that I remain free', is a mysterious figure who may be a
symbol of Laura's chastity, or even a prefiguration of her death. She
is a very different figure from the apparently tame but actually wild
and fickle deer of Wyatt's sonnet (no. 7); and Wyatt is exploiting the
reader's knowledge of the original to make an ironical comment on the
nature of his own lady. In the same way, he exploits his reader's
familiarity with May morning love poetry in his Chaucerean sonnet
'You that in love finde lucke and habundance' (no. 92). He goes even
further in his adaptation of Petrarch's 'Io non fu' d'amar' (LXXXII),
'Was I never yet of your love greved' (no. 9). Petrarch declares that he
would rather have a fine plain tomb than that Laura's name should
be carved in any marble to say that she caused his death. Wyatt makes
the same point, but with such a degree of truculence as to change the
tone of the sonnet completely:

> I will not yet in my grave be buried
> Nor on my tombe your name yfixed fast . . .

Such a development leads inevitably to sonnets which break away
completely from Petrarch in everything except form, and Wyatt
wrote a number of these. One which signals his complete emancipation
from his master is the sonnet number 139, in which he begs his lady, if
she must be fickle, at least to go on being fickle to other lovers as well:

> To Rayle or geste ye kno I use yt not,
>   Though that such cause some tyme in folkes I finde:
>   And tho to chaunge ye list to sett your minde,
>   Love yt who liste, in faithe I like yt not.
> And if ye ware to me as ye are not,
>   I wolde be lothe to se you so unkinde;
>   But sins your faithe muste nedes be so, be kinde:
>   Tho I hate yt, I praye you leve yt not . . .

This is not only a complete denial of Petrarch's idealistic love, and a
return to the spirit of the lyrics; it is a tremendous metrical tour de
force, in which the emphasis falls on the word 'not', repeated as a
rhyme word throughout the first twelve lines. Wyatt is demonstrating
both his mastery of the Petrarchan form and his independence of the
Petrarchan sentiments.

A word in conclusion must be said about the satires which are to

many readers the most successful poems Wyatt ever wrote. Like the
sonnets, they are explicitly humanist, more so than those of Skelton:
the first is based on the satires of the Italian poet Alamanni whose
collected poems had been published four years earlier, in 1532; the
other two are less specific in their sources but go back ultimately to
Horace. All are written in the informal Horatian epistolary style of
satire—'Myne owne John Poynz . . .', 'I thowght forthwith to write/
Brian, to the . . .'; and all are in the familiar Renaissance tradition of
satires directed against the court, although, as we have seen earlier,
Wyatt attacks those who are foolish enough to seek profit there, as
much as the court itself, which he takes for granted as a place of danger
and corruption. In tone they are more urbane than those of Skelton,
and use irony rather than abuse as their basic weapon. They are also
intensely personal, as Wyatt remembers the song of the country mouse
sung by 'My mothers maydes when they did sowe and spynne' (no.
197), or scorns the life at court from the security of his Horatian
country retreat:

> This maketh me at home to hounte and to hawke
> And in fowle weder at my booke to sitt.
> In frost and snowe then with my bow to stawke . . .
> (no. 196)

    Throughout, Wyatt shows a consciousness that he is writing human-
ist satire, and the style is consistently held down at the low level which
the decorum of satire demands. The poems are packed with colloquial
idioms and homely proverbs:

> A chippe of chaunce more than a pownd of witt.

> To set his hay for Conys over Ryvers.

They are full of vivid little scenes which might have come straight out
of a Ben Jonson play about city life:

> Lerne at Kittson that in a long white cote
> From under the stall withoute landes or feise
> Hath lept into the shopp. . . .
> . . . and if he koggh to sore,
> When he hath spit tred owte and please him so.
> (no. 198)

It is no accident that the poems contain many medieval and Chaucerean
phrases, echoes and references—'And drynck goode ale so noppy for

the noyns', 'In lusty lees at libertie I walke'—and when Wyatt protests
that he is incapable of flattery, he does so in an image which evokes
Chaucer, the arch-satirist: he cannot:

> Praysse Syr Thopas for a nobyll talle,
> And skorne the story that the knyght tolld.
>   (no. 196)

In doing this, Wyatt asserts the continuity between the native tradition
and humanist satire, and effects a fusion between the two, more
successfully and with more recognition of the humanist models than
we find in Skelton. As Miss Thomson puts it in her full analysis of
these poems, Wyatt has achieved 'the naturalisation of the classic
satire'. (p. 270)

After Wyatt, Surrey may come as an anticlimax; yet Surrey was the
more often praised in sixteenth-century surveys of English poetry, and
Puttenham couples them together—'Henry Earle of Surrey and Sir
Thomas Wyat, betweene whom I finde very little difference'—
contrasting both with Skelton whom he rates as a mere buffoon.
Puttenham's contempt for Skelton indicates the reason why he fails to
discriminate between such radically different poets as the other two.
By the 1570's, humanistic values were very much to the fore and
Puttenham judged literature by them: all the differences between
Wyatt and Surrey are far outweighed by the one humanist feature
which they have in common, the Petrarchan element in both. Surrey
wrote fewer sonnets than Wyatt, and none of them have the com-
pression and inner struggle which give Wyatt's sonnets their special
quality. If we compare Wyatt's 'The longe love, that in my thought
doeth harbar' (4) with Surrey's 'Love that doth raine and live within
my thought' (4), both of which are versions of Petrarch's 'Amor, che
nel penser' (CXL), it can be seen that Surrey's sonnet is both less
precise in wording and less faithful in content, but at the same time
more fluid in movement. Wyatt's 'preseth with bolde pretence/And
therin campeth, spreding his baner'. is more forceful than Surrey's:

> Clad in the armes wherin with me he fowght
> Oft in my face he doth his banner rest.

just as his original image of love fleeing into 'the hertes forest', with
its underlying pun, is more exciting than Surrey's simple 'to the hert
apace/Taketh his flight'; Wyatt avoids too the tautology of Surrey's
'suffre pain'. His sonnet has a much tighter structure than Surrey's and
even incorporates the final couplet into the rhyming pattern of the

sestet, so that it is virtually Petrarchan in form. Yet the price paid is
that of a ruggedness—'And willes that my trust and lustes negligence'—
which fights with the very conventional conceit around which the
whole sonnet is written: the pressure of Wyatt's sonnet deserves a
better theme, and Surrey's easier, less emphatic version is more of a
piece. The difference springs from the fact that Surrey is using the
looser Shakespearean form with three quatrains on different rhymes
and a final couplet; and Surrey's sonnets are invariably less tortured
by virtue of this fact.

Surrey for the most part avoids Petrarchan sonnets with any concentration of thought and prefers to imitate those consisting of straight
description. This is in part a reflection of his own personal interests;
he had a feeling for nature and a power of natural description which is
unique among the poets of his age:

> The soote season, that bud and blome furth bringes,
> With grene hath clad the hill and eke the vale;
> The nightingale with fethers new she singes;
> The turtle to her mate hath tolde her tale.
> Somer is come, for every spray nowe springes;
> The hart hath hong his olde hed on the pale;
> The buck in brake his winter cote he flinges;
> The fishes flote with newe repaired scale . . .
>
> (no. 2)

Surrey is elaborating on Petrarch in this sonnet, and adding details of
his own; but the simple catalogue, besides encouraging such additions,
also allows a greater freedom in the choice of rhymes than would be
possible if there were a close line of thought to follow, and in consequence Surrey makes of the sonnet a metrical *tour de force*, all on two
rhymes. This is symptomatic of his attitude towards Petrarch's sonnets:
unlike Wyatt he is not greatly interested in love, but he is very interested in the formal possibilities of the sonnet itself, and he chooses
those which allow him to experiment with a more formal yet simpler
rhetoric than that of Wyatt:

> Set me whereas the sonne doth perche the grene,
> Or whear his beames may not dissolve the ise;
> In temprat heat wheare he is felt and sene;
> With prowde people, in presence sad and wyse;
> Set me in base, or yet in highe degree,
> In the long night, or in the shortyst day . . .
> Set me in erthe, in heaven, or yet in hell,
> In hill, in dale, or in the fowming floode; . . .

> Yours will I be, and with that onley thought
> Comfort myself when that my hape is nowght.
>
> (no. 3)

With its three quatrains, each saying the same thing in a different way, and its final couplet rounding off the whole, it shows a perfect correspondence of form to content, and leads straight on to Shakespeare's 'That time of year'.

All of Surrey's poetry looks to the future in this way. Though a less exciting poet than Wyatt, he is of greater historical importance, because he sensed so clearly the deficiencies of the native tradition and gave English verse so radical an overhaul. This is apparent in his translation of Books II and IV of the *Aeneid*, for which he invented the decasyllabic blank verse line to do the job of the hexameter. Surrey's lines are stiff and end-stopped, but they nevertheless established what was to become the authentic High Style of English poetry. The same is true of his notorious Poulter's Measure with its alternate lines of twelve and fourteen syllables, so called after the alleged habits of poulters 'which giveth twelve for one dozen and fourteen for another'. The fourteener and its combinations were old and famous measures which, when split up into Peter Quince's eight and six, formed the traditional medieval Ballad Metre. It was common in the courtly lyric, and Wyatt himself made use of it on occasion, though he usually broke it down into his own short line metres with frequent rhymes:

> O goodely hand
> Wherein doeth stand
> Myn hart distrast in payne;
> Fair hand, Alas,
> In little spas
> My liff that doeth restrayne.
>
> (no. 86)

Surrey uses it frequently, but always in its full extended form to give free play to the strong and rhythmic swing of the line:

> In winters just returne, when Boreas gan his raigne,
> And every tree unclothed fast, as Nature taught them plaine;
> In misty morning darke, as sheepe are then in holde,
> I hyed me fast, it sat me on, my sheepe for to unfold.
>
> (no. 16)

It is a metre of infinite monotony which, by ignoring completely the natural accentual quality of the language, throws up a screen between the reader and the meaning of the verse. Surrey seems almost to have cultivated this quality in placing his Caesuras between the verbs and their objects where they would interrupt the thought sequence to the maximum degree:

> The yong man eke that feeles   his bones with paynes opprest,
> How he wold be a riche olde man, to lyve and lye att rest;
> The ryche olde man, that sees   his end draw on so sore,
> How he wolde be a boy agayne, to lyve so moche the more . . .
> And musinge thus, I thincke   the case is very straunge . . .
>
> (no. 25)

But Surrey was clearly not concerned with the meaning; his materials consist of all the most hackneyed conceits of the period which he can use as a basis for academic experiments in prosody.

He may have been trying to produce an English equivalent of quantitive verse, but what he in fact did was to bring back a knowledge of basic rhythm and show the way to scan in foot and syllable. The reader of Surrey's Poulter's measure can be in no doubt that here is a writer who knows how to scan, and the ruthless repetition of the unvarying foot drives home its nature with inescapable emphasis. The very quality which makes these verses so insufferable nowadays gave the sixteenth-century reader what he most needed after a century of prosodic uncertainty; he was not ready for the precarious and delicate effects of Wyatt, but he could go to school in Surrey's verse and learn again one of the great constituent elements of English prosody. Thanks to Surrey, the sixteenth-century arts of poetry, such as those of Puttenham or Webbe, are full of specimens of scansion complete with their syllables marked long or short; and the poets for a generation after his death practised within the framework he provided. The results can be seen in the attempts of Wyatt's later publisher, Tottel, to reduce his verse to crude regularity; it took thirty years before poetry was ready for the new subtleties of the *Shepheardes Calender* in 1579. The fourteener itself continued to flourish as late as Chapman's Homer in the early seventeenth century, although it had become an anachronism by that time, as can be seen from the way Shakespeare parodies it in Peter Quince's play. Possibly Chapman used it as being appropriate for a great but primitive poet.

Surrey's importance, however, is more than merely historical. When he has a theme in which he is personally involved, he can do very much better. There is, for example, the moving poem which he wrote while imprisoned in Windsor castle where he had spent so many happy days in his youth: he remembers the hunting and tilting, the

tennis played with one eye always 'cast upp unto the maydens towre'
from where the ladies were watching:

> The palme playe, where, dispoyled for the game,
> With dased eyes oft we by gleames of love
> Have mist the ball and got sight of our dame
> To bayte her eyes which kept the leddes above.
>
> (no. 27)

It is as fresh and personal a picture of Tudor life in the big house as
one could wish for, and the contrast moves him to tears:

> And with this thought the blood forsakes my face,
> The teares berayne my cheke of dedlye hewe; ...

He may never have met Wyatt, but he certainly admired him, and
wrote a fine and bitter sonnet about those hypocrites who, having
worked for Wyatt's death, now 'Yeld Cesars teres uppon Pompeius
hedd' (no. 29). His great elegy on Wyatt's death is a magnificent
formal tribute to which there is no parallel until we come to Carew's
Elegy on Donne or Marvell's Horatian Ode upon Cromwell:

> Wyatt resteth here, that quick could never rest;
> Whose heavenly giftes encreased by disdayn
> And vertue sank the deper in his brest:
> Such profit he by envy could obtain.
>
> A hed, where wisdom misteries did frame;
> Whose hammers bet styll in that lively brayn
> As on a stithe, where that some work of fame
> Was dayly wrought to turne to Britaines gayn.
>
> A visage stern and myld; where bothe did grow ...
> A hand that taught what might be sayd in ryme ...
> A toung that served....   (no. 28)

In another mode, he achieves a moving dramatic monologue in the
lament of a woman whose husband is away on the high seas:

> I stand the bitter night
> In my window, where I may see
> Before the windes how the cloudes flee.
> Lo, what a mariner love hath made me! ...

> Thus is my wealth mingled with wo,
> And of ech thought a dout doth growe,
> Now he comes, will he come? Alas, no, no!
>
> (no. 23)

This, however, was a situation which had a personal meaning for him, since he was refused permission to take his wife with him to the French wars. Yet it is typical of Surrey that even here he was experimenting in form and tried to do the same thing, with far less success, in Poulter's Measure (no. 24).

The range and power of these personal poems suggest that if Surrey had lived longer, he might have developed into a poet of real greatness; yet even what he achieved in his short life was of a very startling nature. For Surrey in his own verse achieved a revolution in poetry as momentous as that of Dryden and Waller in the next century, and in many ways similar to it. He pulled verse out of the medieval into the modern world: he banished the aureate and the alliterative once and for all, and established a standard of clear and controlled language which was what the century needed above all else. Read any aureate love poem of the fifteenth century, and then turn to the clarity and unhurried precision of Surrey's six-lined stanza:

> When ragyng love, with extreme payne
> Most cruelly distrains my hart,
> When that my teares, as floudes of rayne,
> Beare witnes of my wofull smart;
> When sighes have wasted so my breath
> That I lye at the poynte of death:
>
> I call to minde the navye greate,
> That the Grekes brought to Troye towne
> And how the boysteous windes did beate
> Their shyps, and rente their sayles adowne,
> Till Agamemnons daughters bloode
> Appeasde the goddes, that them withstode.
>
> And how that in those ten yeres warre,
> Full manye a bloudye dede was done,
> And manye a lord, that came full farre,
> There caught his bane, alas, to sone
> And many a good knight overronne,
> Before the Grekes had Helene wonne.
>
> Then thinke I thus: sithe suche repayre,
> So longe time warre of valiant men,
> Was all to winne a ladye fayre

> Shall I not learne to suffer then,
> And thinke my life well spent to be
> Servyng a worthier wight than she?
>
> Therefore I never will repent,
> But paynes contented stil endure:
> For like as when, rough winter spent,
> The pleasant spring straight draweth in ure,
> So after ragyng stormes of care,
> Joyful at length may be my fare.   (no. 1)

I have quoted this lyric in full because its excellence lies not in single lines but in the cumulative effect and organisation of the whole. In the thirty lines of the poem there are only three sentences, yet it unfolds itself with a clear and ordered logic. It has a form entirely suited to its content, and while never pretending to more feeling than the occasion deserves, it treats a conventional theme with dignity. It is a new form of art, occasional, classical, urbane, and we find nothing comparable until Ben Jonson. The sixteenth century was not yet mature enough for this kind of writing; such Augustan simplicity and restraint were beyond it, and English poetry for the time being went another way. We should not however let the exuberance of Elizabethan poetry blind us to the extraordinary originality of Surrey, for whom, as for no other poet of the time, Humanism meant the austerity of true classicism.

SHORTER FORMS OF ELIZABETHAN POETRY

(1) *Introduction*

The death of Surrey marks the end of the first phase of Tudor poetry. The fact of his execution, and the involvement of Wyatt's son in the rebellion of 1554, halted the poetic movement which they had started, and the troubled reigns of Edward VI and Mary were not conducive to the writing of poetry. The poems of Wyatt and Surrey, however, circulated in manuscript and were published in 1557, in that most influential enterprise of the early days of printing, *Tottel's Miscellany*, or—to give it its proper title—'Songes and Sonettes written by the ryght honorable Lorde Henry Haward late Earle of Surrey, and other'. Tottel was a well-known publisher who, realising the possibilities of the private collections of favourite poems which educated people kept in their scrap-books, conceived the idea in 1557 of publishing such a collection as a popular anthology. His *Miscellany* is the first attempt to popularise serious verse in print, and his choice of materials is calculated to interest as wide a public as possible. The Preface points out that the verse is in 'small parcelles', so that it is easy to read and capable of being sung; the forces of patriotism are invoked to promote the sales of a volume published 'to the honour of the Englishe tong', and the subjects are all drawn from love and the good life, the two great traditional themes of poetry. Every reader would be at home among poems with titles such as 'The lover sheweth his wofull state, and prayeth pitye' on the one hand, or 'Of the wretchedness of this world' on the other; such topics were the commonplaces of Chaucer and Lydgate and the fifteenth-century lyric. Yet these well-worn themes were brought up to date with a veneer of fashionable novelty; the love-lyrics were coloured by the influence of Petrarch, so that the

lovers, though assuming the same postures and enduring the same
agonies as in the past, yet did so with fresh conviction and in terms of
the new poetic conceits; the moral poems, as a result of the Reformation, avoided matters of doctrine and went for wise saws and proverbs
such as suited the more secular and practical morality of the new age.
Whatever was new and fashionable found a place in the *Miscellany*,
and over all was thrown the magic of the new styles and metres which
Wyatt and Surrey had introduced, while Tottel did not hesitate to
regularise even these where he felt that they fell short of contemporary
standards.

The work was enormously popular and had run through nine
editions by 1587. It taught succeeding publishers how to exploit the
new market in poetry and established the miscellany as a popular form
of publication for the next fifty years. The subsequent editors of the
species changed their techniques to meet the demands of a changing
public, and the tendency was, as always, to develop great specialisation.
The Paradise of Dainty Devices, for example, which appeared in 1576,
contains a much higher proportion of didactic verse and was clearly
aimed at a less sophisticated audience than was *Tottel's Miscellany*:
Clement Robinson's *Handefull of Pleasant Delites*, first printed in 1566
but surviving only in the edition of 1584, consists entirely of popular
songs, while the famous *Englands Helicon* of 1600 is all pastoral. As
the Italian tales were translated in greater numbers, and the popular
romances became more varied, the miscellanies had to take more pains
to entertain, in a world where competition was becoming daily more
acute, and the result can be seen in a collection such as *The Gorgeous
Gallery of Gallant Inventions* (1578) with its higher percentage of love
and narrative verse.

Tottel's Miscellany was the dominant influence on poetry for twenty
years after its publication, and the attempts to master the lessons of
Surrey's prosody and develop the Petrarchan conceit gave rise to much
pedestrian verse. There was, however, a good deal of unobtrusive yet
vital experiment within the framework of the fourteener, and though
no major poets appeared, an increasing number of minor ones, writing
indefatigably for the miscellanies, ensured that the lessons of the fourteener had been learnt and that poetry was ready to move on to a new
flexibility. Gascoigne is the most notable poet of the period, and his
moving *Lullaby* has justly found its way into the modern anthologies.
Both for the variety and for the unacademic quality of his verse, he
deserves more space than can be given to him here.

The publication of Spenser's *Shepheardes Calender* in 1579 is generally
held to mark the beginnings of the true Elizabethan poetic renaissance,

but Sidney's eclogues and sonnets, written at the same time though not published until 1591, should share the honour. The immediate inspiration of the new poetry was, as I have already indicated, the work of the Pléiade who had been experimenting in the incorporation of Italian and classical verse forms into the vernacular for the previous thirty years, and who continued to do so until the beginning of the seventeenth century. Du Bellay had died in 1560, but Ronsard lived until 1585 and Desportes, the most prolific of the sonneteers, until 1606. Spenser and Sidney seem to have regarded themselves as the inheritors of the poetic mantle of the Pléiade in England, and to have undertaken the task of doing for English verse what Du Bellay and Ronsard had done for the French. They experimented in new verse forms and were consciously the leaders of a group of new poets which Harvey christened the Areopagus, although they were never so well established a body as the Pléiade. Their early poetry was written according to the latest Renaissance theories, and their Manifesto, Sidney's *Apologie for Poetrie*, defended the vernacular, surveyed the achievements of its literature, and, as Du Bellay had done before, pointed out the superiority of the Ancients.

Sidney, however, died with his works unpublished, and Spenser, having moved to Ireland in 1580, published nothing new for ten years, although the *Shepheardes Calender* ran through several editions in the meantime. In their absence, the new movement was carried on by Lyly and Peele, the earliest of the University Wits, and developed by Greene, Lodge and Marlowe at the end of the decade. By 1590, the eclogue and sonnet were thoroughly established, while such new forms as the elegy, the madrigal, the anacreontic and pindaric had been introduced. English poetry was once more in the great European stream as it had not been since the time of Chaucer. There is scarcely a situation or conceit in the lyrical verse of the 'nineties which had not its counterpart in Italy or France.

Love was the main theme of the shorter forms of Elizabethan verse. The importance of love in Renaissance philosophy has already been indicated, and the vogue of Petrarch owes much to the spread of Neo-Platonic idealism. The European wave of Petrarchism reached England in the 1580's, when it began to sweep through sonnet, lyric and pastoral, bringing with it a flood of obdurate mistresses and protesting lovers who will scarcely ever achieve a kiss. There are other strains in late Elizabethan love poetry, however, and, among them, a rich and passionate sensuality which is deliberately anti-Petrarchan. The longer love poems of the 'nineties are sometimes Platonic, as Drayton's *Endimion and Phoebe*, for example; but more often they are frankly sexual, and mock the usual Petrarchan convention by showing the maid passionately but vainly wooing the man. This is the theme of *Venus and Adonis* or Lodge's poem, *Scillaes Metamorphosis*, to name only two; the extremely provocative love scenes of Marlowe's *Hero and Leander* are a far cry from the sonnet ladies on their platonic pedestals.

Though this note of deeper sensuousness in late Elizabethan verse derived in part from Italy, as the more licentious poetry of the Renaissance became better known, the influence of classical poetry was even more marked. The love poetry of the University Wits reads as if they were the first who turned to classical love poetry in the orginal and not merely to what had filtered through from the continent and the Middle Ages. The classical Renaissance, especially that of Greek, reached England very late, and the spread of Greek studies was an important factor at the end of the century. Classical Greek was as yet scarcely known, but later Greek literature, such as Longus' sophisticated and pornographic story of Daphnis and Chlöe, set the fashion for the Arcadian Romance and provided some pretty models for love-making. In this connection, too, the *Greek Anthology* was very important. This was a traditional collection of Greek poems, some of them extremely licentious, which had been published in Florence in 1494, to which was added a further number of late Greek poems discovered by the French printer Etienne in 1552, and wrongly attributed to Anacreon. From here came the fashion for Anacreontic Odes with their gay, amorous philosophy and their conception of the god Cupid so different from that of the Middle Ages. The medieval god of love was a grown youth whose fierce darts could produce tragedy on the scale of *Troilus and Criseyde*; the new god of the Anacreontics is the sportive little Cupid with his bow and arrows who played with Campaspe at cards for kisses and who shot his bolts at those who took pity on him. He can be seen at large in the lyrics of Lyly or in Sidney's sonnets, and he provided Elizabethan poetry with a great part of its conceits.

Of all classical models, however, Ovid was by far the most important and, after Petrarch, the greatest literary factor in the development of Elizabethan poetry. No longer moralised, as he had often been in the Middle Ages, he was enjoyed for his sophisticated sensuality; and the wider use of classical myth, together with such new forms as the love elegy and the heroic epistle, came from him. It is difficult to overestimate the influence of the *Metamorphoses* on the later sixteenth century; its effects were felt far beyond the range of love poetry and left their mark, as we shall see later, on such essentially English poems as Drayton's *Polyolbion*. It must not be forgotten, however, that there was already a great native tradition of frankly sexual verse which had found its last courtly expression in Skelton, before being relegated to the lower, unprinted levels of popular verse. Occasionally, in a form such as the lyric which built upon popular song, it rose to the surface, to produce such beautiful lyrics as that of Peele which echoes both the new pastoral and the old pagan song of the woman in love:

> Whenas the rye reach to the chin,
> And chopcherry, chopcherry ripe within,
> Strawberries swimming in the cream,
> And schoolboys playing in the stream;
>   Then oh, then oh, then oh, my true Love said,
>   She could not live a maid.
>   (Ault, *Elizabethan Lyrics*, p. 156)

The new Elizabethan verse is less personal than that of the earlier period. The poetry of Skelton or of Wyatt has an unmistakably individual flavour which makes the reader wonder whether a lyric or a sonnet is the record of a personal experience; but the average Elizabethan poem provokes no such conjecture and might be written by any one of a dozen different authors. One thinks of Elizabethan verse in terms of sonnets or pastorals rather than in terms of authors; the divisions are horizontal, into literary 'kinds', rather than vertical, between different poets, and the similarities between poems in the same category are greater than the differences. This results from the force with which the new verse forms seized upon the imagination of the poets, so that the challenge of the form itself was often sufficient to provoke good verse. For this reason it is convenient to discuss Elizabethan poetry in terms of 'kinds' rather than of authors.

C. S. Lewis has christened the poetry of the Elizabethan renaissance 'golden' as opposed to the 'drabness' of the earlier period, and the quality to which he refers is perhaps most clearly defined in Sidney's *Apologie for Poetrie*, written somewhere round 1583. Sidney's justification of poetry is based on his conception of the poet as the 'Maker'; whereas the scientist, the lawyer, the historian are tied to the facts of nature or 'captived to the truth of a foolish world', the right poet is free to invent a world of his own out of his own imagination: 'it is not riming and versing that maketh a Poet,' he says, 'but it is that fayning notable images of vertues, vices, or what else, with what delightfull teaching, which must be the right describing note to know a Poet by...' (p. 160). The peerless poet, therefore,

disdayning to be tied to any such subjection, lifted up with the vigor of his

owne invention, dooth growe in effect another nature, in making things either
better then Nature bringeth forth, or, quite anewe, formes such as never were
in Nature, as the *Heroes, Demi-gods, Cyclops, Chimeras, Furies,* and such like;
so as hee goeth hand in hand with Nature, not inclosed within the narrow
warrant of her guifts, but freely ranging onely within the Zodiack of his owne
wit. Nature never set forth the earth in so rich tapistry as divers Poets have done,
neither with so plesant rivers, fruitful trees, sweet-smelling flowers, nor what-
soever els may make the too much loved earth more lovely. Her world is
brazen, the Poets only deliver a golden . . .   (p. 156)

Not all 'golden verse' was written with Sidney's moral end in view,
but this imaginative quality is an almost universal characteristic until
the end of the century. The new poetry is essentially unrealistic and
fictional: it is set against a background of Arcadia or of classical tale:
if its theme is satirical or moral, it expresses it in terms of pastoral
shepherds or Arthurian knights; if it deals with love, it does so through
Theocritan idyll or Greek myth, or the equally fictional and stylised
attitudes of Petrarchism. The queen is metamorphosed from an ageing
woman to Gloriana or Cynthia; on every progress she was welcomed
by nymphs and woodmen who hailed her as their goddess, and Lyly
could present his play of *Endimion* at Court as a public compliment to
the Mortal Moon herself. There are, of course, exceptions, but the
overwhelming impression is of release into worlds of imagination.
The quality sprang in part from the opening up of the world itself
and the discovery of regions where the distinction between fact and
fiction seemed hardly to exist; it came even more, perhaps, from the
discovery and mastery of the golden world of classical myth. Elizabethan poetry after 1580 often has this quality of myth about it, until
the end of the century, when the great myth of the queen at last begins
to crack under the pressure of religious and political problems, and real
life thrusts itself into poetry again, unveiled and brazen.

(2) *The pastoral*

Something has already been said of the long history of the pastoral, and
its development from the original Theocritan idyll, by way of Virgil
and the allegorical shepherds of medieval Christianity, to the highly
conventionalised forms it took in the Renaissance. The most influential
of Renaissance pastoral writers was Baptista Spagnolo, commonly
known as Mantuan after the place of his birth, whose ten famous
eclogues were published in 1498. These deal with love, with the
neglect of poetry, and with the abuses of religion; and Barclay and
early Elizabethan writers of pastoral such as Googe and Turberville

followed in his footsteps. During the last quarter of the sixteenth century, however, the idyllic quality of the Greek Romances made itself felt increasingly in English poetry, and the pastoral went the same way, tending to lose its satiric function and become more and more an idealised and idyllic picture of the shepherd's life. In this mode it quickly penetrated the lyric, the drama and the prose romance to become one of the most pervasive conventions of later Elizabethan literature.

There are many reasons why the pastoral idyll captured the imagination of the Elizabethans. The tradition was already there in the medieval gardens of love whose unfading beauty prepared the way for the pastoral vision of the Golden Age, but the source of its popularity was not merely literary. In a period of such rapid change as the sixteenth century, when the organisation of society was becoming more centralised, London growing in size with enormous rapidity, and religion and the state making ever-increasing demands upon the individual, the simple shepherd's life stood as an escape from the new responsibilities and as the symbol of a less complicated existence. One of the commonest pastoral themes is the contrast between the city and the country, the court and the shepherd's cottage, but this does not, in the sixteenth century, embody the desire to escape from the town and return to nature which had emerged by the time of the Romantic Revival. The picture which the pastoral gave of country life was never for one moment mistaken for reality; the source of its appeal lay rather in the escape it offered from the responsibilities and worries which afflict 'the head that wears a crown', and it reflects in this the disquiet of a society consciously embarking on a new and more complicated stage of its evolution. Tennyson's English Idylls are closer to the pastoral, and more consciously modelled on it, than are the poems of Wordsworth. It reflects, too, in its nostalgia for the age of innocence, a desire to escape from the obsession with Original Sin which was a quality of the protestant conscience.

It is impossible to deal with all the poets who wrote pastorals, nor is it necessary to do so, for pastoral poetry fell into well-defined kinds, and it is difficult to distinguish the verses of one pastoral poet from those of another. Something, however, may be said about the eclogues which Sidney inserted between the separate books of the *Arcadia*, and those of Spenser's collection, the *Shepheardes Calender*, which really started the pastoral vogue in England. Sidney's poetry is, in some ways, the more interesting, for he never intended to publish it and it therefore exists in the experimental stage, whereas with Spenser we have the finished product. It would appear from the eclogues that Sidney's interest at this stage was mainly in prosody and that he was primarily intent on introducing variety after a generation of Poulter's Measure and the 'rym ram ruf by letter' of the followers of Surrey. De Baïf had been experimenting with classic metres in France, and the four pleasantly flippant letters which passed between Spenser and his Cambridge friend, Gabriel Harvey, show that Spenser was interested in the possibilities of these metres, though he quickly abandoned them. Sidney, on the other hand, tried them out side by side with more orthodox methods to test their possibilities, and, having discovered their inadequancy by practical means, abandoned them for the sonnet form. In the ecologues he tried Elegiacs, Sapphics, 'Exameter verses', Anacreontics and many others, giving a little diagram of the accents in each case to assist the reader, and demonstrating clearly, in spite of one or two successes, that the English language does not lend itself to quantitative verse. Sidney's experiments along more orthodox lines are staggering in their variety and show the influence of the Pléiade. He tried combinations of blank verse and rhyme, interlocking stanzas and echo patterns, fantastic compound rhymes such as 'garrison' and 'tarry soon' which remind one of Gilbert and Sullivan, rhymes which occur in the middle of the line instead of at the end, and occasional excursions back into the fourteener or Rhyme Royal. Most of the verse in Sidney's eclogues is too consciously experimental to be good, but he gave a spring-cleaning to English poetry which helped to liberate it from the old metres and made possible the new and subtler developments of the next decade.

Spenser's *Shepheardes Calender*, published anonymously in 1579, is a much more ambitious affair. It consists of twelve pastoral eclogues, one for each month of the year, together with a long dedicatory epistle and explanatory notes to each poem by a certain E.K. whose identity has not yet been finally settled. The most likely suggestion is that he was Sidney's friend, Fulke Greville. Spenser wrote the work after leaving Cambridge, when he was in London in company with Sidney and the poets who frequented Leicester House; and the epistle is the declaration of his humanist creed. It shows the almost aggressive Humanism which is Spenser's special characteristic. The *Shepheardes Calender* is his first considerable poetic venture; it is therefore in the pastoral vein, writes E.K., because the humanist poet begins with such lowly kinds of verse before advancing to higher ones: 'So flew Theocritus . . . So flew Virgile, as not yet well feeling his winges. So flew Mantuane, as being not full somd. So Petrarque. So Boccace; So Marot . . .' Now an English poet is carrying on the great tradition in the English language, as 'mynding to furnish our tongue with this

kinde, wherein it faulteth . . .' and Spenser is held up as the successor
to Chaucer, christened 'Tityrus, the God of shepheards' in the poem.
Spenser's intention of blending the native with the humanist tradition
is apparent in his choice of Skelton's Colin Clout as his pseudonym
throughout the sequence, and in his claim in the December eclogue
that Colin 'of Tityrus his songs did lerne'. He is not suggesting that he
is attempting to write like Chaucer, but that he now has put on the
mantle of the poet which Chaucer and Skelton have worn before him.

The poems themselves are a piece of humanist virtuosity through
which Spenser's explicit aim is to demonstrate and acclimatise in
English all the functions which the pastoral has ever fulfilled. Thus
May, July and September are allegories of the state of the church:
June and October lament the neglect of poetry; August is a simple
Theocritan singing match between two shepherds; January and April
are love songs; February is a political allegory and November a pastoral
elegy. Puttenham regarded the pastoral as primarily intended 'under
the vaile of homely persons, and in rude speeches to insinuate and
glaunce at greater matters' (I, xviii, p. 38); and E.K. continually warns
us that the poet 'chose rather to unfold great matter of argument
covertly, then professing it . . .' The extent to which Spenser used the
pastoral form as allegory, and the amount of topical allusion within the
poem have been analysed recently in the very important study of
Professor Paul McLane. It would seem that in 1579, Spenser was
deeply concerned with two major public issues: the one was Elizabeth's
apparent intention to marry Alençon, in face of opposition from
Leicester, Sidney, and the greater part of her people: the other was the
systematic plundering of the property of the Anglican church which
Elizabeth countenanced, rewarding her favourites with the revenues of
vacant livings or the bribes received in return for church preferment.
Both issues were dangerous ones and it is not surprising, therefore,
that Spenser took pains to wrap up his criticisms in allegory and to
throw up a smoke screen in the form of E.K.'s often pedantic and
misleading notes, as a means of protecting himself. Without knowledge of the political background, we cannot savour the calculated
tactlessness of Spenser's beautiful song to Elizabeth in the April
Eclogue, the substance of which is the reiterated praise of the 'Mayden
Queene' at a time when she was seriously thinking of changing her
virgin state. On the other level, Bishop Davies of St Asaph, in the guise
of Diggon Davie, is made to lament the notorious plundering of his
See in the September Eclogue. The various pastoral names can be
identified with half of the bishops of England, and Leicester, Sidney,
Gabriel Harvey, Dyer and Spenser himself are there in the poem.

Rosalind, the mistress to whom Colin vainly pleads throughout, is possibly Elizabeth herself, and Spenser, like Skelton fifty years earlier, is lamenting the state of England through his own Colin Clout. The extraordinary quality of the *Shepheardes Calender* is its ability to exist on parallel and separate levels at the same time. It is an exercise in the various modes of the pastoral and quite unexceptionable in terms of Humanism; yet on another level it is a continuous and very daring piece of political propaganda underneath its innocent and traditional exterior.

This is a quality which appealed to the age and to the relatively small clique who were in the know, but the *Shepheardes Calender* has other, more purely literary qualities. The weakness of the pastoral form is its monotony, as a glance at such a miscellany as *England's Helicon* will show. Spenser, however, solves the problem by matching his eclogues to the months of the year, so that their progression is from mournful to gay and back to mournful again, as the year revolves through its seasons. It is the sort of procession that Spenser uses again in the *Mutability Cantos* and hints already at the architectural quality of his imagination. E.K. comments on the 'dewe observing of Decorum' in the poem, and a further point to be noticed is the extraordinary thoroughness with which the rules of decorum are everywhere applied. As befits an English pastoral, the vocabulary consists mainly of archaic or dialect words used, however, not as E.K. erroneously suggests to restore them to current English, but precisely because they were obsolete or yokel and hence suitable for a low kind such as the eclogue. Within the wide range of the eclogues, however, there is an equal and matching range of styles and diction. Satirical eclogues, such as February or July, are doubly low, being both pastoral and satire; and their metres are rougher, their language more than usually colloquial in consequence. February is in irregular Ryding Rhyme, July, full of dialect words and homely saws:

> Syker thou speakes lyke a lewde lorrell,
>   of Heaven to demen so:
> How be I am but rude and borrell,
>   yet nearer wayes I knowe.
> To Kerke the narre, from God more farre,
>   has bene an old-sayd sawe . . .
>   (*Julye*, 93–)

In contrast the song to Eliza in April has a most elaborate stanza and a vocabulary whose archaism consists merely in adding the occasional prefix—'Yclad'—for ornament. The language of the lament for poetry in October reaches out towards the high style of *The Faerie Queene*:

> But ah! *Macoenas* is yclad in claye,
> And great *Augustus* long ygoe is dead:
> And all the worthies liggen wrapt in leade,
> That matter made for Poets on to play:
> (*October*, 61-)

The most remarkable feature of the sequence, however, is the virtuosity of its metres which makes it a milestone in English prosody. Spenser is obviously, even so early in his career, a complete master of his medium and totally emancipated from the pedestrian exercises of the earlier generation. The elaborate lyric metres of April or November anticipate the song patterns of Campion or Dowland twenty years later; and Spenser shows his awareness of his own mastery in August when, in the guise of Colin, he outsings the amateur Perigot (possibly a pseudonym for Sidney) in a quite dazzling piece of virtuosity.

The *Shepheardes Calender* marks the dawn of the new verse and the setting of Poulter's Measure: it also epitomizes all that the pastoral had done and heralds what it was to do during the next three decades. It is the first and also the last expression in English of the full range of the Renaissance pastoral, with the exception of *Lycidas* which crushes all the main pastoral themes into a single poem. The 1580's tended towards exuberant and imaginative expansion rather than to satire, and when the satiric impulse returned at the end of the century, it expressed itself through realism rather than pastoral fancy. Eclogues were written in their thousands, but no other Elizabethan poet used the pastoral as seriously as Spenser did in the *Shepheardes Calender* or in Book VI of *The Faerie Queene*.

The best collection of pastorals outside Spenser's works is Drayton's *Idea, the Shepheards Garland*, published in 1593 and directly inspired by the *Shepheardes Calender* which had by then reached its fourth edition. Drayton acknowledges the debt when, in the third eclogue, Perkin incites Rowland to awake his 'drowsie Muse' and supply the place of 'learned Collin' who 'is to fayrie gone a Pilgrimage'. Drayton writes no satire, but uses the convention to pay formal and sincere tributes to Sidney and to his sister, the Countess of Pembroke, that 'cleere bell of Rhetoricke, ringing peales of love', as he describes her in a fine phrase. He gives a beautiful picture of the Golden Age in the eighth eclogue and follows it up by a genuinely English pastoral to Dowsabell which possibly owes something to Greene's merry milkmaid of Fressingfield in his play *James IVth*:

> Her skin as soft as Lemster wooll,
> As white as snow on peakish hull,
>   or Swanne that swims in Trent.
>   (*The eighth Eclog*)

The native local colour and detail is a pleasant change after *Arcadia*, and one finds that as the pastoral becomes acclimatised, the scenes and occupations it depicts become more and more English. Barnfield's *Daphnis* tempts his Ganymede with 'a pie-bald Curre to hunt the Hare', although the *Affectionate Shepheard* as a whole, for all its local colour, is an obvious imitation and expansion of Marlowe's 'Come live with me'. Breton's charming collection, *The Passionate Shepheard*, printed in 1604, is full of vignettes of English country life:

> Or to heare the Partridge call,
> Till she have her covye all;
> Or to see the subtill fox
> How the villaine flies the box;
> After feeding on his pray,
> How he closely sneakes away,
> Through the hedge and downe the furrow,
> Till he gets into his burrowe . . .
> And the little blacke-haired coney
> On a banke for sunny place,
> With her fore feet wash her face . . .
>   (Pastoral 3)

The many references to fields and hedges in the pastoral support C. S. Lewis' conjecture that the enclosing of land had both improved the English landscape and drawn attention to its beauty. Whatever the reason, the pastoral utters more than conventional praise for the countryside, and is the father of such works as the *Compleat Angler*.

But the pastoral began to decay even at the height of its popularity, and by 1600 two tendencies were already apparent, both ultimately destructive of the convention. On the one hand, the fatal voice o realism was making itself heard in *As You Like It* or Raleigh's famou[s] reply to 'Come live with me and be my love'. On the other, the simple conventions of the traditional pastoral were giving way to something more sophisticated, and the whole genre was beginning to become remote, like the romantic plays of Beaumont and Fletcher. Drayton's exquisite *Muses Elizium* in 1630 is a land of elves and fairies, and the shepherd swains have become shadowy and etherealised. *Lycidas* is the last example of the serious Renaissance pastoral; by the eighteenth century it has declined into decorative idyll or rustic realism. Johnson's attack on *Lycidas* reveals how the pastoral had ceased to be an acceptable convention for the expression of serious ideas.

(3) The sonnet

The term 'sonnet' was used very loosely in the sixteenth century to denote any short love poem. The quatorzaine, as we have seen, had been introduced by Wyatt and developed by Surrey away from the Petrarchan pattern into the three quatrains and a couplet which became the most characteristic Elizabethan form; but the direct cause of the great outbreak of sonneteering in the 1590's was rather the desire to emulate the Pléiade who had been very prolific in this genre. The first systematic collection of English sonnets was Thomas Watson's *Passionate Centurie of Love*, a most unimpassioned and academic century of imitations from the French and Italian which appeared in 1582; but it was Sidney's *Astrophil and Stella*, written probably in the same year and circulated in manuscript after his death, until its publication in 1591, which really started the vogue. The 1590's saw a flood of sonnet cycles, of which the best are Daniel's *Delia* and Constable's *Diana* (1592). Fletcher's *Licia* and Barnabe Barnes' *Parthenophil and Parthenophe* (1593), Drayton's *Ideas Mirror* in the next year, Spenser's *Amoretti* in 1595, and, of course, Shakespeare's sonnets written anywhere between the late 1580's and their publication in 1609.

Puttenham, writing of the 'poesie of amorous affections and allurements', describes it as requiring 'a forme of Poesie variable, inconstant, affected, curious, and most witty of any others . . .' and this is a fair description of the sonnet. It was in essence the verse form of the gentleman amateur, the fashionable thing for the Berownes of the 1590's to give to their mistresses or circulate among their friends, and much of the witty affectation of the form comes from their efforts to outdo one another in the ingenuity of their conceits. The author of *Zepheria* varies the old image of the shipwrecked heart with:

> The *naufrage* of my poor afflicted bark. (Canzon 40)

and in this he speaks with the authentic voice of the young Inns-of-Court man, fresh from his studies and primed with that knowledge of the tongues which Sir Andrew Aguecheek coveted so greatly. The original source of all sonnet cycles was, of course, Petrarch, but no English sonneteer brought to his theme the sincerity, the psychological insight and the sustained feeling which the master had shown. For

most writers, love was the excuse for, not the cause of, sonnets: Giles
Fletcher the elder in his introduction to *Licia* asserts that 'a man may
write of love, and not be in love', and boasts that he only wrote 'to
let my wit blood'; in his opinion the proper people to write love
sonnets are 'the Innes of Court, and some Gentlemen like students in
both Universities, whose learning and bringing up together, with their
fine natures makes so sweet a harmonie . . . and therefore they onelie
are fittest to write of Love' (p. 79).

It was Petrarch's art and his conceits, more than his passion, which
appealed to the Elizabethans, and the sonnet held no very serious place
in the poetical hierarchy. The terms most commonly applied to the
cycles were 'conceitful' or 'sugred', or 'witty amorous toys', fitting for
youth but to be grown out of in maturity, just as Berowne and his
friends in *Love's Labour's Lost* rush off to write sonnets the moment they
first see their mistresses, but eventually forswear their taffeta phrases
and silken terms. Of all verse forms, the sonnet is perhaps the most
explicitly 'artificial', demonstrating in its patterned structure and its
rounded formality the unmistakable stamp of art, and challenging the
writer to meet its obligations. Even where the theme is a serious one,
it is still dressed up in an array of witty rhetoric which belongs to the
very decorum of the sonnet form and provides a legitimate part of the
pleasure it is designed to give. Many sonnets, indeed, consist of this
display alone and are no more than a rhetorical figure worked out to its
full conclusion and finally rounded off. A whole sonnet may be given
up to the establishment of a 'far-fet' comparison, as when, for example,
Constable manages to compare his iron-hearted mistress to Mahomet's
coffin on the grounds that his eyes, 'loves strange exhaling adamants',
have raised her 'to my harts temples height' (*Diana*, IV, iv). Barnabe
Barnes is perhaps the cleverest at this kind of conceit: he has twelve
sonnets comparing the progress of his love to the sun in each of the
twelve signs of the zodiac; or again, he toys with the conventional
comparison of his stony-hearted mistress to a rock, only to reject it on
the grounds that a rock gives back an echo of what is spoken to it,
but her words never echo his. In the same vein Fletcher improves upon
the old ice and fire conceit, by begging that he and his mistress may die
upon the same day, for if he dies first, the heat of his passion will dry
up the Styx, and if she dies first, her frigidity will freeze it; only if they
go together will Charon's boat have a hope of crossing.

This is not to say that the sonnet could not be serious, but that its
moments of deep feeling are expressed through a display of wit which
keeps them below the level of high tragedy. One can see this in Sidney's
moving sonnet to the moon, ' With how sad steps, O Moone, thou

climb'st the skies' (31), or in the brilliant and tortured word play of Drayton's:

> You not alone when You are still alone,
> O God, from You, that I could private be.
> (*Idea*, 1619. Sonnet 11)

or in the extraordinary rhetorical virtuosity of Shakespeare's great sonnet on Lust (CXXIX). Moreover we are apt to mistake for mere conceits statements which in the sixteenth century were accepted as physiologically and psychologically true. The sonnets are full of references to murdering mistresses whose eyes slay and whose eye-beams penetrate like arrows to the very heart; and it is necessary to recognise that these had a basis in what was taken to be fact. When Prospero says of Ferdinand and Miranda, 'At first sight they have changed eyes ... Poor worm, thou art infected,' he is speaking literally. The curious lore behind such statements can be found in Ficino's *Commentary on the Symposium*, much of which is reproduced in Castiglione's *Courtier*. It was believed that the soul controlled all bodily functions by means of the animal spirits which bridged the gap between material and spiritual and were concocted out of the purest of the blood. These spirits, collecting in the heart, were thought to flow out through the eyes in the form of a fine stream of particles which, hitting the eyes of the other person, went down into the heart and set up a disturbance among the animal spirits already there. This disturbance is love, an actual physical infection passing from the one person to the other. Spenser embodies it in his character Corflambo, with his fiery eye, who sets people's hearts aflame; and Milton refers to its operation in *Paradise Lost* when, after the Fall, Eve's eyes dart 'contagious fire' at Adam (IX, 1036). Old people fall in love with young ones rather than young with old, because the animal spirits of youth are more active and powerful; and unsuccessful lovers grow pale and die because they pour out all their spirits and receive none back in return. Happy love, therefore, consists of a literal interchange of the contents of the two hearts in what is in fact a mutual blood transfusion. Castiglione describes the process in the fourth book:

For those lively spirits that issue out at the eyes, because they are engendred nigh the hart, entring in like case into the eyes that they are levelled at, like a shafte to the pricke, naturally pearce to the hart, as to their resting place and there are at rest with those other spirits: and with the most subtill and fine nature of bloude which they carrie with them, infect the bloude about the hart, where they are come to, and warme it: and make it like unto themselves, and apt to receive the imprinting of the image, which they have carried away with

D

them. . . . The eyes therefore lye lurking like souldiers in war, lying in waite in bushment, and if the forme of all the bodie be well favoured and of good proportion, it draweth unto it and allureth who so beholdeth it a farre off: untill he come nigh: and as soone as he is at hand, the eyes shoote, and like sorcerers bewitch, and especially when by a right line they send their glistering beames into the eyes of the wight beloved, at the time when they doe the like, because the spirites meete together, and in that sweete encounter the one taketh the others nature and qualitie . . .   (p. 247)

In the light of such a theory, the common sonnet conceits about eyes take on a new dimension:

> Fayre eyes, the myrrour of my mazed hart,
> what wondrous vertue is contaynd in you,
> the which both lyfe and death forth from you dart
> into the object of your mighty view? . . .
> that your bright beams of my weak eies admyred,
> may kindle living fire within my breast . . .
>   (*Amoretti*, VII)

It is an obvious step to equate these beams with Cupids arrows, and so:

> I mote perceive how, in her glauncing sight,
>   legions of loves with little wings did fly:
> darting their deadly arrowes fyry bright,
>   at every rash beholder passing by
>   (*Amoretti*, XVI)

When the exchange of spirits is mutual, the eyebeams, as in Donne's *Extasie*, do indeed thread the eyes 'upon one double string', but few sonnet lovers are in so happy a position. They are only too well aware, with Wyatt, that:

> . . . an Iye may save or sleye,
>   And stryke more diepe then wepon longe . . .
>   (no. 93)

The most influential and, with the exception of Shakespeare's, the greatest collection of sonnets in the period is Sidney's *Astrophil and Stella*, Star-lover and Star, first published in a pirated edition in 1591, but brought out again in its complete form by Sidney's sister, the Countess of Pembroke, with the rest of his works in 1598. From the time of their first appearance, these sonnets were recognised as containing autobiographical material. Astrophil, the young courtier-politician, bears a clear resemblance to Sidney, and sometimes identifies himself specifically with his creator, as in Sonnet 30, for example, where his reference to 'my father' is unmistakably an allusion to Sir Henry Sidney who had been Governor of Ireland. Stella, on her side, was generally accepted as the pseudonym of Lady Rich, born Penelope Devereux, sister of the Earl of Essex. There is an allusion to her coat of arms: 'roses gueuls ... borne in silver field' in Sonnet 13, and, more significantly, there are bitter puns on her married name of Rich in Sonnets 24, 35 and 37:

> Who though most rich in these and everie part ...
> Hath no misfortune, but that Rich she is.   (no. 37)

These sonnets were omitted from the edition of 1591 but printed in 1598, by which time Penelope was living with Sir Charles Blount who had been at Zutphen with Sidney, and such a compliment from Sidney was no longer out of place.

It is important to consider the extent to which *Astrophil and Stella* is a record of personal history, for it must affect our conception of why the Elizabethans wrote poetry and what they looked for in reading it. The fullest account is to be found in Professor Ringler's edition of Sidney's poems. Penelope's father, the elder Earl of Essex, had expressed a wish for Sidney to marry his daughter in 1576, shortly before he died, but there is no evidence that Sidney became deeply involved with her at any stage, or that his relations with her resembled the story told in the sonnet sequence. In 1578 Essex's widow married Sidney's uncle, the Earl of Leicester, but Sidney may never have met Penelope until she came to court in 1581, at the age of eighteen. She was quickly sought in marriage by Lord Rich, who married her later in the year, and Sidney, who was very much involved in public affairs at this period, is not recorded as showing any signs of distress at the time, although Astrophil declares:

> I might, unhappie word, O me, I might,
> And then would not, or could not see my blisse
> (no. 33)

At the end of 1582 Leicester was trying to persuade Sidney to marry Penelope's younger sister, but without effect, and he married Lady Frances Walsingham in the following year. If any liaison did occur, it was probably between Penelope's marriage at the end of 1581 and the spring of 1582, during the only period when both were together at court. Sidney went off to the Welsh borders in the summer of that year, to join his father who was Lord President of Wales, and it seems likely that he wrote the sonnets at this time, an assumption supported by the political references in Sonnet 30.

In estimating the degree of autobiography in the sonnet cycle, we should remember that Sidney had already made a tentative attempt to deal with the same theme in his 'Certaine Sonets', written as far back as 1577–8. We should also remember the basic argument of his *Apologie*, that the poet is a 'feigner' and poetry by definition is fiction so that a literal transcription of personal history in poetry is almost, for Sidney, a contradiction in terms. We may get a clue as to his intentions if we read his account of the shortcomings of contemporary love poetry at the end of the *Apologie*; he had censured it there on the grounds that it was not true to life:

> But truely many of such writings as come under the banner of unresistable love, if I were a Mistres, would never perswade mee they were in love; so coldely they apply fiery speeches, as men that had rather red Lovers writings, and so caught up certaine swelling phrases ... then that in truth they feele those passions. ...   (p. 201)

Astrophil and Stella is a tragic love story; and tragedy had always been encouraged to use characters taken from real life as an aid to verisimilitude, even though the actions attributed to them were not necessarily true. This is one of the traditional distinctions between tragedy and comedy whose characters were expected to be wholly fictional. Sidney may have been following humanist literary theory in attributing a fictional but credible love affair to real characters, in order to give to his sonnet cycle the verisimilitude which he felt to be lacking in the love poetry of his time.

That Sidney's prime aim was a literary one can be seen from the cycle itself. It is, in the first place, an imitation of Petrarch, much the most ambitious in the whole period, and almost the only one to intersperse the sonnets with songs and longer poems as Petrarch had done. These songs provide variety and at the same time frequently present a moment of action which then becomes the theme of meditation in the succeeding sonnets. Sidney's sequence is more dramatic than Petrarch's, and falls into three clear-cut divisions, like acts, with separate minor scenes within them, the songs serving to mark the divisions. The famous first sonnet is an explicit manifesto of his literary intentions, and it is worth quoting in full:

> Loving in truth, and faine in verse my love to show,
> That the deare Shee might take some pleasure of my paine:

Pleasure might cause her reade, reading might make her know,
Knowledge might pitie winne, and pitie grace obtaine,
    I sought fit words to paint the blackest face of woe,
Studying inventions fine, her wits to entertaine:
Oft turning others' leaves, to see if thence would flow
Some fresh and fruitfull showers upon my sunne-burn'd braine.
    But words came halting forth, wanting Invention's stay,
Invention, Nature's child, fled step-dame Studie's blowes,
And others' feete still seem'd but strangers in my way.
Thus great with child to speake, and helplesse in my throwes,
    Biting my trewand pen, beating my selfe for spite,
    'Foole', said my Muse to me, 'looke in thy heart and write.'

The opening quatrain comes very close to a central passage in the
Apologie in which Sidney is defining what he calls the 'right' poet:

for these indeede doo meerely make to imitate, and imitate both to delight and
teach, and delight to move men to take that goodnes in hande, which without
delight they would flye as from a stranger; and teach, to make them know
that goodnes whereunto they are moved . . .   (p. 159)

   The source of both the poem and the passage from the *Apologie* is,
of course, Horace's advice about persuading through delight, and
Astrophil sits down to compose his poem about real love, 'loving in
truth', with the Horatian advice to poets in his mind. The links between
the sonnet and the *Apologie* are very close throughout: the word
'stranger' in the eleventh line echoes the 'stranger' in the corresponding
passage of the *Apologie* just quoted, and Astrophil's desire to 'paint the
blackest face of woe' follows the *Apologie* in attributing to the poet the
powers of heightened representation which are denied both to the
philosopher and to the historian. His first impulse is to 'imitate' his
poem, and so he turns to 'others' leaves', the product of other poets'
invention, but this does not work. 'Invention' is the first part of
Rhetoric, the method of finding out the proper materials for a given
purpose, and these, in this case, are not to be found in books; Invention
is the child of Nature not of study where love is concerned. His Muse,
therefore, puts him right by telling him to 'looke in thy heart and
write' for that is the place where the real nature of love should be
studied.
   This first sonnet is not a manifesto in favour of making love poetry
a matter of simple personal confession; the advice it gives is the
traditional first rule of rhetoric, to look for your materials in the right
place; and Astrophil proceeds to do this in the next sonnet:

> Not at first sight, nor with a dribbed shot
>   *Love* gave the wound, which while I breathe will bleed: . . .
> I saw and liked, I liked but loved not,
>   I loved, but straight did not what *Love* decreed . . .
>
> (no. 2)

This is a very revolutionary sonnet, for it flouts centuries of love poetry which had always insisted that 'Who ever loved, that loved not at first sight'. Astrophil's love is real, not literary, and comes, as in life, by degrees: moreover, it is accepted very unwillingly by Astrophil who is only writing his poems to persuade himself that love is good in spite of everything, 'To make myselfe beleeve, that all is well.' He underlines the challenge of his own realism in the next sonnet, by an attack on other poets' literary loves: they may ape Pindar 'in phrases fine' and all the flowers of rhetoric, or practise the 'High' style, or dress up hackneyed discussions on love in new metaphors:

> Ennobling new found Tropes with problemes old:
> Or with strange similies enrich each line . . .
>
> (no. 3)

This is not Astrophil's way however: 'Phrases and Problemes from my reach do grow'; he is content to look at Stella's face and in describing it, copies nature herself, the only true form of 'Imitation', as Aristotle defines the term. Sidney constantly plays with the contrasting meanings of 'Imitation': as it is used in the *Poetics*, on the one hand, to mean the imitation of human action in terms of art; and, on the other, in the narrower sense of following the best literary models. In this issue, he is on the side of Aristotle against Horace and the common renaissance use of the term. It is a point Sidney returns to on a number of occasions, notably in Sonnet 15, where he laughs at the 'want of inward tuch' shown by those poets who go on repeating 'poore Petrarch's long deceased woes'; or again in number 6, where he mocks the poetry 'Of living deaths, deare wounds, faire stormes and freesing fires', or those poems which drag in all of Greek myth, 'Broadred with buls and swans, powdred with golden raine'. His way is that of simple reality, and he expresses it in verse which is deliberately colloquial by contrast:

> I can speake what I feele, and feel as much as they,
> But thinke that all the Map of my state I display,
> When trembling voice brings forth that I do *Stella* love.
>
> (no. 6)

This is not to say that Sidney avoids all that is conventional in love poetry: he uses many of the stock situations and conceits, but for the most part keeps to those which are compatible with real love. Lovers in real life are apt to pass sleepless nights or be strangely disturbed by the moon, and so Sidney allows himself the beautiful sonnet to the moon (31), or the conventional pleas for sleep (38, 39). Basically, however, his picture of love is an unorthodox one in relation to Courtly poetry, and Astrophil's debate with himself about love, which comprises the whole first act of the cycle, is in new and contemporary terms. He is torn between the claims made upon him by his career in politics and public life and the excessive demands of love. When, in Sonnet 30, people ask him for the latest news about affairs in Poland or the Low Countries or the Scottish court, he makes some kind of an answer, 'But know not how, for still I thinke of you'; and from time to time he weighs, half dispassionately, the values of love against those of common sense:

> With what sharpe checkes I in myselfe am shent,
>   When into Reason's audite I do go:
>   And by just counts my selfe a banckrout know
>   Of all those goods, which heav'n to me hath lent ...
>   (no. 18)

The sustained image of book-keeping not only reflects Du Bellay's advice that the poet should stock his mind with metaphors drawn from all the trades: it is also singularly appropriate to the problem under discussion, for Astrophil is judging the intangible values of romantic love by the standards of the hard-headed Elizabethan man of affairs, anxious to get on and literally counting the cost of everything. At other times, Astrophil's debate with himself is the more traditional one between reason and passion, and he drags in a veneer of Platonism to prove that loving Stella is the most rational of all activities:

> Reason thou kneel'dst, and offeredst straight to prove
> By reason good, good reason her to love.   (no. 10)

This particular debate about love goes back at least as far as the *Romance of the Rose*, and it is interesting to notice that Sidney keeps to the tradition by introducing the 'Friend' who, in the *Romance*, is the voice of reason vainly trying to dissuade the lover from his siege of the rose. Astrophil's friend plays the same role: in Sonnet 14 he is upbraiding the lover with 'Rubarb' words, trying to persuade him that desire 'Doth plunge my wel-form'd soule even in the mire/Of sinfull thoughts . . .' and in 21 he is urging him to read Plato as a cure for love. Astrophil counters with Neo-Plato against Plato, anticipating Berowne's claim that true learning is to be found in the beauty of a woman's face; and by Sonnet 51, the friend, like his prototype in the *Romance*, has been sent packing:

> Pardon mine eares, both I and they do pray,
> So may your tongue still fluently proceed
> To them that do such entertainment need . . .
> On silly me do not the burthen lay . . . (no. 51)

Passion wins, and the first song, coming after sonnet 63, marks the end of the act and shows, by its forceful and impelling rhythms, that Astrophil's doubts are banished and that he now intends to press forward:

> To you, to you, all song of praise is due,
> Only in you my song begins and endeth.

The first act is meditative, but the second, with all hesitations cast away, is full of action:

> No more, my deare, no more these counsels trie,
>   O give my passions leave to run their race:
>   Let Fortune lay on me her worst disgrace,
> Let folke orecharg'd with braine against me crie . . .
>   (no. 64)

Astrophil's singleness of purpose is quickly rewarded; he sees signs for hope in Sonnets 66 and 67—'Hope, art thou true, or doest thou flatter me?' (no. 67) and by number 69 has won Stella's love, though only on condition that it remains virtuously unconsummated:

> For *Stella* hath with words where faith doth shine,
> Of her high heart giv'n me the monarchie
> I, I, o I may say, that she is mine.
> And though she give but thus conditionly
>   This realme of blisse, while vertuous course I take,
>   No kings be crown'd but they some covenants make.
>   (no. 69)

There is superb irony in the way Sidney makes Astrophil's exultant cry suggest the Io, Io of the traditional marriage song, at the moment when he is protesting the purely spiritual nature of his love. The next sonnet is a jubilant one, unlike the usual woeful ballad of love, as Sidney is careful to point out—'Sonets be not bound prentise to annoy' (no. 70). But retribution is waiting; the virtuous love which seemed enough in the first flush of gratitude leads on to the desire for more, and the physical body suddenly makes its claims. Sonnet 71 is a beautiful piece of dramatic writing in which the complacency of Astrophil's superficial virtue is shattered by the insurrection of Desire:

> There shall he find all vices' overthrow,
>   Not by rude force, but sweetest soveraigntie
> Of reason, from whose light those night-birds flie;
> That inward sunne in thine eyes shineth so.
>   And not content to be Perfection's heire
> Thy selfe, doest strive all minds that way to move,
> Who marke in thee what is in thee most faire.
> So while thy beautie drawes the heart to love
>   As fast thy Vertue bends that love to good:
>   'But ah,' Desire still cries, 'give me some food.'
>   (no. 71)

The calculated brutality of the last line most effectively punctures Astrophil's posturing. From now, Platonic love is not enough, and Astrophil sadly admits that the body will not be controlled by virtue:

> But thou Desire, because thou wouldst have all,
> Now banisht art, but yet alas how shall?
>   (no. 72)

It is inevitable, therefore, that when he finds Stella sleeping, he steals a kiss, an event recorded in the second song which follows; and the next ten sonnets play with the memory of the kiss and the desire it has aroused. There is a brief pause with a simple love song, after Sonnet 83, and then a further burst of action: he is on his way to her house—'Highway since you my chiefe *Parnassus* be' (84)—he arrives—'I see the house ...' (85) and the fourth song which follows at once describes what happens. It is night, and he finds Stella alone writing letters, her mother safely in bed:

> Your faire mother is a bed,
> Candles out, and curtaines spread:
> She thinkes you do letters write:
> Write, but first let me endite:
> Take me to thee, and thee to me.
> 'No, no, no, no, my Deare, let be.

D*

The position is not, however, hopeless for the song is one of those riddling ones like 'No, John', where the final negative becomes almost a positive. The 'No, no' of Stella's protestation changes its function when Astrophil swears that he will die of grief:

> Soone with my death I will please thee.
> 'No, no, no, no, my Deare, let be.'
> (Fourth Song)

The episode makes Stella angry; 'Alas, whence came this change of lookes?' (86) but at this point the text becomes confused and we are uncertain about Sidney's intentions. An assorted batch of five songs is inserted after Sonnet 86, as if everything were included here for which no place could be found elsewhere. Some of them appear to be try-outs or alternative versions which Sidney had scrapped or not decided on, and one pair, Songs 8 and 9, are a pastoral version of the wooing and refusal already treated in the fourth song. The lovers meet 'In a grove most rich of shade', and Astrophil is again refused:

> Trust me while I thee deny,
> In myselfe the smart I try,
> Tyran honour doth thus use thee,
> *Stella's* selfe might not refuse thee.
>
> Therefore, Deere, this no more move,
> Least, though I leave not thy love,
> Which too deep in me is framed,
> I should blush when thou art named.
> (Eighth song)

The pastoral setting of this song and the lament which follows it are out of keeping with the everyday realism of the rest of the drama, but the character of Stella as presented here is not. It is the only time that we see her as a real person, since Astrophil normally holds the stage, and she appears as a three-dimensional character, loving yet refusing out of a sensitive and delicate virtue. She is a long way from the usual stony-hearted sonnet mistress. It would seem that Sidney had not finished off this section of the poem, or that the publisher included materials not intended for the purpose.

This marks the end of the second section; and the last one is full of absence and despair, though these are never allowed to escape from sonnet decorum and become too tragic. The greatest height of Astrophil's grief is expressed in the greatest literary *tour de force* of the whole collection, Sonnet 89, which contrasts presence and absence, joy and grief, in terms of day and night and ends every line on one or the other:

> Each day seemes long, and longs for long-staid night,
>   The night as tedious, wooes th'approch of day;
>   Tired with the dusty toiles of busie day,
> Languisht with horrors of the silent night . . .
>   (no. 89)

In 92 he is asking for news of her; in 101 he learns that she is sick; in 103 he has a happy and unusually Petrarchan memory of her on the Thames; and the cycle ends with a final burst of drama. In the eleventh song, after Sonnet 104, Astrophil is at her window, only to be turned away again:

> Who is it that this darke night,
> Underneath my window playneth? . . .
>
> Peace, I thinke that some give eare:
> Come no more, least I get anger . . .

This is followed by a vivid but tantalisingly brief account in Sonnet 105 of a glimpse of Stella as she passes in her coach at night,

> Curst be the page from whome the bad torch fell, . . .
> Curst be the Cochman which did drive so fast . . .
>   (no. 105)

and the cycle ends on a note of despair.

Astrophil and Stella gives the illusion of telling a true story, yet it makes a very intelligent use of tradition and can be seen to be a great and carefully planned lyrical drama. The nearest equivalents are Shakespeare's sonnets or, close to our day, Meredith's *Modern Love* or even *In Memoriam*. Sidney has followed Petrarch as Shakespeare was to do in treating the sonnet as a meditative, introspective form of verse, recording the effect of actions on the mind rather than the actions themselves. Professor Lever has aptly called the sequence 'a study of the inner conflicts that romance precipitates in the personality of a contemporary man' (p. 74). At the same time Sidney is always conscious of the need for a display of art, which is the other half of the sonnet tradition, and experiments unceasingly in sonnet form. He tries the old pausing twelve-syllable line of Sonnet 1 as well as the usual decasyllabic, and he attempts a great many rhyme schemes, ranging from pure Petrarchan to Shakespearean. He was rarely happy with the final couplet, for his conclusions tend to need three lines, or more

commonly to be expressed in a single punch line as in the first sonnet.
In either case, the units of thought and of rhyme do not coincide as
they invariably do in Spenser's sonnets, for example, and the separate-
ness of the final couplet is often not justified. But the ground which
Sidney broke, as in everything else he wrote, made the way easier for
those who followed him.

A word may be said about one of these later sonnet cycles, to give
some idea of the range of which the form was capable; and the obvious
choice is Spenser's *Amoretti*, published in 1595. Spenser is a love poet
of a very different stamp from Sidney; physical desire may lead to sin,
as it does so often in *The Faerie Queene*, yet sex, for Spenser, is intrinsically holy, blessed alike by God's great creative fiat and by the sisterhood
of the two Venuses. The centre of *The Faerie Queene* is the garden of
Adonis from which comes endless seed to fertilise the great ocean of
Chaos; and the two central characters, Artegall and Britomart, owe
their position to the fact that they are to be the father and mother of a
line of kings. With such a sense of divine plenitude, Spenser sees no
essential struggle between body and spirit, reason and passion; and the
Amoretti is not a dramatic conflict but a sustained lyrical meditation on
the goodness of love.

Furthermore the *Amoretti* together with the *Epithalamium* were
written as a wedding present to Elizabeth Boyle whom he had already
married or was about to marry. They are therefore an elaborate
compliment composed within the Petrarchan convention but offered
to a woman already won, and often one feels that Spenser is celebrating
marriage under the guise of courtly wooing.

> The doubt which ye misdeeme, fayre love, is vaine,
> That fondly feare to loose your liberty;
> when, loosing one, two liberties ye gayne,
> and make him bond that bondage earst dyd fly.
> Sweet be the bands, the which true love doth tye
> without constraynt ...   (LXV)

This could be the language of marriage or of courtship alike. We can
see Spenser's special bent if we compare his treatment of Petrarch's
sonnet about the huntsman and the deer with Wyatt's imitation of it,
'Whoso list to hount'. In Petrarch, it will be remembered, the white
doe was an almost mystical vision of Laura's chastity, singled out by
God and beyond the reach of the poet; in Wyatt, the hind was a
deceitful woman with Caesar's diamonds around her neck and equally

unapproachable for that reason. In the *Amoretti*, however, the weary
huntsman sits down to rest, and to his surprise, the deer comes back:

> There she, beholding me with mylder looke,
>   sought not to fly, but fearelesse still did bide;
>   till I in hand her yet half trembling tooke,
>   and with her owne goodwill hir fyrmely tyde,
> Strange thing, me seemd, to see a beast so wyld,
>   so goodly wonne, with her owne will beguyld.
>   (LXVII)

There is no room for lovers' quarrels or lamentations here, and when
the convention insists that Spenser deal with the lover's complaints,
he is apt to do so with a note of parody which suggests a private joke
between husband and wife. In this way he out-Herods Herod when he
upbraids the lady for her cruelty:

> See! how the Tyrannesse doth joy to see
>   the huge massacres which her eyes do make ...
>   (X)

or drops into the mock heroic when he addresses a poem which his
lady has torn up:

> Innocent paper; whom too cruell hand
> Did make the matter to avenge her yre ...
>   (XLVIII)

Spenser feels none of Astrophil's resentment against love, but loves and
worships with Petrarch's unquestioning idealism:

> More than most faire, full of the living fire,
>   Kindled above unto the maker neere;
>   no eies but joyes, in which al powers conspire,
>   that to the world naught else be counted deare;   (VIII)

His love, however, is more frankly physical than Petrarch's, yet without the sense of guilt shown by Astrophil; and instead of looking
inwards into his own mind, Spenser's gaze is turned outwards upon
the mistress whose sensuous beauty he admires without shame and
which he describes so often in terms of *The Song of Solomon*:

> For loe, my love doth in herselfe containe
>   all this worlds riches that may farre be found,
>   if Saphyres loe her eies be Saphyres plaine,

> if Rubies, loe hir lips be Rubies sound;
> If Pearles, hir teeth be pearles, both pure and round;
> if Yvorie, her forehead yvory weene;
> if Gold, her locks are finest gold on ground;
> if Silver, her faire hands are silver sheene: (XV)

> Goe to my love, where she is carelesse layd,
> yet in her winters bowre not well awake;
> tell her the joyous time wil not be staid ...
> (LXX)

Lust has no place in such sanctified desire, and so:

> Let not one sparke of filthy lustfull fyre
> breake out, that may her sacred peace molest ...
> (LXXXIV)

The cycle has an extraordinary unity of tone which is reflected and produced by the smooth and complex sonnet form which Spenser invented. He uses three quatrains, but each is linked to the next by a rhyme carried over, and the result is something as flexible as Shakespeare's form yet giving the impression of the close-knit unity of Petrarch. The twelve lines are balanced by a final couplet which is self-contained and carries the weight of an epigram. Spenser never forced the sonnet to do the variety of tasks which both Sidney and Shakespeare asked it to perform; but he achieved complete mastery at the level of the sustained lyricism which is his unique quality.

The sonnet was the most widely practised form of poetry during the last decade of the sixteenth century; and its extraordinary but brief efflorescence was undoubtedly encouraged by the cult of worship and ritual which surrounded the virgin queen in her old age. The vogue of the sonnet, however, is of deeper significance than this. The sonnet is the meeting place of old and new, the newest Renaissance values in style coupled with themes and attitudes which are essentially medieval. The Elizabethan sonnet is the last expression of Courtly love, before the marriage ideal absorbed what was best in it and took its place. It is a thin trickle after the great medieval river, but it is recognisably from the same source. Its attitudes and symptoms in love are the old and familiar ones, its images and symbols all traditional. Its lovers besiege the fort of love just as the lover had done in the *Romance of the Rose*, though with less success:

> Retourne agayne, my forces late dismayd
>   Unto the siege by you abandon'd quite ...
> Gaynst such strong castles needeth greater might
>   then those small forts which ye were wont belay ...
> (Amoretti, XIV)

The Elizabethans enjoyed playing with these time-honoured conceptions in pocket form, and still approved of the rituals with which love had been hedged in for three hundred years or more. Shakespeare created the most sympathetic picture of the sonnet lover in his Orsino who is not in love but enjoys going through the motions. 'For such as I am all true lovers are' (II, IV, 17). He languishes at a distance, cherishes his amorous melancholy with the help of music, and is self-consciously changeable in his behaviour to friends because it is a point of honour for the lover to be constant only to his mistress. His relationship with Olivia is a prolonged self-dramatisation in which he plays the role of the lover with a passion which he mistakes for love itself. Even the rebellious Astrophil has his share of these attitudes, although he resents the fact that they are expected of him:

> Because I breathe not love to everie one,
>   Nor do not use set colours for to weare,
>   Nor nourish speciall lockes of vowed haire,
> Nor give each speech a full point of a grone,
> The courtly Nymphs, acquainted with the mone
>   Of them, who in their lips *Love's* standard beare;
>   'What he?' say they of me, 'now I dare swear,
> He cannot love: no, no, let him alone.'   (no. 54)

It was a code which still made its appeal to an educated and leisured class, desirous to be elegant and to avoid at all costs barbarity. As the violence of the age still finds its outlet in the shows of chivalry, so love takes a complementary form—the ladies' faces corresponding to the fierce dragon spleens. The ability to control and to play with the deepest human passions gives a reassuring sense of human dignity and marks the superiority of the civilised man to the barbarian or the beast.

(4) *The lyric*

The Elizabethan lyric was still close enough to oral verse to inherit the traditional association of poetry with music. The relationship was, indeed, revived and intensified in the sixteenth century, partly on account of the revival of the classical lyric which took its name from

the lyre to which it had been sung, and partly owing to the break-up of
the religious foundations and the dispersal of their musicians and singing
men who carried their art into secular life and helped to raise the
general level of musical skill as the century proceeded. The Elizabethan
and the Jacobean years are the great age of English music. It formed an
important part of education, and the Elizabethan gentleman was
expected to be proficient both in song and with the lute, while an
apprentice found a good voice and the ability to read music a sure way
to advancement. It was an age when every barber's shop had a lute
hanging on the walls for the delectation of the customers and when lute
strings were favourite gifts to ladies. Madrigal music was habitually
printed with the separate parts along the four sides of the sheet, so that
the family could sit round the table and sing, and the singing journey-
men in Dekker's *Shoe-Maker's Holiday*, or the shepherdesses who sing
Autolycus' ballads at sight, give a true picture of the general level of
skill and interest. By 1610, the names of Byrd, Morley, Dowland, John
Daniel, Campion and Weelkes, to mention only a few of the great
galaxy, were famous throughout Europe for their madrigals and airs.

For this reason, the lyric is the most ubiquitous of Elizabethan verse
forms, penetrating to all social levels and assimilating all the different
modes of pastoral, sonnet, elegy or hymn into itself. At the beginning
of the century, lyric verse was fairly homogeneous, and Wyatt and
Surrey could use the popular ballad metre for their courtly verses;
but as the century progressed, the courtly lyric became more courtly
under the influence of new Italian models, the popular lyric more
popular and less reputable through its participation in the religious
controversies of the reigns of Mary and Elizabeth, and by 1590, the
courtly and popular lyrics were as clearly distinguished as high-brow
and 'pop' today.

It is necessary, therefore, to consider the lyric at different social
levels. In the first place, the traditional oral ballad was still a living thing
though its days were numbered. A popular writer like Deloney
included many old ballads in the text of his novels, and his own poems
in the *Garland of Goodwill* show that he was still attempting to write
in the traditional form: many of them are narratives with instructions
attached to them such as 'To be sung in the old ancient sort, or else
to the tune of Labandalashot'. The same tradition is still at work, on a
higher level, in Raleigh's 'As you came from the Holy Land' or
Drayton's fine ballad of Agincourt.

In the sixteenth century, however, a new type of ballad emerged with
the advent of printing, namely the broadsheet which is the printed
ballad of the kind that Autolycus was selling. As it was designed to be

sold, it tended to be topical in its appeal, and in drawing its materials
from the more sensational incidents of the time, it fulfilled some of the
functions of the modern cheap press. Autolycus' ballad about the
usurer's wife who was brought to bed of twenty money-bags can be
paralleled in Elderton's account of the monstrous child born at Stony
Stratford or the accounts of the last confessions of such notable
murderers as Mrs Anne Saunders. Some of Elderton's ballads are
lively and amusing, and their circulation must have been enormous;
but, as a whole, the standard of verse was not high, and the upper
levels of the literary profession united in sneering at the 'pot-house
poets' and the 'red-nosed ballet-mongers'.

Not all broadsheets were news ballads, and many were plain love-
songs such as Mopsa and Dorcas sang in *The Winter's Tale*. Clement
Robinson's attractive miscellany, *A Handefull of Pleasant Delites*,
first published in 1566, consists entirely of such songs to which the
tunes are indicated, and it is noticeable that their metres are far more
flexible and interesting than those of contemporary verse written in
less close conjunction with music. At a time when writers were
struggling for regularity with the mechanical help of Poulter's Measure,
Robinson's lyrics, sustained by the movement of their tunes, can
change their rhythm and vary their metre with the greatest confidence.
The influence of the tune is obvious in a complex stanza such as the
following, for example, which varies its rhythm twice in a few lines:

> Now Ladies, be merie
> Because you are werie;
>   leave work I say, and get you home;
> Your businesse is slacking,
> Your lover is packing;
>   Your answer hath cut off his comb.
>   How then?
>
> The fault was in him, sir,
> He wooed it so trim, sir,
>   Alas! poore seelie fellow,
> Make much of thy pillow
> Make much of thy pillow.
>   (*A Handful of Pleasant Delites*, p. 15)

Even the ballad metre itself is capable of taking on a new lilt when
written to the tune of 'Lustie Gallant'.

> Fain would I have a pretie thing,
>   to give unto my Ladie.

> I name no thing, nor I meane no thing,
>   but as pretie a thing as may bee.
>   (Ibid., p. 74)

The livelier rhythms come in from the popular dances, the Almans,
Brawles, Galliards and Canaries which go with the tunes, and it is
interesting to note that popular song has a range of rhythms which are
all its own and scarcely ever appear in the more courtly lyric of the
period. Tunes in triplet measures are very common in the popular song,
corresponding, perhaps, to the hop and skip of a popular dance.
Turkey Loney, Packington's Pound, Cock Lorrel and Light o' Love,
to name only a few of the more famous tunes of the century, are written
in the rhythm of 'The bonnets of bonny Dundee', and this results in a
verse metre based on the anapaestic foot of two short syllables and one
long, such as Byron used in his poem 'The Assyrian came down like a
wolf on the fold', to quote a familar example. Verses such as the
following occur very frequently in the Broadsheets:

> If every I marry, I'll marry a maid,
> To marry a widow I'm sore afraid.
>   (Chappell, p. 95)

sung to Turkey Loney; or the famous ballad of Mary Ambree:

> When Captains Courageous, whom death could not daunt,
> Had roundly besieged the city of Gaunt . . .
>   (Hebel and Hudson, p. 415)

or Desdemona's Willow Song. The only other context in which such
metres appear in any quantity is the *Five Hundred points of Good
Husbandrie* by Thomas Tusser, who used them to describe the whole
farming year:

> Wife, into thy garden and set me a plot,
> With strawberry rootes, of the best to be got.
>   (*September*)

or:

> Good bread and good drinke, a good fier in the hall,
> Brawne, pudding and souse and good mustard with all.
>   (*December*)

Tusser himself had been a singing boy in an ecclesiastical foundation
which was dissolved in 1549. He carried his musical training over into

his farming and wrote what was possibly the most popular book of verse in the sixteenth century. These anapaestic metres stayed below the level of serious verse until the eighteenth century when they rose to the surface and achieved respectability in *The Beggars' Opera* as low life became the fashion.

The popular ballad was there throughout the whole of the sixteenth century, but the courtly lyric decayed in the troubled years after the death of Wyatt and only came to its own again in the general poetic renaissance of the 'eighties. A chronological collection such as Ault's *Elizabethan Lyrics* shows how dramatically the quality and quantity of lyric verse increased with the advent of Spenser, Sidney and the University Wits. The new song contained both the Petrarchan and the erotic strains, and put a rich sensuous vitality into the old icon:

> Have you seen but a bright Lillie grow,
>   Before rude hands have touch'd it?
> Ha' you mark'd but the fall o' the Snow
>   Before the soyle hath smutch'd it?
> Ha' you felt the wooll o' the Bever?
>   Or Swans Downe ever?
> Or have smelt of the bud o' the Brier?
>   Or the Nard in the fire?
> Or have tasted the bag of the Bee?
> O so white! O so soft! O so sweet is she!
> (Ben Jonson, *Her Triumph*, The Underwood, II, 4)

It has a fresh sense of the country which is in part a development out of the medieval spring song but in part, also, an indication of a new interest in the English landscape. Flowers and country matters are the source of many of its settings and images.

The sources of the new poetry have been discussed earlier, but with the lyric, there is something else to consider, namely, the influence of the Italian madrigal and air which affected English music during the last quarter of the century, although Byrd and Dowland did not begin composing them in England until the last decade. The madrigal was essentially a musical technique and had little direct influence on poetry. It is a contrapuntal exercise for a number of voices in which no one melodic line is dominant. The general tone of the poem sets the mood of the music, but as the words are worked over in rotation by the different voices, the original metrical patterns are lost, and verse written for the madrigal has few recognisable characteristics. In subject, it was mainly Petrarchan, since the musical form was evolved in conjunction with the revival of Petrarch's poetry in Italy, round about 1530. But the range of its poetry covers verses from the Bible, English hexameters, stanzas from the *Mirror* or *The Faerie Queene*, sets of hunting calls, and in one case, as a joke, a verse made up of the little prose tags with which the madrigalists concluded their compositions:

> Here is an end of all the songs
> That are in number but four parts ...
> (Fellowes, *English Madrigal Verse*, p. 108)

The only essentials are that the verse must be short enough to allow for extension by the fugal methods of the music, and that it must contain no subtleties of thought, language or emotion, since these would inevitably be lost under the music. There can be no great continuity of thought or image, since the separate phases of the poem are taken out of their context and repeated by the different voices. The madrigal was nevertheless important for its indirect effects on verse, since, at a time when poets were obsessed by the problems of metre, whether the old fourteener or the new classical types, it directed attention away from metre towards the fundamental rhythm. The handling of the same set of words in different rhythms within a single Madrigal encouraged variety and helped to loosen up metres in general. The rhythmic flexibility of later Elizabethan verse owes much to the labours of the musicians.

The air, in contrast, had a more immediate effect on verse form. It was a tune sung to the accompaniment of other voices or of a viol or, particularly in England, of a lute, and it differed from the popular song in that it used the new Italian modes and rhythms. It was a more literary form than the madrigal, and words and tune were precisely matched to each other. 'I have chiefly aymed to couple my Words and Notes lovingly together', wrote Campion in the Preface to his *Two Bookes of Ayres* of which he was both poet and composer, and the verses written for an air were not designed to stand alone. A lyric such as Dowland's ' Weep you no more' has great beauty in its own right and, even in its printed form, gives some indication of the manner in which the music enabled the poet to modulate through a complex series of changing rhythms, to sustain or diminish at will:

> Weep you no more, sad fountains;
> What need you flow so fast?

> Look how the snowy mountains
> Heaven's sun doth gently waste.
> But my sun's heavenly eyes
> View not your weeping,
> That now lies sleeping
> Softly, now softly lies
> Sleeping.
> (John Dowland, *The Third and Last Booke of
> Songs and Aires*, xv. Fellowes, p. 439)

In most cases, however, the printed verse gives little clue to the total effect, and the full structure of the lyric only emerges when lute and voice are there to give it actuality. Much Elizabethan verse which we would take to be narrative or hortatory when we read it in *Tottel* was, in fact, sung: Robert Parson's air, Pandolfo, has for words a most unpromising set of fourteeners:

> Frame else with fyery feends to force on me your furious fates.
> Unless my hurted hart hath help, my hopes are but my hates ...
> Thus restless will I rest, in ruth respecting what remaynes:
> If pittiless, then pleasureless, if pitifull, no payne.

yet when this drab verse is broken down into short sections and each exploited to the full, the crude verbal structure disappears and a most moving oratorio results.

The music takes each several part and develops the emotional implications of every phrase and word, so that the printed verse is no more than the architects' plan for the real building. In this way, very pedestrian poetry can achieve a new dramatic dimension and an astonishing emotional power in conjunction with music specially designed for it. Philip Rosseter's beautiful air, 'Sweet, come again', of which I quote the second verse, is a case in point. The words, possibly by Campion, are conventional enough:

> If true Desire
> Or faithful vow of endless love
> Thy heart inflamed may kindly move
> With equal fire,
> O then my joys,
> So long distraught, shall rest
> Reposed soft in thy chaste breast,
> Exempt from all annoys.

The voice hurries over 'O then my joys' but lingers upon 'So long distraught', drawing each syllable out to many times its normal length; it soars with 'Reposed soft' but sinks and dwells lovingly upon 'thy chaste breast', concluding with a little cadenza upon 'all' in the last line. The lover's desire for his mistress and his even deeper yearning for emotional fulfilment are presented with an almost unbearable intensity of which the words alone give little indication. All good Elizabethan airs combine this full exploitation of the individual detail with the overall unity of mood which the lyric as a whole demands. 'Sweet, come again' pleads with the mistress to return and ends on this note—'To me return again'. To round off the song, therefore, Rosseter concludes with a little flourish on the word 'return', giving it a musical equivalent which epitomises the whole theme of the poem: the voice moves in a circle of notes rising and then returning to the point of departure. John Dowland's 'Sorrow, Stay' ends on a deeply tragic note which is all the more tragic because of the momentary illusions of hope which the music is able to suggest within the general mood of melancholy:

> No hope, no help here doth remain,
> But down, down, down, down I fall,
> Down and arise I never shall.

The music makes a progressive and sombre descent with each repetition of 'Down'; it rises to a hopeful crescendo, which is repeated several times with 'Down and arise', but sinks back again into final despair with 'I never shall'. The effect is of diversity within unity and a variety which never destroys the basic mood.

In many cases the music serves to define the quality of the emotion, giving the key to the degree of seriousness with which it is to be taken and indicating, for example, whether a lover's complaint is genuinely tragic or merely a part of conventional wooing. 'Sorrow Stay' is clearly tragic, but Thomas Morley's 'With my love my life was nested' is turned, by its brisk and vigorous tune, into something less broken-hearted, although its words are not essentially different:

> O true love, since thou hast left me,
> Mortal life is tedious:
> Death it is to live without thee . . .

The tune not only controls the tone but can form a witty counterpart to the words, acting as a running commentary on them and producing effects of humour or even irony. Morley's 'Thyrsis and Milla', for instance, tells a simple enough little tale in itself:

> Thyrsis and Milla, arm in arm together,
>   in merry merry May to the green garden walked,
>   where all the way they wanton riddles talked.
> The youthful boy, kissing her cheeks all rosy,
>   beseeched her there to gather him a posy.
> She straight her light green silken coats up tucked
> And May for Mill and thyme for Thyrsis plucked;
> Which when she brought he clasped her by the middle,
> And kissed her sweet, but could not read her riddle,
> Ah fool! with that the nymph set up a laughter,
> and blushed and ran away, and he ran after.

With the help of the music, however, it grows into a comic and sophisticated drama in which the voice hints at far more than is actually said, and the lute accompaniment, weaving independently in and out of the tune, adds a whole new dimension of innuendo. It begins in a rather declamatory, mock heroic tone, with Thyrsis and Milla marching arm in arm together with a stiff, almost military rhythm; but this is rapidly broken up with 'merry merry may', and even more so with a violent wrench of the rhythm at 'wanton', where the normal accent of the word is distorted, to throw it into rather sinister prominence: 'thĕy wántŏn, wántŏn, wántŏn riddles talked'. The music goes sentimental for a moment at 'The youthful boy', but becomes flippant, with much tinkling of the lute, at 'kissing her cheeks all rosy'; and so on through alternations of feeling and flippancy until the last couplet. This begins with a touch of the mock heroic at 'Ah fool', but develops into a tremendous and sustained gallop, with the lute, so to speak, cheering the runners on—'and ran and ran away, and ran and ran away, and ran and ran away, and he ran after, he ran after, he ran after'. There is little doubt that this wild chase will end in a capture. The amount of drama infused into these verses by the music is remarkable; the simple pastoral boy and girl have been turned into lovers on the brink of passion, and the whole story is told with subtlety and wit for which the music is almost wholly responsible.

It is very necessary to remember, if we are to see Elizabethan poetry in its true perspective, that for the sixteenth century the lyric was still primarily a song, and to recognise this overwhelming importance of the music. For one thing, it enables us to assess more fairly the curious experiments of Spenser, Harvey, Sidney and the rest, in classical metres. These had been first attempted by the Pléiade writers, but always in conjunction with music, for music deals in quantity and has no difficulty in lengthening or shortening syllables against the use of nature, or throwing the stress on to a syllable which is lightly accented in normal use. Gabriel Harvey made fun of the 'new famous enterprise' upon which he and Spenser were embarking, 'for the exchanging of Barbarous and Balductum Rymes with Artificial Verses', and protested that Spenser should never have his consent 'to make your Carpēnter, our Carpĕnter, an inche longer or bigger than God and his Englishe people have made him' (Gregory Smith, I, 117). But the two were exchanging poems for reading not singing, and the song writers found such changes no problem. It is significant that Campion, who was both poet and Composer, wrote extensively in quantitative verse, and some of his compositions, such as the famous 'Rose-cheekt Lawra', still stand in their own right as poems.

Furthermore, a knowledge of song may help us to refute the popular fallacy that there was no passion in the love lyric until Donne put it there. A poem such as *The Sunne Rising* is very novel for the weight of emotion it expresses, but it has an even greater novelty in the fact that it gains its effects by words alone. There are plenty of songs in the period which make as powerful an emotional impact. John Attey's dramatic and passionate air starts from a similar situation, with the lovers waking in the morning:

> On a time the amorous Silvy
> Said to her shepherd: Sweet, how do ye?
> Kiss me this once and then God be wi' ye,
>   My sweetest dear;
> Kiss me this once and God be wi' ye,
> For now the morning draweth near . . .
>   (*First Booke of Ayres*, Fellowes, p. 305)

Again it is the music which does the work. The tune begins rather hesitantly, and wanders off into another key with 'Sweet, how do ye?' as the amorous Silvy sees with dismay her partner still sleeping and the dawn coming. With 'Kiss me this once', the tune moves with a stronger, more confident rhythm, carried on by the sudden flood of her passion, and 'My sweetest dear' is extended to the length of a whole line with a languishing run of notes on 'sweetest', to convey the prolonged kiss. The kiss rouses the lover, for the last two lines move with a joyful vigour, and the hesitation of the opening moments is completely gone. The slightly halting rhythm of 'and then God be wi' ye' is smoothed out by the omission of 'then', and the last line becomes a triumphant cadenza in which 'for now the morning' is repeated three times with joyful acceptance. It is a rather thankless task to try to describe in words effects which are produced through music, though Spenser managed it in his account of the Bower of Blisse. There, the description

of Acrasia's love making against a musical background of airs and bird
songs does convey in words something of the sensuous impact of the
Elizabethan lyric. One feels, after listening to Dowland or Rosseter,
that the Elizabethan with his lute must have been an irresistible wooer.

This is not in any sense to take away from Donne's achievement in
his *Songs and Sonets*. What is happening in the sixteenth century is
the development of two separate lines of lyric, each with its own
decorum—the traditional song in its new humanist forms, and the
lyric for reading made possible by the printing press and the growth of
literature in the strict sense of the term. The sung lyric is public and
hence relatively impersonal; it has immensely complex rhythms but
simple language, and its subtlety comes, as we have seen, from the
interplay of words with music. It may have dramatic continuity, but
it cannot express sustained thought, and if it is in stanza form, each will
be a precise echo in emotion and balance of the one before, so that the
whole lyric forms a pattern of analogies. The lyric for reading, in
contrast, is by its very nature private and introspective, as we have
already seen it in the sonnet cycles; it is relatively pedestrian in rhythms
but capable of far greater verbal complexity.

We can see the two lines emerging clearly by the end of the century
in the Miscellanies: *Englands Helicon* with its simple language clearly
belongs to song, while the *Phoenix Nest* containing so much more
sonnet rhetoric is aimed primarily at the reader. The distinction was
established most clearly by Donne whose complex imagery and subtle
logic would, for the most part, be completely obscured by music.
He learned a great deal from the Air, and his poems on the page with
their stanzas so precisely repeating each other bear a superficial resemblance to the lyrics of the musicians. He was probably hampered to
some extent by the tradition of the sung lyric in his *Songs and Sonets*,
and the necessity of writing in repetitive stanza form, when his actual
mode of progression was by means of logic. Poems such as *A valediction:
of weeping* or *A nocturnall upon St Lucies day* represent a remarkable
degree of intellectual control, in that he has carried out a closely knit
and unbroken sequence of argument through the intricate repetitions
of a series of elaborate stanzas. They would make bad songs, however,
because the verses are not the emotional equivalents of each other, and
the pattern of stresses necessary to bring out the argument in one verse
does not correspond with that in the next. The difference between the
two types of lyric can be seen if one compares Donne's poem, *Lovers
infinitenesse*, with what appears to be the same poem written in the
form of a song, possibly by Donne himself, and called *Love's Exchange*
(Grierson, I, p. 449). The former poem is a sequence of close argument

in which, since the subject is the poet's desire to have the whole of his mistress' love, the predominant rhyme and the key word throughout is 'All'. *Love's Exchange*, on the other hand, though using many of the same arguments and phrases, loses all continuity and decision of statement by chopping up the argument into sections of equivalent weight and size to fit in with the repetition of a tune. It is the clearest illustration of the real difference between the two kinds of lyric, and an object lesson in the dangers of confusing them.

6

HISTORICAL POETRY

The literary judgments of posterity rarely coincide with those of a poet's own time, and we still sing and read the songs and sonnets which the Elizabethans valued as trifles, whereas the historial poems, which they took far more seriously, are nowadays virtually ignored. Yet history was one of the main subjects of Elizabethan verse, and the composition of serious historical poems by Daniel, Drayton and Spenser, the vogue of the historical play, and the effusions of Warner or Deloney at a lower level, all testify to the enormous popularity of the historical mode. The taste for history was a symptom of the Renaissance nationalism which showed itself elsewhere, as we have seen, in the patriotic development of the vernacular. There was a sudden growth of historical consciousness with the accession of the Tudors which found its expression in the great chroniclers and antiquarians of the century, of whom Hall and Holinshed, Leland, Camden, Stow, and the Italian Polydore Virgil, official historian to the court of Henry VII, are the most famous. The sixteenth century was a period of map-making, country histories and regional surveys, and Stow's *London* or Harrison's *Description of England* are typical examples of a very large field.

The study of English history included everything from the ancient Britons to the reign of Elizabeth, but two periods attracted special attention. The first was naturally the Wars of the Roses, still almost a living memory and acting as a terrible warning to a nation not yet wholly unified and often on the verge of renewed civil war. Henry VII and the Tudor line after him made all the political capital they could out of the union of the white rose and the red which had inaugurated an age of peace after 'York and Lancaster's long jars'; and after 1570, when patriotism rose under the stimulus of a Spanish and Papal threat, there was an acute sense of the blessings of unity and an overwhelming fear of internal dissension which formed the driving force behind Shakespeare's history plays. For the same reason, the reign of Edward II was a favourite with the writers because, like that of Richard II, it ended in the deposition of the king.

The second period of special interest to English patriotism was that which covered the fabulous descent of the ancient British kings from Aeneas of Troy. Geoffrey of Monmouth had first propagated the legend which had been elaborated after him and was very hotly debated and sincerely accepted by many sixteenth-century historians. According to the legend, Aeneas, after escaping from Troy, had made his way to Italy where he had founded Rome. His grandson, Brute, led by divine guidance, went to Greece where he collected the remnants of the Trojans still in captivity there, and from thence sailed to Britain, landing at Totnes in Devonshire. From him came the line of British kings which included such illustrious figures as Lud, Lear, Gorboduc and Cymbeline and which reached its peak of greatness under King Arthur. The royal line resisted and survived the Roman Conquest but finally succumbed before the Saxons; and Cadwallader, the last of the British kings, was driven into exile in Brittany. Merlin, however, had prophesied that the British kings would eventually come back to their kingdom, and Arthur himself return to the throne 'when unto a first Succeeds a second she'. The fulfilment of the prophecy came with the Tudors whose ancestor, Owen Glendower, was held to be a descendant of the ancient line, so that Elizabeth, succeeding Mary, was virtually an incarnation of the great Arthur himself. This again was a flattering and useful legend which the Tudors assiduously fostered, and even King James was included in the pattern, as a descendant of Fleance who married into the British line after his escape from Macbeth. It was pleasant to believe that London had originally been Troy Novant, the third Troy founded by the illustrious family of Priam, with Rome, of course, as the second; and for this reason Welsh and Arthurian lore played a very large part in sixteenth-century literature, although there were sceptics like Polydore Virgil who, being an Italian, had no patriotic incentive to believe in it. Even more than the classics, the tales of King Arthur formed the living mythology of the Elizabethan age.

The first poetry to deal with historical themes in a really ambitious way was the *Mirror for Magistrates*. This gigantic compendium began very humbly with a suppressed edition in 1555, but came out successfully in 1559 and from that time grew like a snowball through successive editions throughout the remainder of the century. The preface to the reader in the edition of 1559 tells how the printer had intended to publish Lydgate's *Fall of Princes* but was patriotically offended because the old poet had ignored so many tragedies out of English history. A group of seven well-known scholars, therefore, headed by William Baldwin, a translator and philospher, undertook to supply the deficiency and, by working through the chronicles, to produce a further series of falls of great men which should bring Lydgate up to date. Each of the seven chose a number of figures from English history and, in each case, wrote a poem in which the character concerned told his own story and complained of his unhappy lot. The seven composers then assembled and, with Baldwin in the chair, read out their poems and discussed them afterwards.

The form of the Complaint was perhaps forced upon these writers by the very fact that for the Renaissance, poetry was by definition, a form of 'feigning', and for many people, therefore, a strictly historical poem was a contradiction in terms. If a poet wished to stick closely to the literal fact of history, he was a versifier but no poet, and must choose some period sufficiently vague in detail to allow of elaboration involving fiction, before he could join the ranks of the true 'makers'. It was essential for the purposes of the *Mirror* that the writers should present true history of a recent and familar period, or at least, pretend to do so. The Complaint offered a way out, for as each character tells his story, history is turned into personal drama and truth can be presented through a fictitious occasion.

The poems were tragedies in the Chaucerian sense, that is, accounts of how a great person falls into misery; but whereas Lydgate had designed his tragedies to illustrate the fickleness of fortune, the writers of the *Mirror* had a more practical intention, and one more in keeping with the times. The term 'Mirror' meant the essential type or example, something approximating to the Platonic Idea, while a magistrate, as Baldwin explained in his preface, was any one in a position of authority. The *Mirror* was conceived as a pattern for statesmen, a series of political examples which should teach their own age to avoid the mistakes of the previous one, at a time when the country needed all the political guidance it could get. The seven therefore turned to the Wars of the Roses as a period particularly rich in historical lessons, and chose those figures which drove home a point most forcibly rather than those which were the most illustrious. On occasion, they took advantage of poetic licence to tamper with the facts where a small adjustment made the example more telling.

The series begins with the complaint of Robert Tresilian, the Lord

Chief Justice of Richard II, whose Tragedy illustrates the evils of
'misconstruying the lawes and expounding them to serve the Princes
affections'. Richard II is held up as a 'Kyng that ruled all by lust',
Lord Clyfford as an illustration of the way in which political revenge
recoils back upon the instigator. Throughout the whole, the Tudor
doctrine of Divine Right is emphasised, and Jack Cade's rebellion, for
example, is quoted to prove that:

> When we presume our princes to resist
> We war with God, against his glory to,
> That placeth in his office whom he list.
> (Trag. 12)

The fact that the king may be a bad king like Richard II, or the
rebellion be a sucessful one like that of Bolingbroke, makes no difference. We cannot know God's purposes, and he may have sent a bad
king to try the people's patience or to test the virtue of the ruler himself. The subject is not concerned with the ultimate ends but only with
the rightness or wrongness of his immediate actions. Good is good and
bad, bad, irrespective of the consequences, and no one is justified in
committing an evil deed for a good purpose. The tragedy of Thomas
Montague, Earl of Salisbury, who was slain 'in the middes of his glory'
was intended to teach the very un-Machiavellian moral that:

> God hateth rigour though it furder right,
> For sinne is sinne, however it be used . . .
> (Trag. 9)

The first edition of the *Mirror* is of a competent standard throughout,
but contains two especially remarkable contributions, one by Thomas
Sackville, part author of the play *Gorboduc* which resembles the *Mirror*
in its political intention, and one by John Dolman. Sackville's famous
Induction and his *Tragedy of Buckingham* are such outstanding achievements that Baldwin included them although they did not fit into his
general scheme. Sackville seems to have intended to write a *Mirror*
of his own on thoroughly humanist principles, and his *Induction* was to
have formed the framework for his collection. It begins with a brilliant
evocation of the tragic atmosphere: it is a winter's evening:

> Hawthorne had lost his motley liverye,
> The naked twigges were shivering all for colde.

when the poet meets an old withered woman who is Sorrow, a
personification conceived very much in the Senecan manner:

> . . . in endeles tormentes payned,
> Among the furies of the infernall lake.

She takes him down to a Hades which is a superb fusion of Senecan, Virgilian and medieval elements, and the whole description owes its peculiar richness to the strains of different civilisations which meet and are harmonised within it. The accompanying tragedy of Buckingham is in the same sombre vein, and if Sackville had completed his design, the poem would have been very different from the *Mirror* as it exists, less political in intention, but more profoundly tragic. Sackville was, moreover, a remarkable prosodist who achieved by unobtrusive subtlety the regularity which the writers of the contemporary four-teener sought with so much labour. He replaces the mute 'e', for example, by an extra adjective, turning Chaucer's 'fresshe floures' into 'soote fresh flowers'; and he solves the problem of changing accents by a simple inversion, as when he converts Wyatt's 'sodayn pale colour' with its stress on the last syllable to 'her colour pale'.

In contrast, Dolman, the writer of the twenty-first tragedy of the Lord Hastings, gains his effects by cultivating the very robustiousness of the old style which Sackville avoids. His description of the sea, with its puns and its vocabulary out of the Senecan translations, is un-commonly lively:

> The restless tyde, to bare the empty baye,
> With waltryng waves roames wamblyng forth. Away
> The mery maryner hayles. The braggyng boye,
> To masts hye top up hyes. In signe of joye
> The wavering flagge is vaunsd. The suttle seas
> Theyr swellyng ceasse . . .

His account of life on board ship has the compressed simile and abrupt syntax which takes one forward to the verse of Donne or Chapman:

> In pryson pent, whose woddye walles to passe
> Of no less peryll than the dying was;
> With the Oceane moated, battered with the waves
> (As chaynd at Oares the wretched Galley slaves
> At mercy sit of Sea and enemyes shott,
> And shonne with death what they with flyght may not) . . .

The poem is full of moments of humour and scraps of vivid conversa-tion which bring Richard Crookback with his 'goggle eye' suddenly to life. Sackville and Dolman, indeed, epitomise the two main lines of sixteenth-century verse, which lead on to Milton and Donne respectively.

The later editions of the *Mirror* produced by Higgins and Blenerhasset complete the story of British history from the arrival of Brute to the Norman Conquest. The serious political aim is, however, abandoned and the tragedies abound in such curious moral lessons as that which concludes the history of Kimarus who was eaten by wolves:

> By this appeares that time in Britayne were
> Aboundant store of wolves and vices rife.
> (Trag. 14, Lenvoy, *Parts added to the Mirror*)

The quality of his verse forces us to believe Higgins' confession that 'I have not spent in poetrye my dayes', though Blenerhasset is more competent. As late as 1600, new tragedies were still being added to the *Mirror*, but by that time history was thoroughly established as the theme for serious drama and poetry, and the future of the historical mode had passed from the hands of the compilers to those of individual writers.

The truest historian of all the Elizabethan poets was Samuel Daniel who himself began a prose history of the Wars of the Roses. His *Defence of Rhyme*, which came out in 1602 in answer to Campion's eulogy of classical metres, is not merely a discussion of literary techniques; it is a denial of the supremacy of the classics and a defence of English poetry based on a truly historical perspective with regard to the achievements of the Middle Ages. 'And is it not a most apparent ignorance, both of the succession of learning in Europe, and the generall course of things,' he asks, 'to say, that all lay pittifully deformed in those lacke-learning times from the declining of the Romane Empire, till the light of the Latine tongue was revived by Rewcline, Erasmus and More' (p. 140). He quotes medieval architecture and Philosophy to prove that 'The distribution of giftes are universall' (p. 143), and argues in words which anticipate those of Shakespeare's Cloten, that 'all our understandings are not to be built by the square of Greece and Italie. We are the children of nature as well as they' (p. 139). The study of the chronicles seems to have bred a tolerance for the Middle Ages which is in contrast to the contempt which Bacon and the new scientists felt for them.

Daniel's most considerable historical poem is his *Civile Wars between the two houses of Lancaster and Yorke*, the first four books of which were printed in 1595 and a second four added by 1609, when the poem stopped at the reign of Edward III. The aims of the poem were first to show that the Wars of the Roses were an inevitable result of

Bolingbroke's deposition of Richard II, and secondly to contrast 'the deformities of civile Dissension' with the blessings of Elizabethan peace. Daniel never allows himself to be distracted from these aims; in his determination to 'tell the worst of every raigne', he refuses to be drawn into an account of the victories of Henry V, and he resists the temptation to use fine language since, as he says, 'I versifie the troth, not poetise'. His interest is in the motives rather than the actions of his characters, and he analyses with great shrewdness the selfish calculation which led to the shifting loyalties of the times. The poem conveys well the sense of instability which accompanies usurpation; Henry IV and his son are never sure of themselves and are hampered by never being able to take their royal right for granted. The civil wars develop with inevitable logic out of the initial act as each injustice provokes a greater one, and Daniel supports Divine Right on the grounds of political expediency if nothing else.

The *Civile Wars* was not a popular poem in an age which liked colour and fine language, but Daniel hit the public taste much better in his *Complaynt of Rosamond*, an important and influential poem which was printed in 1592. In form it is an orthodox Complaint in the style of the *Mirror*, the tragedy of the fair Rosamond who became the mistress of the aged Henry II and was finally poisoned by his jealous queen. Its importance lies in the fact that it exploits history for other than historical purposes; the fact that it deals with historical characters is only incidental, for it is primarily a love story told in appropriately conceited language; and in crossing the historical 'Complaint' with the traditional lament of the forsaken woman, Daniel created what was virtually a new 'Kind' of poetry. The Complaynt is dramatically effective; Rosamond is a living and pathetic figure with her guilty conscience and her joyless relationship with an old man. History is made an effective teacher of private as well as public morality.

The most voluminous writer of historical poetry was Michael Drayton, whose favourite period was the reign of Edward II, and who never tired of revising and rewriting his poems through edition after edition until the final version of most of them appeared in 1619. His first batch of historical poetry, written between 1593 and 1596, shows the same deliberate exploitation of history as we have seen in *Rosamond*. His poems *Piers Gaveston, Matilda, The Tragical Legend of Robert, Duke of Normandy* and the longer *Mortimeriados, The Lamentable civell warres of Edward the second and the Barrons*, all reveal by their very extensive rhetoric, their amorous laments, their emphasis on character and dramatic situation, their experiments in form, that Drayton had found in history a new and popular subject capable of serving almost

E

any literary purpose. The plundering of history was most successful in
Drayton's deservedly popular collection, *Englands Heroicall Epistles*,
which first came out in 1597 and passed through countless editions
before 1619. The work, which is modelled on Ovid's *Heroides*, consists
of pairs of love-letters supposedly written between famous lovers of
English history. Drayton begins the series with letters between
Rosamond and Henry II, and King John and Matilda, from whence
he moves on to the Wars of the Roses, with Queen Isabel and Richard
II and with Edward IV and Jane Shore, for example. He finishes up in
the Tudors with Surrey and his Geraldine and the ill-fated couple,
Lady Jane Grey and her husband, Guildford Dudley. The combination
of a new humanist poetical form, a strong love interest and a glimpse
into the private lives of great ones proved as irresistible to the public
then as it would now, but the poems are worth reading for their own
sakes. The letters really answer each other, and the pairs of lovers are
selected with skill and treated with variety. Thus Rosamond is clearly
an honest and well-meaning woman and King Henry achieves real
pathos when he complains that the whole nation expects his favours
but that he alone is denied the right to ask for favours in return. In
contrast, King John, pursuing the chaste Matilda, is drawn as a cynical
lecher who underestimates the passionate virtue of his mistress and,
when she retreats into a nunnery to escape him, woos her with sonnet
conceits which are little short of blasphemy in the circumstances:

> Holy Matilda, Thou the Saint of mine,
> Ile be thy servant, and my Bed thy Shrine.
> When I doe offer, be thy Brest the Altar,
> And when I pray, thy Mouth shall be my Psalter . . .
> (p. 83)

His flippant suggestion that even the Phoenix is chaste only because she
is alone, and:

> had our Mother Nature made them Two,
> They would have done as Doves and Sparrowes doe;
> (p. 151)

shows a real misconception on his part of Matilda's character. In
contrast again, Jane Shore is a pretty picture of hypocrisy, the seem-
ingly virtuous wife who is in reality only too anxious to be seduced by
her king, while Geraldine is a young and modest virgin, Lady Jane Grey
a pathetic child writing under the shadow of the scaffold. The character-
isation is vivid, and the poems have the precision of Browning's

dramatic monologues. Drayton's strong historical imagination enables him to create characters who are genuinely involved in the minor events of history which surround them, and whose reactions, in consequence, have a verisimilitude which rivals that of the drama. The verse has a springy regularity very different from that of contemporary satire, and often anticipates the movement of the later Augustan couplet:

> But if that Love, Prince Edward doth require,
> Equall his Vertues, and my chaste desire;
> If it be such as we may justly vaunt,
> A Prince may sue for, and a Lady graunt . . .
> That Faith I send, which I from you receive:
> The rest unto your Princely Thoughts I leave.
> (*Alice, Countesse of Salisburie*, p. 155)

By 1605, however, a curious change has come over Drayton's attitude to history. His revised version of the *Mortimeriados*, which he brought out in 1603 under the title of the *Baron's Warres*, is a reversion to the manner of Daniel's *Civile Wars*, with much of the dramatic material omitted and a closer adherence to the chronicle materials. The same is true of his *Legends* of Robert of Normandy, Matilda and Gaveston, which are revised versions of his earlier poems and have a new one, that of the Great Cromwell, added to them. Drayton is at pains to describe the four as 'Legends', which he defines as a 'species of an Epick or Heroic Poeme' in the manner of the individual books of *The Faerie Queene*. The best of them is the legend of Cromwell which contains a new critical attitude to the reign of Henry VIII, and one which was impossible while Elizabeth was still on the throne. Drayton was perhaps the first man to laugh at the great king for having six wives. All four of the poems, however, show a more serious attitude to history, a more sober use of rhetoric and a closer approximation to the original ideals of the *Mirror*.

The reason for the change lay in the ending of a great era and the dawn of a new, less certain one with the accession of James. Drayton is not the only writer to sense the loss of unity and to deplore the decline of the old heroic patriotism in the new century. He is never tired of criticising the new Iron Age which has replaced the old one of gold, and he can see in the new dispensation only a growing passion for money, a loss of social responsibility on the part of citizen and landlord alike, and an increasing effeminacy at court. Poetry itself is becoming harsh gibberish, making a 'viler noyse, than carts upon the stones' (*Polyolbion*, XXI, 174), or debased by the popular press. Drayton's satire, *The Moone-Calfe*, written about 1607, is one of the most bitter attacks of the period, and although much of the acid may be attributed to personal disappointment, the poem clearly reflects a wide-spread disenchantment and a general feeling of disintegration.

For this reason, the old historical parables took on new vitality, and in his historical verse, the *Miseries of Queene Margarite* and the *Battaile of Agincourt* printed in 1627, Drayton turned back to point the old morals once again. The two are companion pieces, the one a picture of the miseries of civil war, and the other of the glories of patriotic unity. Written as they were with the next bout of civil war almost in sight, they form a grim and prophetic warning to the times. The *Battaile of Agincourt* is a deeply felt account of a great national triumph. Drayton knows as well as anyone that war is cruel, and that the motives behind Henry V's attack on France were largely unworthy ones. He shows the Church fostering the campaign to divert the King's attention from reform, and the Commons rising to the bait hysterically; he makes no secret of the fact that many of the English ports only sent ships in the hope of gaining further trade out of the expedition, and that the soldiers quarrelled over the amount of the ransoms on the very field of battle. And yet, in the blazons of all the troops and the ships which assemble from all parts of England, and in the unfolding of the great plan of battle which finally routs the French, there is the purest heroism, as patriotism transcends all personal motives in the heat of the fight. The poem is full of vivid and unforgettable scenes such as the description of the French horses galloping away with their rears stuck full of English arrows:

> Upon the Horses as in Chase they flye,
> Arrowes so thick, in such aboundance light,
>   That their broad buttocks men like Butts might see,
>   Whereat for pastime Bow-men shooting be.
>
>   (p. 1493)

It is in the light of this that we must read Drayton's great *Polyolbion*, that 'Topo-chrono-graphicall Poeme', as Wither christened it in his prefatory verses to the second part. Begun early in the century, the first part was published in 1612 with explanatory notes by the antiquary John Selden, to be followed by the second part in 1622. The poem, which drew its materials largely from Camden's *Britannia*, consists of a trip round Britain and Wales in company with the Muse. Rivers play an especially prominent part in Drayton's topography; every stream is a nymph or a swain, and every confluence a marriage in the manner of Spenser's wedding of the Thames and Medway, though without the symbolic significance which he attached to it. The lovely Bry in Somerset, for example, sets his affection on 'beauteous Avalon' and cannot be seduced from it:

> Though many a plump-thighed moore, and full-flanck't marsh do prove
> To force his chaste desires, so dainty of his love.
>
> (III, p. 326)

The woods are full of satyrs, and every fountain is a nymph metamorphosed. The poem is a rich example of Elizabethan myth-making which is only excelled by Spenser; in it the *Metamorphoses* has become acclimatised to England; the maps which accompany the Songs are dotted with naiads, while Neptune and his herds sport themselves in the British seas.

There are some fine topographical descriptions in the poem, especially of country which Drayton himself knew well. The Peak with its frowning cliffs and gloomy caverns is described with something of the Gothic fervour of the Romantics, and Drayton does full justice to the bird-song of the Forest of Arden, or the rich flocks of the Cotswolds, or Lincolnshire with its fishermen on stilts and its 'foule woosie' marshes. There are famous anthology descriptions of hawking or coursing the hare, or hunting the stag; yet the poem as a whole is far less descriptive than historical. Drayton has something of Kipling's feeling for England; it has been fought over and conquered by many races and every one of them has left something precious and enduring behind. The frontispiece to the poem shows Britannia in the centre with her horn of plenty, while at the four corners are the figures of Brute, Julius Caesar, Horsa and Henry VII. It is with the deeds of the kings and their subjects that the poem is really concerned. There are lists of great soldiers and seamen, catalogues of English battles and English saints, blazons of all the counties, tales of Robin Hood or Guy of Warwick and the rolls of all the British and Saxon kings.

As in the *Battaile of Agincourt*, the intention is plain. In an age which exports all its own produce in exchange for foreign goods, and chops down its own forests to feed the forges and the 'smokie citties', Drayton is reminding his countrymen of their glorious heritage, and of the greatness which has been and might be again. *Polyolbion* is the swan-song of the Elizabethan age, and Drayton speaks with the voice of Shakespeare's dying John of Gaunt. It is the voice of a man out of sympathy with the new modern world of the seventeenth century and looking back nostalgically to the age of 'globe-engirdling Drake'.

Drayton was the last of the Elizabethan historical poets; already, by the time of *Polyolbion*, the taste had changed, and Donne was complaining of the mendacity of 'Hollensheads or Halls or Stowes'. Drayton himself, in his Preface to Part II of the poem, denounced those 'outlandish, unnaturall English' who can find 'nothing in this Island worthy studying for'. One reason for the neglect, had he but known it, was the influence of such men as Selden who wrote the historical notes for him. For Selden, with his passionate curiosity into the origins of things, quietly yet systematically undermines the authority of the myths which he is elucidating. He is a man of the new science, sceptical of the Arthurian fable and suggesting that the bones of the old giants are perhaps only the bones of animals after all. He allows poetry a liberty to play with myths which he will not allow to history, and in doing so, he relegates it to the level of a polite entertainment, the relaxation of an idle hour but unworthy the serious attention of a man of science. Ben Jonson praised him truly when he wrote:

> What fables have you vext! what truth redeem'd!
> Antiquities search'd! Opinions dis-esteem'd.
>
> (*Epistle to Selden*)

A further reason for the decay of historical verse was the intensification of religious feeling. The man of the seventeenth century was more concerned to save his soul than to preserve national unity. As *The Faerie Queene* with its all-embracing analysis of personal and social morality was naturally couched in terms of the Arthurian legends, so was it equally inevitable that Milton should abandon an Arthurian epic for one based on the Bible.

7

THE FAERIE QUEENE

Spenser had already begun *The Faerie Queene* by 1580, as we learn from his correspondence with Gabriel Harvey, and the work must have been under discussion when he was in London, moving in the Leicester-Sidney circle: it is a product of the same thinking which produced the *Arcadia* and the *Apologie for Poetrie*. The work was, however, written mainly in Ireland, where Spenser went in 1580 as Lord Grey's secretary and where, apart from occasional visits to England during the early 1590's, he lived until finally driven out of his estate at Kilcolman by the Tyrone rebellion in 1598. His neighbour was Sir Walter Raleigh, a great Irish landlord, who encouraged him in the writing and publication of the poem and to whom he addressed the letter 'expounding his whole intention in the course of this worke' which was appended to the first three books. These were published in 1590, to be followed in 1596 by an edition of the whole six books, the last stanzas of Book III being modified to establish continuity with Book IV. Spenser died in England at the beginning of 1599, and in 1609 the Folio edition of the poem was printed, comprising the six books, together with two cantos of a further book on Constancy, commonly known as the *Mutability Cantos*.

There is no certainty about the precise date or order of composition of a work which took so long in the making, but it has been plausibly argued that it began with fragments of Books III and IV in the mode of Ariosto, and that the allegory of Arthur and Gloriana was developed at a later date. This would, of course, parallel the development of Sidney's *Arcadia* which began as straight Romance but was moralised in the revised version. In his letter to Raleigh, Spenser declared his

intention of producing a first poem of twelve books on the 'twelve
private morall vertues, as Aristotle hath devised', and if that were 'well
accepted', perhaps a similar work on the political virtues. In sonnet
LXXX of the *Amoretti*, printed in 1595, he remarks that he is 'halfe
fordonne', having completed six books, and is entitled to a rest before
going on to 'that second worke'. Whether he still had in mind the
original total of twenty-four books, or whether the reference to the
'second worke' implies that he had cut down each project to six cannot
be decided with certainty; but it can be argued, as we shall see, that
the poem as it now stands is Spenser's completed poem dealing with
the moral virtues, and that the original plan was discarded as too
formidable an undertaking.

The systematic humanism which we have seen to be so distinct a
feature of the *Shepheardes Calender* is a characteristic of all of Spenser's
poetry; and while writing *The Faerie Queene* he tried his hand at a
number of other Renaissance humanist 'kinds' to supply the deficiencies
of the English language 'where it faulteth'. His *Muiopotmos* published
in 1590, for example, is an exercise in the Mock-Heroic; his *Daphnaida*
of 1591, a formal Elegy; his *Mother Hubberds Tale*, published in the
same year, a satire imitated from native models. He brought out his
Petrarchan sonnet sequence and his *Epithalamion* in 1595, his *Fowre
Hymnes* on Love and Beauty the year after. *The Faerie Queene* is the
culminating example of this process of humanist experiment; and as in
the *Shepheardes Calender* he wrote as the English heir to the pastoral
tradition, so in *The Faerie Queene* Spenser saw himself as the successor
to the great line of heroic poets: 'In which I have followed all the
antique Poets historicall, first Homere . . .: then Virgil . . .: After him
Ariosto . . . and lately Tasso . . .' As a heroic poem, *The Faerie Queene*
deals with history, but with a period sufficiently remote and misty
to allow of the 'feigning' which the Renaissance considered the essence
of poetry, while at the same time giving the authenticity which belongs
to a record of real people. It enshrines a great national hero, as the
heroic poem had always done, and Spenser's initial plan for twelve
books is his acknowledgment of the traditional epic pattern.
He was writing, however, at a time when critical opinion was
deeply divided over the question of epic structure; whether the
heroic poem should follow the plan of classical epic with its single
hero and action, or whether it could have the more complex unity of
Ariosto's Romance, with its multiple structure of interlocking tales.
The Faerie Queene is a good deal nearer to the *Orlando Furioso* than
to the *Aeneid*, with its proliferation of heroes and stories interwoven,
dropped and taken up again; and Spenser clearly enjoyed the game

of narrative hide-and-seek which the method makes possible:

> Now turne againe my teme thou jolly swayne,
> Backe to the furrow which I lately left;
> I lately left a furrow, one or twayne
> Unplough'd, the which my coulter hath not cleft:
> (VI, IX, 1)

Yet above the twelve separate heroes Spenser placed his single all-embracing hero designed to pull the whole poem into epic unity and reconcile the forms of epic and romance. Arthur is not sufficient to unify the whole poem in terms of literal story, but we shall see that he carries a much stronger unifying force in terms of the underlying moral allegory.

The structure of the poem indicates Spenser's knowledge of the latest theories concerning the nature of the heroic poem, but the fact that he included both epic and romance writers in his line of heroic poets shows that for him the similarities between the two kinds were more import-ant than the differences. The significant thing about them all was that they celebrated heroes, and this, for Spenser, was the highest task of poetry. Only poets can raise great men to the level of gods and set their names among the stars; poets have the key to the one kind of immortality possible upon earth:

> But fame with golden wings aloft doth flie,
> Above the reach of ruinous decay,
> And with brave plumes doth beate the azure skie,
> Admir'd of base-borne men from farre away:
> Then who so will with vertuous deeds assay
> To mount to heaven, on *Pegasus* must ride
> And with sweete Poets verse be glorifide.
> (*Ruines of Time*, 421–)

The idea is a commonplace of the period and one which Spenser echoes frequently. By immortalising virtue, the poet gives mankind the ideal images by which it needs to live and so justifies the renaissance claim that the poets were the first priests and civilisers of the race.

Spenser's choice of a hero was almost inevitable; not only was Arthur the British hero *par excellence* of popular lore but he was also, in terms of the Tudor myth, a descendant of the line going back through Aeneas to ancient Troy and even remoter heroic vistas, and in the other direction, ancestor of the Tudor line which culminated in Gloriana, the most mythical of them all. Both by epic tradition and by literal genealogy, Arthur took his place among the poetical heroes. The choice of Arthur as the central figure inevitably dictated the use of the Romance form for the poem, and this provided Spenser with a very convenient framework for his purposes. The world of the Romance is a world of moral blacks and whites, of noble knights and wicked magicians, which offered the poet a set of ready-made and familiar symbols for his moral allegory. Moreover the loose framework of the romance allows anything to happen without the need for explanation or analysis: a giant appears from nowhere, pursued by a strange knight, or Launcelot suddenly comes upon a lady 'naked as a needle' in a bath of boiling water from which he alone can release her. There is no need to comment or explain what happened before or after and this inconsequentiality gave Spenser a medium in which the allegory could dominate the narrative in a manner impossible in a more demanding form such as that of the novel.

Spenser insists in the letter to Raleigh that *The Faerie Queene* is a 'continued Allegory, or darke conceit', and in this respect the poem is a typical product of an age in which allegory was a normal mode of expression, everywhere accepted and understood. The Renaissance conception of the universe in terms of different levels of correspondencies encouraged the mental habit of discovering relationships and expressing one thing in terms of another. This led not only to the metaphorical use of language but to all forms of allegory, both verbal and iconographical, as demonstrated, for example, in the innumerable emblem books of the period. Professor Wind has shown how extensive and elaborate is the allegory underlying the pictures of Botticelli or Titian, to name only two; and the same processes were at work on more popular levels. When Queen Elizabeth visited Elvetham, she was met by a number of virgins who were busily removing blocks from the road in front of her, which blocks, we are told, had been placed there by the person of Envy. In the same way Mercy removes the 'bushy thornes and ragged breares' which hinder Red Cross' passage to the Holy Hospital in the House of Holiness (I, X, 35). Or again, when in the *Arcadia* Dorus pretends to woo the stupid Mopsa but is in reality aiming his declarations past her at her mistress, Pamela, he produces a jewel 'made in the figure of a Crab-fish, which, because it lookes one way and goes another, I thought it did fitly patterne out my looking to Mopsa, but bending to Pamela' (*Arcadia*, 1590, II, 3). Spenser's readers enjoyed such conceits, nourished as they were on a tradition of allegorical expression which penetrated every field of life and reached back into the Middle Ages. Spenser could draw not only on the Renaissance sensibility in all its varied manifestations of allegory, but on a literary tradition which included the *Romance of the Rose*, the Morality play and the modes of allegorical interpretation to which both the Bible and the classics had been subjected for centuries. The traditional four-fold interpretation of the scriptures was still familiar enough in Spenser's time for Sir John Harington to apply it in his interesting Preface to his translation of *Orlando Furioso* in 1591:

> The ancient Poets have indeed wrapped as it were in their writings divers and sundry meanings, which they call the senses or mysteries thereof. First of all for the litterall sence (as it were the utmost barke or ryne) they set downe in manner of an historie the acts and notable exploits of some persons worthy of memorie: then in the same fiction, as a second rine and somewhat more fine, as it were nearer to the pith and marrow, they place the Morall sence profitable for the active life of man, approving vertuous actions and condemning the contrarie. Manie times also under the selfesame words they comprehend some true understanding of naturall Philosophie, or sometimes of politike governement and now and then of divinitie: and these same sences that comprehend so excellent knowledge we call the Allegorie, which Plutarch defineth to be when one thing is told, and by that another is understood.
>
> (Gregory Smith, II, 201–2)

He goes on to apply the method to the myth of Perseus and the Gorgon, taking both his example and his interpretations from Leone, who took them from Boccaccio, and concluding very instructively: 'The like infinite Allegories I could pike out of other Poeticall fictions, save that I would avoid tediousnes.'

Harington is working within the traditional framework of the four-fold interpretation, but his treatment indicates a development beyond it. In terms of Renaissance euhemerism the myth was a statement of historical fact: Perseus, a historical hero, killed Gorgon, a historical tyrant of the ancient world: yet for Harington, the myth is also a mode of literary expression, an extended metaphor or allegory through which the poet conveys a variety of simultaneous meanings. What in the Middle Ages had been accepted as true on both literal and symbolic levels is now becoming a 'poeticall fiction', a conscious literary device which instructs through delight, according to the Horatian definition. Harington's account of poetic allegory clearly defines what Spenser was doing in *The Faerie Queene*, with its historical fable used as a mode of literary allegory; and such a development resulted when the older tradition of symbolism fused with the new revival of interest in allegory as the extended metaphor of rhetoric. It is the fact that allegory belongs both to the worlds of religion and rhetoric which gives to Spenser's allegory its conviction and its enormous flexibility.

The rhetorical nature of Spenser's allegory is immediately obvious at the level of the individual images which have the logical defining quality characteristic of all metaphor in the period. The little iron wedges which the blacksmith, Care, is manufacturing in IV, V, 35 are a very accurate image to define the 'unquiet thoughts' which, in the manner of little wedges, open up the way for bigger fears; and the fact that Care's hammers keep Scudamore awake all night extends and applies the metaphor. A set piece such as the description of the Palace of Pride in I, IV consists of a single extended metaphor in which the architectural and moral statements unfold themselves synonymously:

> A stately Pallace built of squared bricke,
>   Which cunningly was without morter laid,
>   Whose wals were high, but nothing strong, nor thick,
>   And golden foile all over them displaid,
>   That purest skye with brightnesse they dismaid:
>   High lifted up were many loftie towres,
>   And goodly galleries farre over laid,
>   Full of faire windowes and delightfull bowres;
> And on the top a Diall told the timely howres.
>
> It was a goodly heape for to behould,
>   And spake the praises of the workmans witt;
>   But full great pittie, that so faire a mould
>   Did on so weake foundation ever sit:
>   For on a sandie hill, that still did flit,
>   And fall away, it mounted was full hie,
>   That every breath of heaven shaked it:
>   And all the hinder partes, that few could spie
> Were ruinous and old, but painted cunningly.
>
> (I, IV, 4–5)

Here every detail helps to define the essential nature of pride, its glittering attractiveness and its underlying instablity. The bricks are showy but insecure; the walls impressively high but thin, and the gold is only foil, and only on the front where it shows. Its deceptive glitter rebelliously challenges the 'purest sky' even while the whole structure is shaken by 'every breath of heaven'. Its ultimate fall is prophesied by the dial on top which marks the passing of time, and its fundamental weakness comes from the fact that it is built not on the Biblical rock but on the sand. The sin is systematically analysed in terms of a familiar and memorable image which, it must be noted, is aimed at the reader rather than at Red Cross who cannot see the back parts as we

can. *The Faerie Queene* forces us to read it with a strenuous and un-
flagging attention to detail, and to weigh, at the same time as we
enjoy, the images. The Bower of Blisse subjects us to the whole range
of physical sensations through soporific metres and near-pornographic
description, but the signposts are always there forcing us, if we use our
minds, to evaluate these sensations in moral terms. To read *The Faerie
Queene* is to experience in vicarious literary form the very temptations
which beset the heroes of the books, and if we read honestly, to be
forced to pit our minds against them as the characters themselves have
to learn to do. The two naked damsels wrestling in the little lake are
as tempting to the reader as they were to Guyon when he went by;
but we are warned that they only 'seemed' like Venus rising from the
sea (II, XII, 65), and that their little lake is protected from the sun by
shady laurel trees (63). We are told, in other words, that the sex which
they offer is not of the true and fruitful kind, and their proximity to
the allegorical forest shade identifies them as temptations to be resisted. The poem is carefully designed to move the reader to virtue
by fostering in him moral discrimination.

There is nothing intrinsically unpoetical in such allegory. That it
forces us to think does not prevent it from expressing complex con-
cepts in truly imaginative form. On the way to the Bower of Blisse,
Guyon passes by the Rock of Vile Reproach, which is Spenser's
symbol for the spite, callousness and hostility of the world towards
those prodigals who have squandered their wealth in riot and gluttony:

> Forthy this hight *The Rocke of vile Reproch*,
>   A daungerous and detestable place,
>   To which nor fish nor fowle did once approch,
>   But yelling Meawes, with Seagulles hoarse and bace,
>   And Cormoyraunts, with birds of ravenous race,
>   Which still sate waiting on that wastfull clift
>   For spoyle of wretches, whose unhappy cace,
>   After lost credit and consumed thrift,
> At last them driven hath to this dispaireful drift.
>
> (II, XII, 8)

The bare rock sticking out of the sea, and the hoarse squawking of the
sea birds as they hiss at the passing boat form an extraordinarily powerful
picture in its own right and at the same time a terrifying image of one
of the most hateful of human traits. The double meaning of the word
Cormoyraunt—at once the name of the greediest of seabirds, and a
slang Elizabethan term for the moneylenders upon whom the young
prodigal will be wrecked—brings the image and the underlying mean-

ing together with a most satisfactory snap. The pleasure in reading *The Faerie Queene* comes from carrying in one's mind simultaneously a lively story and an allegorical meaning which follows the tale in every detail of its logic and, as C. S. Lewis says, fits it like a hand into a glove. The unique quality of the poem is its sustained power of maintaining simultaneous and parallel levels of meaning.

It should be emphasised that *The Faerie Queene* is not merely concerned with the allegorial presentation of abstract virtues and vices: a passage such as the following reveals a more complex intention. It comes early in Book I, where Red Cross is fighting Error in the specific form of heresies, and it is the turning point of the conflict, when he succeeds in throwing off the swarm of crawling little monsters which assail him:

> The same so sore annoyed has the knight,
> That welnigh choked with the deadly stinke,
> His forces faile, he can no longer fight:
> Whose corage when the feend perceiv'd to shrinke,
> She poured forth out of her hellish sinke
> Her fruitful cursed spawne of serpents small,
> Deformed monsters, fowle, and blacke as inke,
> Which swarming all about his legs did crall,
> And him encombred sore, but could not hurt at all.

> As gentle Shepheard in sweete eventide,
> When ruddy *Phoebus* gins to welke in west,
> High on an hill, his flocke to vewen wide,
> Markes which doe byte their hasty supper best;
> A cloud of combrous gnattes do him molest,
> All striving to infixe their feeble stings,
> That from their noyance he no where can rest;
> But with his clownish hands their tender wings
> He brusheth oft, and oft doth mar their murmurings.
>
> (I, I, 22–3)

The stanzas tell us a good deal about the nature of these heresies—that they are black as ink from the 'bookes and papers' of verse 20, that they are sent from the 'feend', and that they cannot harm the Christian. More important, however, is the contrast between the two stanzas: the first, by its picture of these horrible creatures swarming up Red Cross' legs, gives an impression of fear, nausea and disgust; the second stanza, in contrast, conveys an overwhelming sense of physical relief after the suffocating horror of the first. The horrible creatures attacking the lower members are suddenly metamorphosed into harmless gnats buzzing around the head, to be brushed away with the back of one's

hand. The operative word effecting the change is, of course, 'shepheard'
—Christ, the good shepherd, the recollection of whom renders the
most horrible heresies impotent in the light of faith. They may trouble
his lower nature, but Red Cross has only to use his head to see them in
their true perspective and fear them no more. Spenser has made a
comment, therefore, on the relationship between faith and heresy, and
on the unthinking ignorance which alone makes heresy to be feared.
He has also, however, conveyed a sequence of emotions; he has
expressed, in two stanzas, what it feels like to be troubled by terrifying
doubts and then to regain the serenity and innocence of faith again.
The sense of relief is that of Red Cross at having escaped; the allegory
is of inner states of mind which colour the general statement and
infuse personal feeling into it.

This is one of the keys to the understanding of *The Faerie Queene*. It
is based upon psychological allegory by which the qualities and movements of the mind are projected as external forms, and the inner conflicts and moods are given objective personification. The tradition of
such allegory goes back to classical times, but can be seen most obviously
in the *Romance of the Rose:* the lover's pursuit of the lady is symbolised
by his attempt to pluck the rose in the walled garden; and the rose has
its defenders and betrayers, consisting of those qualities in the lady which
are hostile or favourable to the lover's suit. Thus Pite, Fraunchise and
Kinde welcome him in but are constantly opposed by Fere, Drede and
Daunger representing all the instincts of modesty and stand-offishness
in the lady's character. The conflict within the mind of the lady is
shown as a battle between these oppoing personifications, and the
lover's progress depends upon the outcome. This is Spenser's basic
method of allegory, although his use of it is infinitely more complex.
Each book of *The Faerie Queene* has as its centre a hero or heroine
whose task it is to learn a particular virtue by facing, falling before but
ultimately discovering how to master, the specific vices which beset it.
As in Bunyan, the central character is a real person who has to face
allegorical temptations: Red Cross goes through the Pallace of Pride,
falls before Orgoglio, the giant of deadly sin, and nearly succumbs to
Despair, just as Christian has to pass by Vanity Fair or Doubting Castle
or Giant Despair. He sets out, however, in company with characters
who personify those aspects of his own nature which are relevant to
his quest, and as the story develops and new passions arise in him,
these too appear in the guise of new characters. The hero is surrounded
by projections of himself which act out in front of us an allegory of
what is going on within the mind, so that in Book I, for example,
where this method appears in its purest form, there is really only one

character, Red Cross himself, and the rest, apart from Arthur and the inmates of the House of Holiness, are all aspects of his own personality. The action takes place primarily within the mind, and by thus anatomising it, Spenser is able to trace and demonstrate the sources of virtue and of vice.

Spenser's psychology throughout the poem is the traditional three-fold one of Mind, Soul and Body. Mind is man's purely spiritual part and its instrument is what Milton called 'Right Reason', the 'erected wit' which involves conscience and an intuitive sense of right and wrong; it is the divine spark which Adam forfeited at the Fall but which God of his Grace in part restored to him, as Milton describes in *Paradise Lost* (III, 194–6). The body is, of course, material, the seat of the instincts, which are not necessarily bad but irrational, brute and therefore easily misdirected. Between these two comes the soul, part spiritual and part material, acting as mediator and having as its quality the power of practical reason. In the truly temperate person, right reason rules the body through the medium of the rational soul, but this happy state of inner hierarchy is rare since the Fall.

Book I exemplifies the method. Red Cross set out on life's journey with his quota of qualities: Una, his right reason; the dwarf, representing the powers of the soul; and the bodily instincts, demonstrated at first by the unruly horse he rides and later, in Canto III, by the lion. But all is not well with the trio. Una, since the fall of man imprisoned her in the corrupt flesh, is veiled, so that her full beauty is invisible to Red Cross and she herself cannot see as clearly as she once could. She rides on her white ass, suggesting, of course, the ass on which Christ rode, but instead of leading the procession as the Palmer does at the start of Book II, she lags woefully behind Red Cross whose steed perpetually charges ahead. Moreover Una is dependent on the dwarf who bears 'her bag/Of needments at his backe' (6), and he lags even further behind when he should in fact come second. The improper order of this little procession with which the poem opens would not be lost upon the Elizabethan reader, accustomed to such moral pageantry, and would indicate at once that all is not well with Red Cross. It explains why, although wearing the full Christian armour, he is yet 'too solemn sad', as Spenser doubly underlines it in the second stanza. Right reason is not in full control, and so he is unable to understand the true happiness which his faith implies.

Inevitably, therefore, he is drawn off his way into the allegoric forest of temptation:

Whose loftie trees, yclad with sommers pride,

Did spred so broad, that heavens light did hide . . .

(7)

and distracted from his quest by his delight in all the innocent variety
of the world, symbolised by the multitude of trees and their functions,
he follows the beaten track into Error's den. It should be noticed that
'full of fire and greedy hardiment', the 'youthful knight' insists on
fighting Error against the advice of both Una and the dwarf (13).
The Christian need not seek out heresies which are impotent to harm
him, and Red Cross attacks 'As Lyon fierce', by instinct and against
reason. When the monster seizes his shield of faith, his right reason
reminds him of the strength which lies in his armour: 'Add faith unto
your force,' Una cries (19), and he is saved, but at a price. Spenser
always insists that the mortal body is too frail to waste its energies in
resisting temptations which need never have been encountered, for a
tired body liberates the passions and reduces the control of right reason.
This is what happens in Book II where Guyon, in the absence of his
Palmer and mainly out of curiosity, wears himself out by the magnificent
but quite irrelevant exercise of virtue in Mammon's cave. As a result
he faints when he reaches the unaccustomed air again, and all the
unruly passions at once gallop up to seize him. So with Red Cross, as
soon as the fight with Error is over, he is met by Archimago, the
satanic voice of his whole lower nature inviting him to have a rest;
and in the literal and allegorical sleep which follows, his physical
passions assert themselves. The erotic dreams which Archimago
conjures up from the underworld, of a Una now only too visible
through her veil, represent the way of life the average sensual man would
prefer to have, a more indulgent mistress than the austere Una with
which he began. Red Cross is horrified at his own desires at first, but,
envious at the pleasures of life which he feels he is missing, he storms
out as George Herbert threatens to do for the same reason in his poem
'The Collar'. He forsakes Una, his eye of reason blinded, and at
once finds a guide more to his liking. He is not yet without faith; he
can still beat Sans Foy; but Duessa is an Una adulterated by sensuality
and therefore the guardian of a more sensual faith, that of the Roman
Catholic not the true church.

Inevitably he goes to the Pallace of Pride, though not without
moments of uneasiness on the way which he is not clear-sighted
enough to understand; but even here he can defeat Sans Joy, although
he cannot kill him, having lost his right reason which alone can show
him the gospel way to do it. Sans Joy remains alive to trouble Red
Cross obscurely and to rise again eventually in the guise of Despair.

F

He still has enough of the habit of virtue to escape from the Pallace of Pride, though he does so by the prudential calculations of the dwarf on seeing the skeletons in the cellar, rather than by an absolute knowledge of the sinfulness of pride: so a non-Christian might profit by reading the *Fall of Princes* or the *Mirror for Magistrates*. He has not escaped by his right reason, and Duessa is still with him, so that relaxing after his victory by the well of Sloth, he takes his Christian armour off and is struck down by the full force of sin, Original and acquired. Orgoglio is not a single sin, like the six who draw Lucifera's carriage in Canto IV; he is the personification of the Fall itself, and once seized by him, Red Cross is spiritually dead. Spenser has shown the gradual decline of Red Cross, through a counterfeit faith to a state of no faith at all; and as Una loses her control of him so Archimago gains it. He puts on the Christian armour and counterfeits Red Cross because Red Cross has become a counterfeit Christian, and he loses it to Sans Loy when Red Cross ceases to wear it altogether. Although the literal Red Cross often disappears from the picture, he is always firmly there in the person of his own qualities, and we must not interpret Una or Archimago as separate characters with their own story.

The rest of the book analyses the process by which right reason, through the Grace of God, gradually reassumes control in Red Cross, so that he is able to rise again. At first, with the soul eclipsed by the flesh, right reason is left with instinct alone: with the dwarf away, Una has only the lion, and lacking the interpreter, she can neither guide nor be guided by him. Thus they wander into the house of Blind Devotion, and though even the lion is ennobled by her presence, his virtue can only be instinctive, like that of Red Cross himself when not guided by Una, and he falls before Sans Loy. But God does not abandon the sinner so lightly, and Una battles on to save her lover, the voice of right reason and conscience still making itself heard, however obscurely, in the heart of Red Cross. Spenser traces the stages of regeneration in great detail. First, by 'Eternall Providence' the wood-folk come to the rescue; and these, though inhabitants of the forest, are yet above the beast: the half-human satyrs worship Una without understanding her significance, and symbolise the first yearnings in the fallen soul of Red Cross for a virtue which he can not yet comprehend. From this follows Satyrane, born of the satyrs yet above them and dedicated to taming the beast within: he is the desire for virtue crystallising into a moral purpose and thus struggling with Sans Loy though not yet able to defeat him. Out of this inner moral struggle comes knowledge, and the dwarf therfore returns to Una. Red Cross is not yet in a state of faith, but he is now aware of his own fallen condition, as is made clear in the account of the whole sad sequence which the dwarf gives to Una in I, VII, 26. Red Cross has achieved a degree of knowledge and humility comparable to that of Adam and Eve at the end of Book X of *Paradise Lost* where they confess their fault, or of Samson at the beginning of *Samson Agonistes*. He has acknowledged his sin and is fit for redemption, so that Una is able to call to Arthur for help. In this context, Arthur is the symbol of Christ offering redemption to those who believe in him and rescuing them from the prison of sin. He embodies the doctrine of Justification by Faith. The conquest of Orgoglio is an allegory of Red Cross' intellectual acceptance of faith by which his eye is unblinded and the burden of sin falls from his back as it does for Bunyan's Christian. He is now in a state of Grace again, but he still has to use his powers against the arch-enemy of the gospels, Despair, to which in his new-found awareness of sin he is especially prone. The arguments with which Despair assails him are the arguments with which his own guilty conscience would persuade him that he is unworthy to be saved, and the whole episode is the projection, once more, of an inner dialogue. It is interesting to note that Despair attacks with scraps of theological argument divorced from their context: his first assertion that 'he should die, who merites not to live' (I, IX, 38) is, of course, the pronouncement of the Law without the Gospel; it is the source of Faustus' Despair when he remembers that the reward of sin is death. When Red Cross argues that a man cannot simply kill himself because he wants to, Despair counters with the doctrine of Predestination—'When houre of death is come, let none aske whence, nor why' (42). Right reason is strong enough to counter these doubts with the naked assertion of gospel faith. 'In heavenly mercies hast thou not a part?' (53), but Red Cross is clearly confused over the intellectual bases of his belief, and hence his visit to the House of Holiness is necessary, and his instruction by Fidelia in the basic dogmas of the faith, 'Of God, of grace, of justice, of free-will' (I, X, 19). Now at last he is ready to fight the dragon.

I have analysed Book I in detail because it reveals an essential Spenserean method in its naked purity: the battle of faith is fought within the mind, so that all the action of the book takes place there. All evil springs ultimately from man's own fallen nature, so that all conquest of sin throughout *The Faerie Queene* involves some degree of inner conflict and self conquest. Even in Book I, however, the inner quality is related to its external manifestation in society, as Una is linked with the true Church, Duessa with the false; and in later books of the poem the external symbol at times receives more emphasis than its inner cause. The hero may seem to represent an achieved virtue opposing vices in other people, but a careful reading of the poem will show that this is never the whole picture and that the outer battle involves an inner one as well. In Book II the psychological nature of the allegory is unmistakable, and the characters are those we have met in Book I, though seen from a different angle. Guyon has his Palmer, right reason, to guide him, and his bodily instincts, in the form of his well-controlled horse at the beginning, and his boatman at the end who remains by the boat when Guyon and his Palmer go forward to meet temptations against which bodily vigour will be a hindrance more than a help. Guyon has his fluctuating passions in the guise of Pyrochles and Cymochles; he has impulses to relax related to these, in the form of Phaedria; and last of all he has the witch, Acrasia, who, like Archimago, would blind the eye of reason another way. By lulling men into a state of sensuous contentement, she would remove the sense of sin and with it the knowledge of the need for Grace.

It is easier to lose sight of the psychological level of allegory in Books III and IV under the proliferation of stories, especially in Book IV, where Spenser is demonstrating at philosophical and social as well as psychological levels the concord resulting from love, both human and divine. Britomart, however, is the essential character, and as both books are concerned with the control of her sexual nature, this is personified in its different aspects. Amoret is the symbol of her pro-creative instincts, what the Middle Ages called 'Kinde', the human embodiment of the Platonic Venus Dione: Belphoebe symbolises the idealism which alone can sanctify the physical nature; the love of divine beauty which must precede the desire to propagate it, as Venus Urania is the elder of the two sisters. Besides these, there is Busyrane, the power of fantasy to distort our sexual attitudes and surround them with unnatural fears; and there is Lust and all the varieties of perversion which have their place in the heart of man. Britomart's quest is to learn the use and mastery of these explosive qualities within her own nature, before she is fitted to be the mother of a line of kings and heroes.

Book V would seem to be the most objective, the least psychological of all the books of *The Faerie Queene*: Artegall, backed by Talus, is engaged in battles with oppression, fraud and all the external evils of society. Yet Talus is not simply a symbol of Law; he is the rational and just use of force, and Artegall has to learn to master and employ the violence in his own nature before he is the truly just man. It is revealing of Spenser's own nature that he makes the greatest temptation that of not employing rather than employing unjustly our own powers of compulsion. Artegall falls through a misplaced impulse of pity which makes him spare Radegund when he should have killed her. It is the

temptation to which Guyon was subjected on his way to The Bower
of Blisse when he heard the maiden lamenting and was moved to
'foolish pitty' (II, XII, 27-9). In Book VI the allegory is the subtlest and
most elusive of all. There are no personifications of inner qualities:
instead, the great image of the Graces dancing expresses the vision of
unfallen beauty which the poet alone sees clearly and which ordinary
men get a hint of in the world around them and pursue in their blunder-
ing way, as Calidore breaks in upon the Graces' dance without knowing
what they are. Book VI goes beyond the realm of analysable allegory
into a world of psychological symbolism where states of mind are
projected through long sequences of action, Innocence and Experience,
pre-lapsarian nakedness and the sense of the shame which came with
the Fall. These great contrasts make up the book and invest its action
with a special radiance or a special horror.

There are many levels of allegory within *The Faerie Queene*, since an
inner conflict results in an outer one, and all battles on the psychological,
historical, political or religious levels are simultaneous manifestations
of the same thing. For this reason, it is necessary to recognise that
underneath his panoply of knights and quests, Spenser is dealing with
the most common and daily human experiences, of feeling tired and
impatient, angry or sentimental. The presentation is inevitably in terms
of consecutive narrative, but the true logic of the story is that of cause
and effect, each new encounter following as an inevitable psychological
result of the one before. On his way to The Bower of Blisse, Guyon,
having rowed hard past an assorted batch of temptations, is assailed
by the syrens who woo him in verse of infinite seduction to take a rest.
His Palmer drives him on, however, and immediately they are over-
whelmed in the dark fog full of bats and birds of ill omen. If we
translate this into terms of simple realism we can see that it presents an
inevitable sequence: Guyon, wearied with the effects of sustained
resistance, wants to relax but feels forced to drive himself onwards:
his exhaustion, therefore, manifests itself in a mood of black doubt
from which only his reason and his bodily health can rescue him. It is
a sequence with which we are all very familiar in our daily lives, and
it represents the basic level at which *The Faerie Queene* operates. Spenser
is very much of his age in this respect; he shares the passion of Shakespeare and the drama to explore the springs of human nature, the
subtle interaction of body and mind, the infinite powers of sels
deception, perversion and also heroism within human nature. There if
no other work in the language which presents so systematic and full
an anatomy of human behaviour in all its respects as this infinitely
capacious poem. We shall do the work greater justice if we link it to

the great psychological novels such as those of Proust or Joyce, than if we analyse it merely in terms of moral emblems.

A discussion of the methods of *The Faerie Queene* inevitably covers much of the content, and it only remains, therefore, to try to indicate briefly the moral scheme in terms of which the poem is set. In his letter to Raleigh, Spenser declares that his aim is 'to fashion a gentleman or noble person in vertuous and gentle discipline', and by the word 'fashion' he means to 'represent' the image of a gentleman and perhaps, too, to fashion his reader to the likeness of the image. In its literary intention, the poem belongs to the great class of Renaissance books of improvement of which Elyot's *Governor*, Castiglione's *Courtier* and Machiavelli's *Prince* are examples. It is obvious, however, that Spenser's Gentleman is something less specialised than the Governor or Courtier or the Gentleman as we think of him today. The poem is concerned throughout with the nature, the cause and the cure of the deadly sins, and Spenser's central preoccupation is with the problem of the Fall. *The Faerie Queene* sets out to instruct the reader how to repair the ruins of the Fall and, as the basic part of this, to answer the question 'What shall I do to be saved?' The Fall brought sin and death into the world, and the poem explores the psychology of the former and the philosophy of the latter, offering what is ultimately a theological answer to both.

It is difficult to pin Spenser down to any precise position in the sixteenth-century controversy over the nature of Justification. He clearly believed in Justification by Faith and that only by faith do good works become possible; but he never makes it clear whether good works are a cause or a result of salvation. Similarly, although *The Faerie Queene* deals with the area between the state of potential redemption into which man is born and the actual redemption which he finally learns to achieve, Spenser never commits himself wholly to any precise statement of the extent of human responsibility for this development. The heroes are continually faced with agonising moral choices to which only the use of right reason can give the answer, yet God himself sends the right reason without which man would be helpless, and the will is in one sense free but in another not. We cannot be sure whether, in Spenser's opinion, God surrounds man by temptations and gives him absolute free will with which to stand or fall, or whether God leads man through the world of temptations letting him fall as a part of his moral education. There is a stronger sense of God's guiding love throughout *The Faerie Queene* than there is through *Paradise Lost*, where Milton invests Adam's seed with magnificent but terrifying independence. Spenser never commits himself as thoroughly as this, and his attitude is deliberate in a poem intended for all mankind, not merely for a sect. He stresses the points which all Christian creeds have in common, and there is nothing in the poem which would offend the sensibilities of either a reforming Catholic or a reasonable Calvinist.

For Spenser, the world is irrevocably fallen and human nature inescapably prone to sin. Salvation depends, therefore, on Grace—the grace which restored some degree of right reason to Adam's seed and offers redemption through Christ to those who believe. Since this is the basis of all human virtue, it is dealt with at the beginning of the poem; Book I shows man how to value and use the faith into which he is christened. Holiness is not a state in which the Christian no longer sins, for that is impossible since the Fall; it is a state in which man sins continually but is always able to rise again through faith. Arthur, who plays the role of the Redeemer towards Red Cross, is in himself the example of true holiness; and in his fight with Orgoglio, therefore, he too falls before the giant and is only saved by the blow of the club which in striking removes the veil from his shield. Even he is a sinner but is redeemed through his sin, as Adam's sin was the reason why Christ the Redeemer came into the world. Red Cross has to learn this certainty, and by Canto XI he has done so. In his fight with the dragon he falls twice, as he had done earlier; but now he falls under the Tree and into the Well of life, symbols of the flesh and blood of his redeemer, so that after each fall he arises again stronger than ever, his faith fortified by the trial. This is only the beginning: he will go on falling, which is why Spenser places his climax in the eleventh canto and leaves the final one for the return of Duessa and Archimago. The rest of *The Faerie Queene* is an account of all the subsequent ways of sin which are possible to mankind, and yet with this start, no fall need be final. Christ has made it possible for man always to come back into the fight again, and hence he must go battling on in his quest no matter what happens.

Book I clarifies the mystery and the nature of faith, and establishes the availability of Grace for all who will take it. Una is, therefore, the figure of the Virgin with her eyes turned towards heaven. Book II is the complementary study, showing how to control the lower nature and keep the eye of reason unblinded, so that the human being may always recognise and avail himself of the powers of Grace. The Palmer is thus the figure of wisdom guiding Guyon in the ways of Temperance. Temperance, however, was initially a classical virtue with all the weight of Aristotle's golden mean behind it. Guyon, as he sets out on his quest, is drawn essentially as a classical hero, an Odysseus or Aeneas who swears a pagan oath by the dead body of Amavia, or like Aeneas, recounts his story to Medina from the height of his 'Lofty siege' (II, II, 39). Guyon's main lesson, indeed, is to learn what classical temperance ignored, that man is a fallen creature in need of Grace. His failing is pride, the Christian name for the classical sense of self-sufficiency: his horse is under control; he rashly frees Pyrochles; he guides himself by the light of 'his own vertues and praiseworthie deedes' when he has lost his Palmer, and he ventures into Mammon's cave when he could have stayed out of it; Braggadochio is a real part of his nature. His fall comes from a virtuous indignation which is itself a form of excess. The mortal body has only limited powers of resistance which must be husbanded for the right occasion, and Guyon's over-confidence leads him to ignore this aspect of his own mortality. His intemperate passions take over when he is too tired to control them any longer; and Spenser underlines the moral in his account of Arthur's fight with Maleger, in Canto XI. Arthur, too, pursues his enemy with too much zest and, but for the Grace of God, would be overcome by the two hags, Impatience and Impotence, who are waiting for just such an occasion. Guyon falls, but that he learns his lesson is indicated by the speedy way in which he profits by what Red Cross has already demonstrated. There is no falling into despair for Guyon: the angel of Grace restores his Palmer to him who at once calls on Arthur to save (Canto VIII) and the burden of sin slips from his shoulders. From now on he takes his Palmer's advice to control the passions before they get a proper hold and to avoid all unnecessary occasion of temptation. It is significant that when Guyon finally defeats Acrasia, he does so only by avoiding a great many temptations on the way. If he had not followed the Palmer's advice in this, he would never have reached the Bower at all but stayed for ever on Phaedria's island. The real Homeric Odysseus was less cautious, but he also took a good deal longer over his journey than his Christian-ised counterpart.

This, then, is Spenser's account of what God will do for man and what man may do for himself: together they form Spenser's answer to the problem of generic sin. But the Fall brought death into the world, physical as well as spiritual, and that too must be answered. The Bower of Blisse poses a double problem, of spiritual and of physical death as well, for Acrasia's love is sterile: the Genius at her gate is explicitly not that Genius who, in the *Romance of the Rose*, is Venus' agent of procreation. The answer lies in sex, the eternity by succession through which the human race can alone preserve itself, and this,

therefore, is the subject of Book III. The central character is appropriately Britomart, mother-to-be of the line of British kings, and the
central symbol is the Garden of Adonis, the phallic source of an endless
cycle of fruitfulness whence the seeds flow out to fertilise chaos
and produce those dying generations which always replace themselves.
Britomart has to discover her own sexual nature and release the Amoret
within her for her proper function. Her story is that of growing up from
romantic adolescent dreams to physical maturity. The House of
Busyrane is Spenser's symbol for the exciting yet terrifying emotions
surrounding the subject of sex, especially for those brought up on a
diet of Courtly love Romances and sonnet agonisings. Amoret is
imprisoned here and Britomart has to break her way in and
destroy it all before Amoret can fulfil herself in the embraces of
Scudamore, which is how Book III ends in the first version.
Fellini has treated a similar theme more flippantly in his film *The
White Sheik*, where the young girl after getting lost in the world of
her romantic dreams comes home very gladly to her prosaic but at
least real husband.

But sex as a reality presents new dangers. It is at once the most
essential and the most unruly of the passions, the cause of the fall of
both Red Cross and Artegall. Once Britomart has taken Amoret to
her bed, she too is in the same danger, and when she falls asleep, the
monster Lust makes his appearance. This, of course, happens in Canto
VII, immediately after she has met Artegall face to face, and her
imagined lover has become a real one. Amoret is carried away, making
only a feeble protest, and Lust is able to use her body as a protection
against the pursuing spear of Timias because it is the body which
comes between the human being and virtue. Britomart needs educating
in some other quality to protect her procreative instinct from the
dangers inherent in it, and this is what Spenser treats in Book IV under
the title of Friendship. Friendship is love independent of sex: between
man and woman, therefore, it is the idealised love expressed by the
higher Venus, the love of divine beauty which precedes, inspires and
justifies the desire to propagate it. Belphoebe is the figure embodying
this quality and it is she alone who can redeem the Amoret in Britomart's nature from the clutches of Lust. Since, as we have seen earlier,
God's contemplation of his own perfection was the source from which
all goodness and all creation stemmed, so from the idealism of Belphoebe comes all the human nobility of *The Faerie Queene*. By means
of her, Britomart's physical desire is given sanction; and it is her vision
of human responsibility which provides the rationale for the whole
human quest:

G

Who seekes with painfull toile shall honor soonest fynd:
In woods, in waves, in warres, she wonts to dwell,
    And wil be found with perill and with paine;
    Ne can the man that moulds in ydle cell
    Unto her happy mansion attaine:
    Before her gate high God did Sweat ordaine,
    And wakefull watches ever to abide ...   (II, III, 40–1)

In this knowledge, Britomart can perfect her sexual nature and be
truly prepared, with Artegall, to propagate the line of kings and
heroes.

In these four books Spenser has dealt with the problems of the Fall
as they affect the individual: he has shown a way of life in which the
effects of the Fall can be in part limited by a group of virtues and
ultimately neutralised by divine Grace. But man does not live by himself; he exists in society and is faced with his own sins as they occur in
other people and which he must put down in others as well as in himself, if the true concord of love is to be maintained. For this task, since
Astraea was driven from the world by human sin, force is necessary,
and Justice is the virtue with which it must be used, the virtue of
giving to each person what is fairly his, to oneself as well as to others.
Artegall learns this rational use of force, in society the force of the law,
in himself, force governed by right reason. Yet justice by its very nature
breeds further evils beyond its own control, the hatred, envy and
backbiting of those whom force has justly conquered. As soon as
Artegall has conquered Grantorto, the Blatant Beast appears in company
with Detraction and Envie, and this is inevitably so since Artegall's
victory has created them. Some further virtue is necessary to meet the
evils bred by force, and this is the task performed by Courtesy.

Spenser conceives of Courtesy as springing from an inner vision of
love and beauty, embodied in the dance of the Graces which the poet,
Colin, can see clearly but which the earthly nature of Calidore prevents
him from understanding. Calidore is able to glimpse it, at his own
lower level, in his vision of pastoral beauty which he has to learn to
apply as a positive principle of life rather than as an escape from the
evils of a fallen world. The Graces traditionally symbolised generosity,
and courtesy is an essentially generous virtue. It woos rather than
forces, and its specific quality is not to crush but to rescue and lift up.
It rescues Serena from among the cannibals, and the child from the
bear; it restores Pastorella to her rightful heritage as daughter of a king.
In its power to raise up it is the most Christ-like of all the virtues,
and Calidore rescuing Pastorella from her dark and symbolic prison,
bursting open the doors 'with huge resistless might' and scattering

the brigands like flies, is a type of Christ harrowing hell and routing Satan. It is Una's virtue, the final virtue by which fallen man can become one with Christ through love. The Gospels of Book VI succeed the Law of Book V, and we have worked round to Book I again in a circle of which Christ is the beginning and the end.

For this reason, I feel that Book VI completes the education of the gentleman, and that the *Mutability cantos* are an epilogue rather than an unfinished fragment. Mutability, daughter of the rebellious Titans and symbol of all the change, decay and rebellious pride of the world, challenges Jove and claims that she is the mistress of the whole creation. She is the voice of fallen man claiming that all is irrevocably fallen, and she speaks for all that is multitudinous and chaotic within the whole poem. Yet the very presentation of her claim carries with it its own refutation. The witnesses whom she summons to testify to her supremacy are infinite in number; yet they file past great Nature's throne in an orderly procession, marshalled by Order himself—the seasons, the hours, the planets in their motions, all witnessing to an unchanging and regular order of death and rebirth which underlies the seeming anarchy of their being. This is why Nature can look up 'with chearefull view' and assert that Mutability is the servant not the master: she is only the means by which all things:

> ... their being doe dilate,
> And turning to themselves at lengthe againe,
> Doe worke their owne perfection so by fate:
> (VII, VII, 58)

As Mutability symbolises both sin and death in her rebellious role, so Nature's pronouncement applies equally to both aspects of the fall. Through death the flowers of the world wither, but returning to the Garden of Adonis, can through love be reborn again and so make possible the infinite variety of the creation. Through sin and temptation, the heroes discover the powers they were born with, as Red Cross learns the true value of his Christian armour only by taking it off. Sin, time, the fallen world of mortality are, in the end, God's means of educating mankind and repairing the ruins of the Fall; it is Cupid, the God of love himself, who sets Mirabella her penance of tears in Book VI, and Mutability herself is beautiful.

Spenser's poem, therefore, is a tremendous affirmation of the goodness of all things. There is no facile optimism in the poem: Spenser has more than any other poet a sense of the ubiquity of sin, its subtlety in penetrating the most hallowed impulses and perverting them to its own purposes. Yet this vision of evil is balanced and outweighed by a certainty that love is the ultimate law of nature and that all things fulfil God's benign purposes. The introduction of Arthur into each book in the double role of Christ the Redeemer and the human hero in a state of achieved virtue reminds us throughout of what God has done for man and what man may thereby do for himself to make love and virtue prevail. Like Milton, Spenser is concerned to justify God's ways to man, but his answer stems from a stronger, more buoyant faith than that of his successor. The battle will never be over; there can be no respite until all things are 'firmly stayd/Upon the pillours of Eternity'. The unfinished state of the poem with its loose ends, its central quest uncompleted, is symbolic of the nature of the world itself. Arthur will not achieve his Gloriana and the knights return to their feast at the Court of Maidenhead, their quests finally completed, until the day of Judgment when the earth is made anew. In the meantime, Spenser enjoys the quest and celebrates its heroes, conscious that in doing so he is fulfilling the truly heroic role of the poet.

8

CONCLUSION: THE END OF THE CENTURY

The Faerie Queene is the epitome of the whole Elizabethan age, not least in that it ends with the *Mutability Cantos*. The last years of the sixteenth century were heavy with the expectation of change, and Mutability could have included in the procession of her witnesses most of the traditional 'kinds' of poetry, as time-honoured conventions began to be overthrown. One reason for the changes in literary sensibility lay, perhaps, in the larger number of outlets open to the poet, so that what in earlier generations had found expression as simple poetry was now more likely to be channelled off into courses offering greater profit. In this way the 'Complaint' as used in the *Mirror for Magistrates* was superseded by the history play, and Spenser's allegorical pageantry found increasing expression through the Court Masque. One has only to read Ben Jonson's *Hymenaei* or his *Masque of Blackness* to see how the descent of Cambina in her chariot or the wedding of Thames and Medway have been transmuted into dramatic form. The fact of the drama itself encouraged a greater immediacy of treatment, the influence of which can be felt on non-dramatic forms of literature such as the lyrics of Donne, for example.

A more important factor in the production of change was the mounting political and religious pressures of the period which demanded a directer form of literary treatment than had been necessary before. For Sidney's generation, the essence of poetry was an exuberant fiction emancipated from the truths of a foolish world and expressing its own deeper truths through images and settings far removed from everyday life. This is true of *The Faerie Queene* or the *Arcadia*, or *Tamburlaine* or the romances of Greene and Peele. By the end of the

century, however, the veils of fiction were beginning to get in the way
of those who wished to see the truth clearly. The golden age was
giving way to one of baser metal, as the glamour of the Armada years
wore off, and the mounting religious pressures from Calvinism and
Counter-Reformation coincided with increased political tension over
Monopolies. Above all, the Queen herself was an old woman without
an heir. In the *Mutability Cantos*, Mutability invades the sphere of
Cynthia herself, where she sits attended, symbolically, by the evening
star, and is only deterred from pulling her from her throne by the
messenger of Jove. At such a time, when the Queen's mortality could
be so sadly and openly acknowledged, the myth and ritual surrounding
the court became more difficult to sustain and, on a wider level, the
traditional literary fictions no longer satisfied.

The result of these various factors was a mounting chorus of protest
against some of the most characteristically Elizabethan forms of poetry,
and a dissatisfaction with verse which 'doth but champ that which
another chewd'. The first book of Hall's *Virgidemiarum* (1597), for
example, is a systematic attack on favourite Elizabethan 'kinds': on
erotic Ovidean tales based on the *Metamorphoses*; on 'worme eate
stories of olde times', always excepting those of 'renowned Spenser';
on Complaints in the manner of the *Mirror for Magistrates*, and on
sonnets to the poet's 'durtie ill fac'd bride'. It is interesting to note that
Marston, in his *Certaine Satyres* a little later, attacked Hall's criticisms
on the grounds that they denied to poetry its essential quality of
fiction:

> For tell me *Crittick*, is not *Fiction*
> The soule of Poesies invention?
> Is't not the forme? the spirit? and the essence?
> (*Certaine Satyres*, IV, 87–)

Yet in 1598 Marston too joined in the attack with his *Scourge of Villanie*:

> Here's one must invoke some lose-legg'd dame,
> Some brothell drab, to helpe him stanzaes frame, ...
> Another yet dares tremblingly come out,
> But first he must invoke good *Colyn Clout* ...
> (*Satyre*, VI, 33–8)

The modes of statement once acceptable as poetic conventions are now
seen as fictions distorting reality.

This change of sensibility was not a simple turning to realism, nor
was it anti-humanist; it expressed itself through a different selection of

humanist models, those which allowed a closer approximation to real life as a part of their essential decorum. Ben Jonson called his comedies 'poems' because they were fictions, yet he turned away from the romantic fiction of contemporary comedy to the 'deeds and language such as men do use' of his Everyman plays, while at the same time establishing himself as the most thorough-going exponent of humanist comic theory. A further example of the same process can be seen in the great outburst of satire which culminated in the burning of satirical books at the order of the Archbishop of Canterbury in 1599. There had been humanist satire earlier, but since the time of Wyatt it had expressed itself mainly through the pastoral convention, as in the case of the *Shepheardes Calender*. The new satires of Hall, Marston and Donne, however, turned back to the formal satire of Juvenal, Persius and Horace, or the epigrams of Martial, with their direct realistic picture of recognisable social types. Spenser's allegorical shepherds are replaced by Donne's witty and scathing portraits of the ceremonial courtier or Hall's complete gallery of contemporary rogues and fools: the upstart gentleman buying himself a noble pedigree and adopting as his ancestors any old 'rain-beat' statues he can find in the local churchyard; the young Inns-of-Court lawyer going home to pontificate over his father's tenants; the rack-renting landlord battening off his abbeylands, without which, 'Who now's a monke, had been a Mendicant', the monopolist and all the rest who come under the lash of Jonson's plays or Dekker's pamphlets. Once more the movement is from the more to the less fictional model, although the decorum of humanist satire is strictly adhered to. The metres are deliberately rough, the imagery calculated to debase, and the style racy or, in Marston's case, based on a curious mixture of colloquial and latinate designed to take the place of the combination of dialect and medievalism which Spenser had used for his shepherds.

We can see the same pressures to break the moulds of fiction at work in a poem which is itself one of the most elaborate pieces of fiction in the period, namely, *Hero and Leander*. The first two sestiads were written by Marlowe probably a short time before his death in 1593, the remainder by Chapman round about 1598, and the two parts form a record of transition which is not explicable merely in terms of the difference between the two authors. Chapman was not essentially a more serious writer than Marlowe, and the contrast must in part be attributed to the changing sensibility of the times. The story of Hero and Leander is one of tragic and immoral love and both writers recognise this fact. Marlowe implicitly acknowledges the simple carnality of the love affair when he makes Hero meet Leander as she is sacrificing

in Venus' temple, the walls of which are covered with the same images
as those which decorate the tapestries in Malecasta's castle:

> There might you see the gods in sundrie shapes,
> Committing headdie ryots, incest, rapes; . . .
> Jove slylie stealing from his sisters bed,
> To dallie with Idalian Ganimed,
> And for his love Europa, bellowing loud,
> And tumbling with the Rainbow in a cloud: . . .
>
> (I, 143–)

But Marlowe avoids all the serious implications of the story and keeps
the whole thing at the level of Ovidean flippancy, just as Chaucer
glosses over the tragic nature of his *Knight's Tale* by the swift and
brilliant manner of his treatment. Marlowe turns his story into a piece
of mythology into which the human values are never allowed to
intrude, and produces what could almost be another episode of the
Metamorphoses. If he had finished it, he must have done so in a vein of
mythology: Leander would have been wooed by the sea nymphs or by
Neptune himself to live for ever in the depths of the sea, and no hearts
would have been allowed to break. For Marlowe, the delight in myth-
making and in the imaginative pleasures of fiction are enough.

Chapman, in contrast, is at pains to apply his story to life and to
bring out the human tragedy which Marlowe had so brilliantly
suppressed. He warns us of his intention at the beginning of the
third sestiad:

> New light gives new directions, Fortunes new
> To fashion our indevours that ensue,
> More harsh (at least more hard) more grave and hie
> Our subject runs, and our sterne Muse must flie . . .
>
> (III, 1–)

and in talking of Leander's 'Hero-handled bodie' he at once uses a
phrase which, for its immediacy, could have had no place in Marlowe's
version. Hero is turned into a real woman tormented by her regrets
and passions:

> Sweet Hero left upon her bed alone,
> Her maidenhead, her vowes, Leander gone,
> And nothing with her but a violent crew
> Of new come thoughts that yet she never knew,
> Even to her selfe a stranger; . . .
>
> (III, 199–)

Leander, complacent in his conquest and about to set out on his last
fatal swim, is described in terms which could have come straight out of
a Donne satire on courtiers:

> As short was he of that himselfe he prisde,
> As is an emptie Gallant full of forme,
> That thinks each looke an act, each drop a storme,
> That fals from his brave breathings; most brought up
> In our Metropolis, and hath his cup
> Brought after him to feasts; and much Palme beares,
> For his rare judgement in th'attire he weares,
> Hath seene the hot Low Countries, not their heat, ...
>
> (VI, 108-)

Chapman is no puritan; his criticism of the lovers springs from his
sense of human dignity: Leander has dispended the sanctified gift of
love 'like a greedie vulgar Prodigall' instead of with the ceremony
proper to a human being—'To loves sweet life this is the courtly carv-
ing' (III, 58). Chapman is anticipating Lear's defence of the retinue,
ceremonies and clothes which alone distinguish the man from the
'bare forked animal'. He brings Marlowe's pair of mythological lovers
to the bar of human civilisation and turns simple fiction into tragedy.

   In these developments of the 1590's Donne plays an important but
ambiguous role. He has often been held up as the great revolutionary
heading the reaction against the artificialities and rituals of Petrarchism
and bringing love poetry back to nature and sexual realism. He is
certainly an anti-Petrarchan, as are Marlowe, Marston and the other
writers of Ovidean erotic poetry in the period, and his *Elegies* differ
from these not so much in the attitude to love they reveal as in the
choice of literary model: whereas the others draw on Ovid's *Metamorphoses*, Donne bases his *Elegies* on the more realistic *Amores*. Once
more it is a case of turning from a less to a more realistic literary 'kind'.
In his 'Elegie upon the death of the Deane of Pauls, Dr John Donne',
Carew praises him not for his realism but for throwing away the lazy
seeds of 'servile' imitation, and fears that with the poet's death, all the
old gods and goddesses of the *Metamorphoses* will come flocking back
into love poetry once more:

> They will repeale the goodly exil'd traine
> Of gods and goddesses, which in thy just raigne
> Were banish'd nobler Poems, now, with these
> The silenc'd tales o'th' Metamorphoses
> Shall stuffe their lines, and swell the windy Page,

Till Verse refin'd by thee, in this last Age,
Turne ballad rime, ... (63-69)

Donne's Elegies, for all their apparent realism, are among the most literary and humanist poems he ever wrote.

His greatest innovation is not here but in the *Songs and Sonets* which, in many ways, are still very much in the tradition of the Elizabethan love sonnet. Poems such as 'Communitie' or 'The Indifferent', although voicing un-Petrarchan attitudes towards love, are doing so in terms of the flippant rhetoric in which the conventional sonnet specialised. 'The Dissolution', for example, works out a syllogism with precisely the kind of mock solemnity to be found in the sonnets of Sidney or Barnabe Barnes:

> Shee'is dead; And all which die
> To their first Elements resolve;
> And wee were mutuall Elements to us,
> And made of one another.
> My body then doth hers involve, ...

It follows therefore that her death replenishes in him the four elements:

> My fire of Passion, sighes of ayre,
> Water of teares, and earthly sad despaire,
> Which my materialls bee, ...

and he might as a result of her death be expected to live all the longer. In fact, however, 'my fire doth with my fuell grow', and he will burn up all the more quickly on account of the extra material, so that his soul may even hope to overtake that of his mistress as one bullet does another, 'the pouder being more'. This is admirable sonnet-type fooling, and Donne's shorter love poems abound in this sort of thing. 'The Legacie', to take another example, parodies the common sonnet theme of lovers changing hearts, the neatest expression of which is Sidney's 'My true love hath my heart, and I have his.' When Donne's lover searches his breast to find a heart to give in exchange, he can only find:

> ... something like a heart,
> But colours it, and corners had, ...
> It was intire to none, and few had part.

The exchange has, in fact, already taken place and what the lover finds is that misshapen and divided organ which is all that his mistress has to offer. Even a serious and passionate love poem such as 'A Valediction:

of weeping' is based on a *tour de force* of extended metaphor such as we commonly find in the sonnet. On the eve of a long sea voyage, the lover lies weeping in his mistress' arms: his tears, reflecting the image of his mistress whose face is so near to his own, are turned to little worlds, just as a workman turns a blank globe into a world by stamping on it the shapes of Europe, Africa and Asia. When she too weeps, therefore, and her tears flow over his, they drown 'This world, by waters sent from thee, my heaven dissolved so'. He can thus logically compare his mistress to the moon as it governs the tides, and conclude with a more-than-sonnet hyperbole in which the tears and the great seas themselves can be brought together within a single image:

> O more than Moone,
> Draw not up seas to drowne me in thy spheare,
> Weepe me not dead, in thine armes, but forbeare
> To teach the sea, what it may doe too soone;

This is sonnet rhetoric, and yet the result is like nothing which has gone before. Donne uses all the sonnet conceits, but with a difference; his method is not to reject them but to put new blood into their face. Shakespeare's way is to disown them in the interests of truth and realism:

> My mistress' eyes are nothing like the sun;
> Coral is far more red than her lips' red:
> If snow be white, why then her breasts are dun;
> If hairs be wires, black wires grow on her head . . .
>   (Sonnet CXXX)

Donne's is to restate them with such conviction that they become true. He calls the bluff of those who mock at sonnet hyperbole, by insisting that to the lover who loves strongly enough, his mistress' eyes really *are* like the sun. It is Longinus' point, that a hyperbole ceases to seem hyperbolic if it has enough passion to carry it. A lover who really loves is not exaggerating when he says:

> She 'is all States, and all Princes, I,
>   Nothing else is.
> Princes doe but play us; compar'd to this,
> All honor's mimique; All wealth alchimie.
>   (The Sunne Rising)

In 'The Canonization', he plays with the stock similes which have been

applied to lovers: 'Call us what you will,' he says, 'we are made such
by love;'

> Call her one, mee another flye,
> We'are Tapers too, and at our owne cost die,
> And wee in us finde the'Eagle and the Dove.
> The Phoenix ridle hath more wit
> By us, we two being one, are it.

For the conventional sonnet lover these are just conceited hyperboles,
but for himself they are no more than the truth, so that even the sonnet
may be made to house a real love again:

> We'll build in sonnets pretty roomes;
> As well a well wrought urne becomes
> The greatest ashes, as halfe-acre tombes, . . .

The sovereign-mistress conceit with all the accompanying play of
images about kings and subjects is a common and a commonplace
sonnet feature, whether in Shakespeare's 'Being your slave . . .' (LVII)
or Sidney's 'Like some weak lords . . .' (29). Donne can use it with
a totally new conviction in 'The Anniversarie':

> Here upon earth, we'are Kings, and none but wee
> Can be such Kings, nor of such subjects bee;
> Who is so safe as wee? where none can doe
> Treason to us, except one of us two.

He can only do so because the experience he is describing has enough
weight to carry the comparison and redeem it from frivolity:

> Only our love hath no decay;
> This, no tomorrow hath, nor yesterday,
> Running it never runs from us away . . .

Donne is therefore bringing the love song back to nature as Sidney
had set out to do a generation earlier, but he takes the process a stage
further than Sidney whose love lyrics, however much of his own actual
experience they contain, yet express it through the dramatic mask of
Astrophil. Donne dispenses with the mask altogether, or creates a
lover in his poems who is indistinguishable from himself. There is
little room for the 'I' in a pastoral or a stock Petrarchan sonnet:
Donne brings it back again to a place it had not held since the time of
Wyatt—'I hate extremes', 'I hate dead names', 'For God's sake hold

your tongue and let me love'. Moreover he replaces the stock Petrarchan situations by new ones carrying a greater sense of authenticity—the lover in bed with his mistress, being wakened by the morning sun, or so close that he can see his image reflected in her eyes. It is from this that Donne's lyrics gain their unique quality of immediacy and revitalise the witty conceit so that it can become a vehicle for passion.

Donne's real novelty can perhaps be seen better if we compare him with Spenser, who treats love as seriously as Donne himself, than if we compare him with the relatively flippant sonneteers. The two poets are often dealing with the same range of experience: Spenser's Garden of Adonis has, at its heart, a psychological experience which is shared by many of Donne's lyrics. Writing of the Mons Veneris which is Venus' Bower in the Garden, Spenser describes the pleasure he has had there:

> But well I wote by triall, that this same
>   All other pleasaunt places doth excell, ...
>   (III, VI, 29)

and this sexual experience is for him an escape from time, a moment of timelessness in which past and future are lost in the present but which, in its consequences, projects the new life out into the world of time again:

> For here all plentie, and all pleasure flowes,
> And sweet love gentle fits emongst them throwes,
> Without fell rancor or fond gealosie;
> Franckly each paramour his leman knowes,
> Each bird his mate; ne any does envie
> Their goodly meriment, and gay felicity.
>
> There is continuall spring, and harvest there
> Continuall, both meeting at one time;
> For both the boughes doe laughing blossome beare,
> And with fresh colours decke the wanton Prime,
> And eke attonce the heavy trees they clyme,
> Which seeme to labour under their fruits lode: ...
>   (III, VI, 41-2)

There is no sense of time, no distinction of season at this moment, though the imagery of harvest, of course, leads back into the world of time and of the future. Spenser is recreating in his own terms the medieval garden of love, an ordered and idyllic plot where it is always spring and where age and mutability are excluded. This is one of the

basic experiences of love, and the one about which Donne perhaps felt
most deeply; but he dispenses with myth and describes it in direct
subjective terms. He is continually contrasting the world above and
beyond time which lovers create between them with the everyday
world of time and change outside. In 'The Sunne Rising' he mocks
the busy morning sun which would drag him out into the business of
the day, and prefers the world of mutual completeness which he and
his mistress share:

> Love, all alike, no season knowes, nor clyme,
> Nor houres, dayes, moneths, which are the rags of time.'

In 'The Good-morrow', the lovers create a world of their own which
escapes all the penalties of the Fall: it is a world symbolised by the two
hemispheres of their own eyes reflecting each other's images:

> My face in thine eye, thine in mine appeares,
> And true plain hearts doe in the faces rest,
> Where can we finde two better hemispheares
> Without sharpe North, without declining West?

For Donne the moment of the rose is a moment where time is withdrawn, and he never tires of playing with the paradox of double time,
or of an eternity created within time itself. He is as conscious of the
ruins of time as Spenser is, and the thought of death is continually with
him in his treatment of love. The little universe which the lover
creates out of his tears in *A Valediction: of weeping* is of the same salt
water as the ocean which may drown him, and the idea of death steals
even into so triumphant a love poem as 'The Anniversarie':

> Two graves must hide thine and my coarse,
> If one might, death were no divorce: . . .

'The Will', 'The Funerall', 'The Blossome' or 'The Relique' indicate
by their titles alone Donne's awareness of the transitoriness even of
love, and he has none of the real, if sometimes melancholy, comfort
which Spenser gains from the thought of the succeeding generations
to which that love will give being. Love, for Donne, stands in its own
right as a human relationship and needs no justification in terms of
religion or society: the very absence of such justifications creates the
especial intensity of the experience itself which makes love, for Donne
of the *Songs and Sonets*, the only barrier against chaos. For this reason
Donne's love lyrics have none of the generalised quality which is to

be found in Spenser's equally passionate and personal *Epithalamion*.
Spenser is celebrating the goodness of all love, not merely his own, and
so inevitably turns to the traditional form of marriage song for his
medium: for Donne, the value of love lies in the uniqueness of every
experience which only a unique form of expression is able to convey
in each case.

The same is true of Donne's religious poetry which often begins in
the same material as Spenser's but effects the metamorphosis into the
personal vein. Donne's battle with despair:

> Despaire behind, and death before doth cast
> Such terrour, and my feeble flesh doth waste
> By sinne and it, which it towards hell doth weigh:
> Onely thou art above, and when towards thee
> By thy leave I can looke, I rise againe . . .
>   (Holy Sonnets, I)

is a personal statement of Red Cross' passage through the cave of
Despair, and is as precise in its theology: 'By thy leave', for example,
echoes Spenser's assertion that 'all the good is Gods, both power and
eke will' (I, X, 1). It can be argued that the lyrical and allegorical
forms which the poets use result from an entire difference of intention;
but this, although obviously true, does not explain why the two poets
put similar materials to such different uses. It is obvious, of course, that
the two poets are not merely different in sensibility but start from
different centres of gravity and belong to virtually different civilisations.
The Tree of Knowledge plays a fair part in *The Faerie Queene*, but we
cannot conceive of Spenser using it as Donne does when he writes in
the seventh *Elegie*:

> I planted knowledge and lifes tree in thee,
> Which Oh, shall strangers taste?

So too when Donne attempts something comparable to Spenserean
allegory, it turns out very different from *The Faerie Queene*. The theme
of Donne's third satire, for instance, the search for the true religion, is
one relatively close to Spenser in content and in method:

> . . . On a huge hill,
> Cragged, and steep, Truth stands, and hee that will
> Reach her, about must, and about must goe;

and Spenser would certainly have approved of Donne's advice to the
seeker:

> Be busie to seeke her, beleeve mee this, . . .
> To stand inquiring right, is not to stray;
> To sleepe, or runne wrong is.

Yet the unlovely collection of girls who present themselves each as the bride of Christ are very different and far more alive than Spenser's more objective definitions by means of Una or Duessa:

> . . . her onely, who at Geneva is call'd
> Religion, plaine, simple, sullen, yong,
> Contemptuous, yet unhansome: . . .
>   (*Satyre*, III)

In the same way, Donne makes of his bride of Christ in Holy Sonnet XVIII something more like a real mistress than an allegory of the various churches:

> Show me deare Christ, thy spouse, so bright and clear.
> What! is it She, which on the other shore
> Goes richly painted? or which rob'd and tore
> Laments and mournes in Germany and here?
> Sleepes she a thousand, then peepes up one yeare? . . .

The realism of the metaphor overpowers the allegoric content, as is never the case with Spenser, so that by the end of the poem, Donne is able to extend his metaphor to a point at which the image, though logically relevant, carries overtones which clash violently with the literal meaning. It is good for the church to be embraced by as many men as possible, but hardly so for the bride under whose image the church is prefigured:

> Betray kind husband thy spouse to our sights,
> And let myne amorous soule court thy mild Dove,
> Who is most trew, and pleasing to thee, then
> When she'is embrac'd and open to most men.
>   (Holy Sonnet XVIII)

Donne has first dramatised his allegorical figure and then exploited the clash between image and meaning with a flippancy which is decorous in the sonnet form as it would not have been in the satire.

Donne is here seeking a very calculated effect which marks the same radical development as that apparent in the rest of his poetry. He is using allegory less as a mode of objective definition than as a means of self-expression. What comes from this sonnet is an impression of Donne's own scepticism, a sense that perhaps there is no true church at all, though we are compelled to go on 'like adventuring knights' in search of one. The poem once more brings us back to the individual experience of the individual writer and makes us aware of Donne himself within his poems. When we read Sidney or Spenser we are primarily aware that we are reading Renaissance poetry: the individual voice is there, but it is absorbed and transmuted by the literary medium, so that we are more conscious of differences in the treatment of a genre than of the different personalities of the writers. This is not true of Donne: he exhibits his individual mind as the Jacobean dramatists explore the solitary consciousness of a Hamlet or a Bosola. In his later *Anniversaries* he was to regret that each man now 'alone thinkes that he hath got/To be a Phoenix', yet in these sixteenth-century Songs and Sonets it is above all the Phoenix quality he displays. His appeal to us today comes largely from this modern note, yet it should not be forgotten that he, too, was a humanist, and that much of his strength derives from the security of his traditional framework. It is often only by restriction that intensity can be generated; and the pressure in Donne's verse comes not only from the ferment within but from the firm control of those established patterns which, as we have seen, played such a significant part in sixteenth-century poetry.

BIBLIOGRAPHY

The following selection of books will be found useful as a basis for further study.

GENERAL

BRADBROOK, M. C., *Shakespeare and Elizabethan Poetry* (London, 1951)

CRAIG, HARDIN, *The Enchanted Glass* (Oxford, 1950)

HEBEL & HUDSON (ed.), *Poetry of the English Renaissance* (New York, 1957)

LEWIS, C. S., *English Literature in the Sixteenth Century* (Oxford, 1954)

DE SOLA PINTO, V., *The English Renaissance.* Introductions to English literature. Vol. II (London, 1951)

Stratford upon Avon Studies, No. 2, *Elizabethan Poetry* (London, 1960)

TAYLER, E. W., *Nature and Art in Renaissance literature* (New York, 1964)

TUVE, ROSEMOND, *Elizabethan and Metaphysical Imagery* (Chicago, 1963)

CHAPTER I

BURCKHARDT, JACOB, *The Civilization of the Renaissance in Italy*

BUSH, DOUGLAS, *Mythology and the Renaissance Tradition in English Poetry* (New York, 1963, revised edition)

CASPARI, FRITZ, *Humanism and the social order in Tudor England* (University of Chicago, 1954)

CASSIRER, KRISTELLER and RANDALL (ed.), *The Renaissance Philosophy of Man* (Chicago, 1963)

HOOPES, ROBERT, *Right Reason in the English Renaissance* (Cambridge, Mass., 1962)

HUNTER, G. K., *John Lyly* (London, 1962)

KRISTELLER, PAUL O., *Renaissance thought: The Classic, Scholastic and Humanist strains* (New York, 1961)
Renaissance thought, II. *Papers on Humanism and the arts* (New York, 1965)

LEWIS, C. S., *English Literature in the Sixteenth Century* (Oxford, 1954)
The Allegory of Love (Oxford)

MAJOR, JOHN M., *Sir Thomas Elyot and Renaissance Humanism* (University of Nebraska, 1964)

MASON, H. A., *Humanism and Poetry in the early Tudor period* (London, 1959)

NUGENT, E. M. (ed.), *The Thought and Culture of the English Renaissance* (Cambridge, 1956)

ROSS, J. B., and MCLAUGHLIN, M. M. (ed.), *The Portable Renaissance Reader* (New York)

WEISS, ROBERTO, *The Spread of Italian Humanism* (London, 1964)

CHAPTER 2

ATKINS, J. W. H., *English Literary Criticism: The medieval phase* (Cambridge, 1943)
English Literary Criticism—the Renascence (London, 1947)

SMITH, G. GREGORY, *Elizabethan Critical Essays*. 2 Vols. (Oxford, 1964)

TUVE, ROSEMOND, *Elizabethan and Metaphysical imagery* (Chicago, 1963)

YATES, FRANCIS, *The French Academies of the Sixteenth Century* (Warburg Society, London, 1947)

CHAPTER 3

EDWARDS, H. L. R., *Skelton* (London, 1949)

FISH, STANLEY, E., *John Skelton's Poetry* (New Haven, 1965)

GORDON, I. A., *John Skelton* (Oxford, 1938)

NELSON, W., *John Skelton, Laureate* (New York, 1939)

CHAPTER 4

CASADY, E., *Henry Howard, Earl of Surrey* (New York, 1938)

FOXWELL, A. K., *A study of Wyatt's poems* (London, 1911)
The Poems of Sir Thomas Wyatt. Vol. II (London, 1913)

FRYE, NORTHROP, *Anatomy of Criticism* (Princeton, 1957)

LEVER, J. W., *The Elizabethan Love sonnet* (London, 1956)

MASON, H. A., *Humanism and Poetry in the early Tudor period* (London, 1959)

MUIR, KENNETH, *Life and letters of Sir Thomas Wyatt* (Liverpool University, 1963)

PETRARCH, *Sonnets and Songs*. Trans. Anna Maria Armi (New York, 1946)

STEVENS, JOHN, *Music and Poetry in the early Tudor period* (London, 1961)

THOMSON, PATRICIA, *Sir Thomas Wyatt and his Background* (London, 1964)

CHAPTER 5

DONNO, ELIZABETH S., *Elizabethan Minor Epics* (New York, 1963)
ING, CATHERINE, *Elizabethan Lyrics* (London, 1951)
JOHN, L. C., *The Elizabethan Sonnet Sequences* (New York, 1964)
LEE, SIR SIDNEY, *The French Renaissance in England* (Oxford, 1910)
LEVER, J. W., *The Elizabethan Love Sonnet* (London, 1956)
McLANE, PAUL, E., *Spenser's Shepheardes Calender* (Notre Dame, 1961)
PATTISON, B., *Music and Poetry of the English Renaissance* (1948)
RENWICK, W. L., *Edmund Spenser: an essay on renaissance poetry* (London, 1925)
SIDNEY, SIR PHILIP, *The Poems* ed. W. A. Ringler (Oxford, 1962)
SMITH, HALLETT, *Elizabethan Poetry* (Cambridge, Mass., 1952)

CHAPTER 6

CAMPBELL, L. B., *Shakespeare's Histories, Mirrors of Elizabethan Policy* (1947)
SWART, S. J., *Thomas Sackville. A study in Sixteenth Century Poetry* (Groningen Studies in English)
TILLYARD, E. M. W., *The English Epic and its background* (London, 1954)

CHAPTER 7

BENNETT, JOSEPHINE WATERS, *The Evolution of The Faerie Queene* (Chicago, 1942)
BERGER, HARRY, *The Allegorical Temper* (New Haven, 1957)
FOWLER, ALISTAIR, *Spenser and the Numbers of Time* (London, 1964)
GREENLAW, EDWIN, *Studies in Spenser's Allegory* (Johns Hopkins University, 1934)
HAMILTON, A. C., *The structure of Allegory in The Faerie Queene* (Oxford, 1961)
HOUGH, GRAHAM, *A Preface to The Faerie Queene* (London, 1962)
LEWIS, C. S., *The Allegory of Love* (New York)
MILLICAN, C. B., *Spenser and the Table Round* (Cambridge, Mass., 1932)
MUELLER, W. R., and ALLEN, D. C. (ed.), 'That Soveraine Light' (Johns Hopkins University, 1952)
NELSON, WILLIAM, *The Poetry of Edmund Spenser* (New York, 1963)
NELSON WILLIAM (ed.), *Form and Convention in the poetry of Edmund Spenser* (New York, 1961)
RATHBONE, ISABEL E., *The Meaning of Spenser's Fairyland* (New York, 1937)
SEZNEC, JEAN, *The Survival of the Pagan Gods* (New York)
The Spenser Variorum (Johns Hopkins University)
TILLYARD, E. M. W., *The English Epic and its Background* (London, 1954)
WHITAKER, V. K., *The Religious Basis of Spenser's Thought* (Stanford, 1950)
WIND, EDGAR, *Pagan Mysteries in the Renaissance* (New Haven, 1958)

CHAPTER 8

ALVAREZ, A., *The School of Donne* (London, 1961)

BUSH, D., *English Literature in the Earlier Seventeenth Century* (Oxford, 1945)

ELIOT, T. S., *Selected Essays* (London, 1932)

GARDNER, H. (ed.), *John Donne. The Elegies and Songs and Sonnets* (Oxford, 1965)

KERMODE, F. (ed.), *Discussions of John Donne* (Boston, 1962)

LEISHMANN, J., *The Monarch of Wit* (London, 1951)

MAHOOD, M., *Poetry and Humanism* (London, 1950)

STEIN, A., *John Donne's Lyrics. The Eloquence of action* (University of Minnesota, 1962)

TUVE, ROSEMOND, *Elizabethan and Metaphysical imagery* (Chicago)

EDITIONS QUOTED

Arber, E., *An English Garner* (8 vols). (For sonnet sequences)

Ascham, Roger, *The Scholemaster*, ed. Mayor (London, 1934)

Ault, N., *Elizabethan Lyrics* (New York, 1960)

Barclay, Alexander, *Eclogues*, ed. Cawood (E.E.T.S. Original Series, 175, 1961)

Barnes, Barnabe, *Parthenophil and Parthenophe*, Arber's *English Garner*, vol. v.

Barnfield, Richard, *Poems* (Fortune Press, 1936)

Breton, Nicholas, *Works*, ed. Grosart (1879)

Brown, Carlton, *Religious Lyrics of the Fifteenth Century* (Oxford, 1939)

Campion, Thomas, *Works*, ed. Perceval Vivian (Oxford, 1909)

Castiglione, B., *The Book of the Courtier* (London)

Caxton, William, *Prologues and Epilogues*, ed. Crotch (E.E.T.S. Original series, 176, 1928)

Chapman, George, *Hero and Leander*, *Sestiads III–VI*. In *Elizabethan Minor Epics*, ed. Donno (New York, 1963)

Chappell, W., *The Ballad Literature and Popular Music of the Olden Times* (2 vols., 1859)

Chaucer, *Poems*, ed. F. N. Robinson (Oxford)

Constable, Henry, *Poems*, ed. Grundy (Liverpool University, 1960)

Daniel, Samuel, *Poems and a Defence of Ryme*, ed. A. C. Sprague (London, 1950)

The Civile Wars, Vol. II, complete Works of S. Daniel, ed. Grosart (1885).

Davison's Poetical Rhapsody, ed. A. H. Bullen (1890)

Deloney, Thomas, *Works*, ed. F. O. Mann (Oxford, 1912)

Donne, John, *Poems*, ed. Grierson, 2 vols (Oxford)

Drayton, Michael, *Works*, ed. J. William Hebel, K. Tillotson and B. H. Newdigate, 5 vols (Oxford, 1931)

Du Bellay, Joachim, *The Defense and Illustration of the French Language*, in *The Great Critics*, ed. Smith and Parks (New York)

Dunbar, William, *Poems*, ed. W. Mackay Mackenzie (London, 1932)

Elyot, Sir Thomas, *The Book named the Governor* (London)

Englands Helicon, ed. Hugh Macdonald (London, 1950)

Erasmus, D., *Colloquies*, trans. Bailey (London, 1877, 2 vols)

Erasmus, D., *Concerning Freedom of the Will*, selections in *The Portable Renaissance Reader*, ed. Ross and McLaughlin (New York)

Fellowes, E. H., *English Madrigal Verse* (Oxford, 1950)

Ficino, Marsilio, *Commentary on Plato's Symposium*, trans. Sears Reynolds Jayne (University of Missouri studies XIX, 1, 1944)

Fletcher, Giles, the Elder, *English Works*, ed. Berry (University of Wisconsin, 1964)

Gascoigne, G., *Complete Works*, ed. J. W. Cunliffe (Cambridge, 1907)

The Gorgeous Gallery of Gallant Inventions, ed. T. Proctor (1578) In *Heliconia*, Vol. I

Greene, R., *Plays and Poems*, ed. Churton Collins (Oxford, 1905)

Hall, Joseph, *Poems*, ed. A. Davenport (University of Liverpool, 1949)

A Handfull of Pleasant Delites, ed. Clement Robinson. In *Heliconia*, Vol. II.

Hawes, Stephen, *The Pastime of Pleasures*, ed. W. E. Mead (Early English Text Society. Original series, 173, 1928)

Hebel and Hudson, *Poetry of the English Renaissance* (New York, 1957)

Heliconia, ed. T. Park (1815). (For poetical miscellanies)

Jonson, Ben, *Collected Poems*, Vol. VIII. Complete Works, ed. Herford and Simpson (Oxford, 1947)

Lee, Sir Sidney, *Elizabethan Sonnets* (London, 1904)

Leone Ebreo, *The Philosophy of Love*, trans. F. Friedeberg-Seeley and Jean H. Barnes (London, 1937)

Lodge, T., *Collected Works*, ed. E. Gosse (Hunterian Club, Glasgow, 1883)

Luther, Martin, *The Bondage of the Will*. Selections in the *Portable Renaissance Reader*, ed. Ross and McLaughlin (New York)

Lyly, J., *Complete Works*, ed. R. W. Bond (Oxford, 1902)

Mantuan, *The Eclogues of Baptista Mantuanus*, ed. Mustard (Johns Hopkins University, 1911)

Marlowe, *Complete Works*, ed. C. F. Tucker Brooke (Oxford, 1910)

Marston, J., *Poems*, ed. Davenport (Liverpool, 1961)

Meres, Francis, *Palladis Tamia* (Gregory Smith, Elizabethan critical essays Vol. II)

The *Mirror for Magistrates*, ed. Lily B. Campbell (Cambridge, 1938)

More, St Thomas, *Utopia and A Dialogue of Comfort* (London)

Nugent, E. M., ed., *The Thought and Culture of the English Renaissance* (Cambridge, 1956)

Parts added to the *Mirror* by John Higgins and Thomas Blennerhasset, ed. Lily B. Campbell (Cambridge, 1946)

The Paradise of Daynty Devises, ed. H. E. Rollins (Cambridge, Mass., 1927)

Percy, W., *Coelia*, Arber's *English Garner*, Vol. VI.

The Phoenix Nest, ed. H. E. Rollins (Cambridge, Mass., 1931)

Pico della Mirandola, Giovanni, *Oration of the Dignity of Man*. In *Portable Renaissance Reader*. Also in *The Renaissance Philosophy of Man*, ed. Cassirer, Kristeller and Randall (Chicago)

Portable Renaissance Reader, ed. James B. Ross and M. M. McLaughlin (New York, 1964)

Puttenham, George, *The Arte of Englishe Poesie*, ed. Gladys Doidge Willcock and Alice Walker (Cambridge, 1936)

Robbins, R. H., *Secular Lyrics of the XIV and XV Centuries* (Oxford, 1952)

Sidney, Sir Philip, *Poems*, ed. W. A. Ringler (Oxford, 1962). *An Apologie for Poetrie* (Gregory Smith, Elizabethan Critical Essays, vol. I)

Skelton, John, *Poems*, ed. Philip Henderson (London, 1948)

Smith, G. Gregory, *Elizabethan Critical Essays*, 2 vols. (Oxford, 1950)

Spenser, Edmund, *Works* (Oxford)

Surrey, Henry Howard, Earl of, *Poems*, ed. Emrys Jones (Oxford, 1964)

Tottel's Miscellany, ed. H. E. Rollins (Cambridge, Mass., 1929)

Tusser, Thomas, *500 points of good Husbandrie*, ed. W. Payne, English Dialect Society (London, 1878)

Watson, Thomas, *Poems*, Arber's *English Reprints* (1870)

Whetstone, George, *The Rocke of Regard*, ed. J. P. Collier (1870)

Wilson, Thomas, *Arte of Rhetorique*, ed. Mair, Tudor and Stuart Library (Oxford, 1909)

Wyatt, Sir Thomas, *Collected Poems*, ed. Kenneth Muir (London, 1949)

Wyatt, Sir Thomas, *Unpublished Poems*, ed. from Blage manuscript ed. Kenneth Muir (Liverpool, 1961)

Zepheria, 1594, Arber's *English Garner*, vol. V.

INDEX

Aeneid, 78, 136
Affectionate Shepherd, 94
Against a Comedy Coistrown, 49, 50
air, the, 112, 115, 116–19, 121
Alamanni, 75
Aldus, 10–11
Alençon, 91
allegory, 32, 42, 56, 88, 91, 135, 138, 139, 141, 143, 144, 145, 147, 148, 149, 157, 159, 167, 168
alliteration, 36, 39, 40, 81
Amores, 161
Amoretti, 95, 98, 108, 109, 111, 136
Anacreon, 86
Anacreontics, 85, 86, 90
animal spirits and the love conceit, 96–8
anti-Petrarchism, 85–6, 161
Apologie for Poetrie, 14, 22, 26, 85, 87–8, 100, 101–2, 135
Arcadia, 89, 135, 138, 157
archaism, 10, 25, 92
Areopagitica, 13
Areopagus group, 85
Ariosto, 25, 28, 61, 135, 136
Aristotelian Mean, 49
Aristotle, 11, 12, 26, 29, 50, 102, 136
Art of Rhetoric, 30
Arte of English Poesie, 26, 31, 61
Arthur, Prince, 43
Arthurian lineage of Tudors, 124, 137
As You Like It, 94
Ascham, R., 14, 19

Astrophil and Stella, 95, 98–9, 101–7
Attey, J., 120
Ault, N., 87, 115
Aureate Diction, 40, 44–5, 81
Autolycus, 112, 113

BACON, F., 128
Baif, de, 90
Baldwin, W., 125
ballad, 112–15
ballad metre, 72, 78, 112, 113
Barclay, A., 41–3, 48, 56, 64, 88
Barnfield, R., 28, 32, 94
Barnes, B., 33, 95, 96, 162
Battaile of Agincourt, 132, 133
Beggars' Opera, The, 115
Bellay, J. du, 25, 27, 28, 71, 85, 103
Blage Manuscript, 63
Blount, Sir C., 99
Boccaccio, 90, 139
Boleyn, Anne, 62–4, 67
Book of the Courtier, 13
Bouge of Court, 42, 45, 46, 48, 64
Boyle, Elizabeth, 108
Brant, S., 41–2
Breton, N., 94
Britannia, 132
broadsheets, 112–14
Browning, R., 12, 130
Bunyan, J., 21, 22, 143, 147
Byrd, W., 112, 115

CALVINISM, 13, 19, 20, 158
Cambridge, 25, 90
Camden, W., 123, 132
Campion, T., 93, 112, 116, 117, 128
Canterbury Tales, 23, 27, 41, 44, 59
Carew, T., 80, 161
Castiglione, B., 13, 14, 16–17, 66, 97–8, 150
Catherine of Aragon, 62
Caxton, W., 25
Certain Notes of Instruction, 41
Certaine Satyres, 158
Chapman, G., 79, 127, 159–61
Chaucer, G., 15, 26, 27, 28, 29, 39, 40, 41, 44, 49, 50, 52, 53, 59, 60, 71, 76, 83, 85, 91, 127, 160
Cheke, J., 25, 47
Chesterfield, Lord, 13
Church, Anglican, 20–1, 91
Church, Roman Catholic, 11, 19–22, 41, 49
Cicero, 10, 25, 30
Civile Wars between the two houses of Lancaster and Yorke, 128–9, 131
classical metres in English, 39, 85, 89–90, 119–20, 128
classical models, 26 ff., 86, 88, 128, 136, 161
Colet, J., 10
Colin Clout, 46, 55–8, 59
comedy, 100, 159
Commentary on Plato's Symposium, 14, 97
Complaint of Chastitie, 32
Complaint, The, 125, 129, 157, 158
Complaynt of Rosamond, 129
Compleat Angler, 94
conceit, 31, 77, 84, 95–7, 98, 162–5
Constable, H., 31, 35–6, 95, 96
Constantinople, 10
Cornysshe, 45
Counter-Reformation, 158
Courtly love, 17–18, 29, 45, 53, 65, 66–8, 102–3, 110, 153
Cromwell, T., 65, 80, 131
Crowly, 41

DANCE, rhythms and poetry, 114
Daniel, J., 112
Daniel, S., 23, 95, 123, 128–9, 131
Dante, 24, 61
Daphnaida, 136
Darrell, Elizabeth, 62
Davison's *Poetical Rhapsody*, 28

De Vulgari eloquentia, 24
Decorum, 35–7, 55, 92, 96, 121, 159
Defence of Rhyme, 128
Defense et Illustration de la langue Francoyse, La, 25, 71
Dekker, T., 112, 159
Delia, 95
Deloney, T., 112, 123
Description of England, 123
Desportes, 85
Devout Trental for old John Clarke, A, 44
dialect, 47, 92, 159
Dialogue of Comfort, 21
Diana, 31, 35, 95, 96
Disposition, 30, 31, 33
Divine Right, 126, 129
Dr Faustus, 21
Dolman, J., 126, 127
Donne, J., 18, 32, 33, 80, 98, 121, 127, 134, 157, 159, 161–9
Dowland, J., 93, 112, 115, 116, 118, 121
Drayton, M., 85, 86, 93, 94, 95, 97, 112, 123, 129–34
Dryden, J., 81
Dunbar, W., 40, 44, 47, 53
Dyer, Sir Edward, 91

Education of a Christian Prince, 60
Edward II, 124, 129
Edward III, 128
Edward IV, 130
Edward VI, 83
Elderton, 113
Eleanor of Aquitaine, 67
Elegiacs, 90
Elizabeth I, 21, 91, 92, 112, 123, 124, 131, 138, 158
Elocution, 30, 31, 34
Elyot, Sir T., 13, 14, 19, 24, 25, 29–30, 60, 150
emblems, 138, 150
Endimion and Phoebe, 85
England's Helicon, 84, 92, 121
England's Heroicall Epistles, 130
Epistle to Selden, 134
Epithalamium, 108, 136, 167
Erasmus, D., 11, 19, 20, 41, 60, 128
Essex, Earl of, 99
Etienne, 86
Euhemerism, 139
Extasie, 98

Fairie Queene, The, 15, 21, 22, 23, 28, 34, 93, 108, 116, 131, 134, 135–56, 157, 164–8
Fall of Princes, 41, 44, 125, 146
Ficino, M., 14–18, 97
Five Hundred points of Good Husbandrie, 114
Fletcher, G., 94, 95, 96
fourteener, 78, 79, 84, 90, 116
Fowre Hymnes, 136
Fox, Bishop, 19
Foxwell, A. K., 71–2
Frye, Professor N., 40

Garland of Goodwill, 112
Garland of Laurel, The, 44, 52, 58–60
Gascoigne, G., 41, 84
Geoffrey of Monmouth, 124
Glendower, O., 124
Googe, B., 88
Gorboduc, 126
Gorgeous Gallery of Gallant Inventions, The, 84
Governor, The, 13, 19, 24, 25, 150
Gower, J., 26, 52, 59
Greek Anthology, 86
Greek Language, 9, 10, 11, 12, 19, 24, 26, 48, 86
Greek Romances, 89
Greene, R., 85, 93–4, 157
Greville, F., 90
Grey, Lord, 135
Grocyn, 11

HALL, J., 158, 159
Hampton Court, 58
Handefull of Pleasant Delites, A, 84, 113
Harington, Sir J., 22, 139
Harvey, G., 85, 90, 91, 119, 120, 135
Hawes, S., 40, 41
Henry II, 129, 130
Henry IV (Bolingbroke), 126, 129
Henry V, 129, 132
Henry VII, 43, 123, 133
Henry VIII, 43, 48, 61–2, 63, 65, 66, 67, 131
Herbert, G., 53, 145
Hero and Leander, 86, 159–61
heroic poem, 34–5, 131, 132, 136–8
Heroides, 130
high style, 34–5, 40, 44, 78, 102
historical poetry, 123–34

Hoccleve, 39
Holinshed, R., 123
Homer, 28, 136
Horace, 26, 29, 42, 55, 75, 101, 159
House of Fame, 59
Howard, Catherine, 62, 65
Howard, Henry (Earl of Surrey), 41, 61–2, 71, 76–82, 83, 84, 90, 95, 112, 130
Howard, Thomas (Duke of Norfolk), 61–2
Humanism, *passim*; see especially, 9–23, 24–9, 40, 42–3, 47–8, 53, 54, 55, 56, 59, 71, 75, 76, 82, 90, 91, 92, 121, 136, 158–9, 161, 162, 169
Humphrey, Duke of Gloucester, 11
Hymenaei, 157

Idea, the Shepheards Garland, 93, 97
Ideas Mirror, 95
Imitation, 27, 28–9, 73, 81–2
Induction, 126–7
Inkehornisms, 24–5
Invention, 30, 31, 33

JAMES I, 124, 131
James IVth, 93–4
John, King, 130
Johnson, Dr, 27, 95
Jonson, B., 25, 55, 75, 82, 115, 134, 157, 159
Justification, 20–1, 150–1
Juvenal, 29, 58, 159

KINDS, the, 26–7, 38, 53, 55, 87, 129, 136, 157, 158
Kipling, R., 133
Knight's Tale, 15, 160

Lamentable civil warres of Edward the second and the Barrons, The, 129
Langland, J., 49
language changes, 24–6, 40, 47, 52
Latin language, 9–11, 19, 24, 26, 40
laureate, 43
Leicester, Earl of, 91, 99, 135
Leland, J., 123
Leone Ebreo, 14, 16, 18, 139
Lever, J. W., 65, 107
Lewis, C. S., 10, 57, 87, 94, 142
Licia, 96

Linacre, T., 11
Locke, J., 13
Lodge, T., 85, 86
London, 25, 28, 89, 90, 124, 135
Longus, 86
Lovers infinitenesse, 121
Love's Exchange, 121-2
Love's Growth, 18
Love's Labour's Lost, 17, 96
low style, 36-7, 47, 55-6, 75
Lullaby, 84
Lupset, 11
Luther, M., 19-20
Lycidas, 27, 93, 94-5
Lydgate, J., 26, 39, 40, 41, 44, 52, 59
Lyly, J., 85, 86, 88
lyric, courtly, 65-71, 78, 112
lyric, popular, 45, 86-7, 112-14
lyric, sung and read, 121-2

Macbeth, 32
Machiavelli, N., 150
McLane, Professor P., 91
madrigal, 112, 115-16
Magnificence, 47, 48-9, 59
Malory, Sir T., 12
Mannerly Margery, 45
Mantuan (B. Spagnola), 25, 27, 28, 42, 88, 90
Marlowe, C., 21, 85, 86, 94, 159-60, 161
Marot, C., 28, 90
Marston, J., 158, 159, 161
Martial, 159
Marvell, A., 80
Mary I, 83, 112, 124
Mason, H. A., 65
Masque of Blackness, 157
Medici, Cosimo de, 14
Memory, 30
Meres, T., 29
Merry Tales of Skelton, 43
Metamorphoses, 86, 133, 158, 160, 161
metaphor, 32-3, 50, 103, 138, 139-40, 163, 168
middle style, 35-6
Milton, J., 12, 13, 27, 97, 128, 134, 144, 150, 156
Mirandola, Pico della, 18
Mirror for Magistrates, 37, 116, 124-8, 131, 146, 157, 158
miscellanies, 83-4, 92, 121

Mock-Heroic, 136
Modern Love, 107
Moone-Calfe, The, 132
More, Sir T., 13, 19, 21, 41, 49, 128
Morley, T., 112, 118
Mortimeriados, 129, 131
Mother Hubberds Tale, 136
Muiopotmos, 136
Muir, Professor, 63
Muses Elizium, 94
music and poetry, 41, 45, 111-22
Musophilus, 23
Mutability Cantos, 92, 135, 155, 157, 158
My Darling Dear, 45
myth, 88, 133-4, 139, 158, 160, 161

Narrenschiff, The Ship of Fools, 41, 42
Nashe, T., 26
Neo-Platonism, 14-18, 21, 85, 104
nocturnall upon St Lucies day, A, 121
Nonne Preestes Tale, 50
Noodt, Van der, 28

Orlando Furioso, 22-3, 136, 139
Othello, 16
Ovid, 9, 51, 86, 130, 160, 161
Oxford Reformers, 11, 48

Palladis Tamia, 29
Paradise Lost, 97, 144, 147, 150
Paradise of Dainty Devices, The, 84
Paradise Regained, 12
Parthenophil and Parthenophe, 95
Parts added to the Mirror, 128
Passionate Centurie of Love, 95
Passionate Shepheard, The, 94
Pastime of Pleasure, 40, 41
pastoral, 37, 42-3, 55-7, 87, 88-95, 106, 136, 159
patriotism, 24-5, 124, 131, 132
Peele, G., 85, 87, 157
Pembroke, Countess of, 93, 98
Penitential Psalms, 65
Persius, 159
Petrarch, 10, 17, 25, 27, 28, 45, 51, 59, 61, 62, 71, 73-4, 76-7, 83, 85, 86, 90, 95, 96, 100, 102, 108, 109, 110, 115, 116
Petrarchism, 45, 85, 88, 161
Philip Sparrow, 43, 46, 50, 52, 59
Philosophy of Love, The, 14, 15, 16

Phoenix Nest, 121
Piers Gaveston, 129
Piers Plowman, 41
Pindaric, 85
Plato, 11, 12, 14, 17, 60, 104
Platonic revival, 9, 14-18
Plautus, 48
Pléiade, 85, 90, 95, 119
Plotinus, 15
Poetaster, 25
Poetics, 26
Polyolbion, 86, 131, 132-4
Poulter's Measure, 41, 78-9, 81, 90, 93, 113
Praise of Folly, The, 41
Prince, The, 150
printing, 10-11, 26, 112-13, 121
pronunciation, changes in, 40-1
prosody, 39-40, 41, 45-6, 71-3, 77-9, 84, 89-90, 93, 113-14, 127
Proust, M., 150
pun, 33, 50
Puttenham, G., 26, 30-1, 32, 34, 35, 36, 37, 41, 61, 76, 79, 91, 95

QUINTILIAN, 29, 30, 48

RALEIGH, SIR W., 94, 112, 135, 138, 150
Reformation, 19-22, 41, 43, 49, 84
Religious Treat, The, 11
Renaissance, 9-23, 24, 25, 26, 27, 28, 29, 37, 40, 85, 86, 87, 88, 123, 136, 139, 150, 169
Replication, A, 54-5
Rhetoric, colours of, 29, 37
Rhetoric, figures of, 31-2, 96, 162-4
Rhetoric, parts of, 30, 31, 33, 101
Rhetoric and poetry, 29-38
Rhyme Royal, 44, 90
Rich, Lady (Penelope Devereux), 99
Rich, Lord, 99
Richard II, 124, 126, 130
Robinson, C., 84, 113
Romance, 137-8
Romance of the Rose, 70, 103-4, 110, 139, 143, 152
Romantic revival, 37, 89
Ronsard, 28, 85
Rosseter, P., 117-18, 121
Ruines of Time, 137
Ryding Rhyme, 41, 92

SACKVILLE, T., 126-7
Samson Agonistes, 147
Sapphics, 90
satire, 29, 37, 41-3, 52-9, 61, 64, 65, 74-6, 88-9, 92, 93, 131-2, 136, 159, 161, 167-8
Scholemaster, The, 13-14, 19
Scillaes Metamorphosis, 86
Scourge of Villanie, 158
Selden, J., 132, 134
Shakespeare, W., 18, 25, 27, 32, 78, 79, 95, 96, 97, 98, 107, 110, 111, 124, 128, 149, 163, 164
Shelley, P. B., 32
Shepheardes Calender, 25, 28, 38, 79, 84, 85, 89, 90-3, 136, 159
Shoe-Maker's Holiday, 112
Sidney, Sir H., 99
Sidney, Sir Philip, 12, 14, 22, 26, 28, 31, 32-3, 54, 85, 86, 87-8, 89, 90, 91, 93, 95, 96-7, 98-108, 115, 119, 135, 157, 162, 164, 169
Skelton, John, 39-60, 61, 62, 65, 70, 75, 76, 87, 91, 92
Song of Solomon, The, 109-10
Songs and Sonets, 121, 162-6
Sonnet, 29, 35-6, 37, 65, 71, 72, 73-5, 76-7, 80, 84-5, 86, 87, 90, 95-111, 136, 153, 158, 162-9
Speak Parrot, 44, 48, 53-5
Spenser, E., 12, 13, 21, 25, 28, 31, 35, 55, 56, 59, 60, 84, 85, 95, 97, 108-10, 115, 119, 120, 123, 132, 133, 135-56, 158, 159, 164-5, 166-8, 169
Stow, J., 123
Sunne Rising, The, 120, 166
Surrey, Countess of, 59
Sylvius, Aenius, 42

Tamburlaine, 157
Tasso, 28, 136
Terence, 10
Theocritus, 28, 42, 90
Thirty-Nine Articles, 20
Tottel's Miscellany, 28, 72, 79, 83-4, 117
tragedy, 125-8, 160, 161
Tragedy of Buckingham, 126, 127
Tragical Legend of Robert, Duke of Normandy, 129
Tretis of the tua mariit Wemen and the Wedo, 53
Troilus and Criseyde, 17, 27, 44, 86

Tuberville, G., 88
Tunning of Elinour Rumming, The, 50, 52, 53
Tusser, T., 114–15
Tuve, R., 32

UNIVERSITY WITS, 85, 86, 115
Utopia, 13, 21, 41
Utterance, 30

Valediction: forbidding Mourning, 33
valediction of weeping, A, 121, 166
Venus and Adonis, 86
vernacular language, 24, 25, 26, 85, 123
Vinsauf, G. de, 29, 50
Virgidemarum, 158–9
Virgil, 9, 10, 25, 27, 28, 29, 40, 42, 51, 60, 88, 90, 136
Virgil, Polydore, 123, 124

Vulgate Bible, 53

WALLER, E., 81
Walsingham, Lady Frances, 99
Warner, W., 123
Wars of the Roses, 49, 123–4, 125–6, 128–9, 130
Watson, T., 95
Webbe, W., 41, 79
Why come ye not to Court?, 47, 49, 50, 53, 57–8
Wilson, T., 30
Winter's Tale, The, 113
Wolsey, Cardinal, 43, 48, 49–50, 53, 54, 58
Wyatt, Sir T., 41, 61–81, 83, 84, 87, 95, 98, 108, 112, 115, 127, 159, 164

Zepheria, 95